NATION BRANDING
AND INTERNATIONAL POLITICS

Nation Branding
and International Politics

CHRISTOPHER S. BROWNING

McGill-Queen's University Press
Montreal & Kingston • London • Chicago

© McGill-Queen's University Press 2023

ISBN 978-0-2280-1890-2 (cloth)
ISBN 978-0-2280-1891-9 (paper)
ISBN 978-0-2280-1945-9 (ePDF)
ISBN 978-0-2280-1946-6 (ePUB)

Legal deposit fourth quarter 2023
Bibliothèque nationale du Québec

Printed in Canada on acid-free paper that is 100% ancient forest free (100% post-consumer recycled), processed chlorine free

McGill-Queen's University Press in Montreal is on land which long served as a site of meeting and exchange amongst Indigenous Peoples, including the Haudenosaunee and Anishinabeg nations. In Kingston it is situated on the territory of the Haudenosaunee and Anishinaabek. We acknowledge and thank the diverse Indigenous Peoples whose footsteps have marked these territories on which peoples of the world now gather.

Library and Archives Canada Cataloguing in Publication

Title: Nation branding and international politics / Christopher S. Browning.

Names: Browning, Christopher S., 1974- author.

Description: Includes bibliographical references and index.

Identifiers: Canadiana (print) 20230446795 | Canadiana (ebook) 20230446825 | ISBN 9780228018902 (cloth) | ISBN 9780228018919 (paper) | ISBN 9780228019459 (ePDF) | ISBN 9780228019466 (ePUB)

Subjects: LCSH: National characteristics—Political aspects. | LCSH: Branding (Marketing)—Political aspects. | LCSH: World politics.

Classification: LCC JC311 .B76 2023 | DDC 659.2/991—dc23

This book was typeset by Marquis Interscript in 10.5/13 Sabon.

Contents

Tables and Figures vii
Acknowledgements ix

Introduction 3
1 Brand(ing) States 10
2 Competition States 30
3 Anxious States 57
4 Good States 87
5 Peaceful States 119
6 Stigmatised States 154
Conclusion: Nation Branding and the Remaking of International Politics? 182

Notes 193
References 199
Index 225

Tables and Figures

TABLES

4.1 The Good Country Index 99
5.1 Propaganda, public diplomacy, and nation branding compared 135
6.1 Geopolitical nation branding strategies in response to stigmatisation 159

FIGURES

2.1 Anholt's hexagon of nation branding 47
5.1 SNASK's redesign of the Democratic People's Republic of Korea, reproduced with permission of SNASK 120

Acknowledgements

This book has developed over a number of years and has benefited from the input and support of many colleagues and friends. I want to especially thank Richard Baggaley for taking interest in this project and for procuring two helpful reviews of the manuscript. I would also like to thank the McGill-Queen's University Press team for getting the manuscript ready for production.

My interest in nation branding has been cultivated in many contexts. However, I am particularly indebted to fellow colleagues working on the 'Nordic Branding' project at the University of Oslo, especially to the project directors Malcolm Langford and Eirinn Larsen. Engagement in this project rekindled what had previously been a 'side hustle' into a core focus of my research. The project's multiple seminars and workshops were highly instructive, and I am grateful and appreciative to all who participated but are too numerous to name. Special thanks, though, go to Kristian Bjørkdahl, Antoine de Bengy Puyvallée, Marko Lehti, Johann Strang, Inger Skjelsbæk, Mads Madsen, Halvard Leira, and Sidsel Roalkvam for their insights and for providing contexts especially in which to explore notions of 'good state branding' and 'peace branding' that are central to key parts of the book. Thanks are also due to Jenifer Chao and Jiang Jiehong, in particular for our discussions on nation branding in London, Venice, and Birmingham, but also to the UK Arts and Humanities Research Council (UK) for funding our project on 'Art Diplomacy and Nation Branding: The Visual Politics of Reinventing China'.

I am also indebted to my two former student research assistants, Antonio Ferraz de Oliveira and Steven Chaljub. Both have now gone on to bigger and better things, but Steven was invaluable in providing insight into the Colombian context, while discussions with Antonio resulted in two co-authored articles and a co-edited special issue of *Geopolitics* that were key in helping me think through an initial conceptual framework for the book.

I am also indebted to Louis Clerc, Nikolas Glover, Paul Jordan, César Jiménez-Martínez, Sabina Mihelj, Dan Sage, Rebecca Adler Nissen, Kristin Eggeling, and Paul Beaumont for inviting me to present my work at workshops and conference panels. Through these various events I had the opportunity to meet and engage with key people in the field. Specifically, though, my thanks go to Paul for the opportunity to discuss his excellent manuscript on status dynamics in international politics and to Kristin with respect to her work on nation branding in soft authoritarian states. I would also like to thank the SNASK branding consultancy for providing permission to use their images with respect to their innovative offer of re-branding North Korea, and Juliette Schwak for directing me to this case.

Throughout my intellectual journey, I have benefited from the insight, benevolence, and friendship of many colleagues and to all a massive thank you. Much of the theoretical framing of this book, centred as it is on ontological security and status dynamics has been tried out in different contexts. The ontological security community within the discipline is everything you would want to find in an academic community – open, generous, supportive, and inclusive. I am indebted to you all, but I would particularly like to mention and thank Brent Steele, Catarina Kinnvall, Jenifer Mitzen, Bahar Rumelili, John Cash, Ted Svensson, Jakub Eberle, Ty Solomon, Joseph Haigh, and Ilke Dagli. I should also like to thank current and former colleagues and PhD students, in particular Andre Broome, George Christou, Eun-jeong Cho, Nikolai Gellwitzki, Charlotte Heath-Kelly, Alex Homolar, Elisa Lopez Lucia, Trevor McCrisken, Matt McDonald, Ed Page, Owen Parker, Charlie Price, Nick Vaughan-Williams, and Johanna Vuorelma. All have contributed to this book in ways they might not immediately recognise. Special mention, though, must go to James Brassett, who has listened to my arguments at length, provided novel insights, but also much light relief in conversations reminding me that international politics (including nation branding) is also often quite funny!

Most importantly, this book is dedicated to my wife, Tess, and daughter, Abigail. They are a constant source of patience, support, and love. The feeling of home and belonging I am filled with around them is something I cherish dearly. Specifically, I would like to thank Abigail for producing figure 2.1 when all my own efforts to do so had failed. Apparently, it was 'easy'!

NATION BRANDING
AND INTERNATIONAL POLITICS

Introduction

But the great prize for this country – the opportunity ahead – is to use this moment to build a truly Global Britain. A country that reaches out to old friends and new allies alike. A great, global, trading nation.

UK Prime Minister Theresa May (May 2017)

If Global Britain comes to be perceived as a superficial branding exercise, it risks undermining UK interests by damaging our reputation overseas and eroding support for a global outlook here at home.

House of Commons Foreign Affairs Committee, 2018

Sometimes we can forget just how big our reputation is – that the world over the letters 'UK' stand for unique, brilliant, creative, eccentric, ingenious. We come as a brand – and a powerful brand ... If we lost Scotland, if the UK changed, we would rip the rug from our own reputation. The fact is we matter more in the world if we stay together.

UK Prime Minister David Cameron (Cameron 2014)

On 17 January 2017, more than six months after the British public narrowly voted for the country to leave the European Union, Prime Minister Theresa May finally made a speech setting out the government's 'Plan for Britain'. The delay, of course, reflected the fact that there had been no plan. Since the Leave campaign was never expected to win, the Brexit vote came as a profound shock to the governing political and social elite in the UK. And since the Leave campaign also expected to lose, it too lacked a plan, its campaign instead centring around nostalgic sound bites of sovereignty, independence and 'taking back control'. May's speech, however, did not so much lay out a plan as try to hit an aspirational and reassuring tone, captured in its own sloganeering sound bite or strapline, 'Global Britain', a phrase invoked eleven times in the speech and then hammered home in subsequent government communications.

Straplines like 'Global Britain' have become commonplace in international politics in recent decades, but while they are most usually associated with tourism advertising campaigns ('Malaysia truly Asia', 'Incredible India', 'Maldives – the sunny side of life', 'Jamaica – Get All Right', 'I feel S*lov*enia') they have also been increasingly deployed as short-hands for making more substantive claims about nation-states. 'Global Britain' is one such example, imbued as it is with implied claims about Britain's *being*, its role and identity, its attributes and values. To this extent, 'Global Britain' has all the hallmarks of a 'nation brand'.

The idea of nations as brands is relatively recent, however, since its claimed coining in 1998 by the branding consultant Simon Anholt (1998), the *nation brand* concept, and related idea and practice of *nation branding*, has proliferated globally. Nation brands and nation branding are now a part of everyday political discourse, and, as indicated by the above quotes, it is not just consultants who today think of nations in these terms, political leaders do too. Yet the idea of 'branded' (and more particularly of 'branding') nations is also often frequently derided as lacking seriousness. The second of the above quotes reflects such a sentiment, with the Foreign Affairs Committee of the House of Commons, barely a year after the prime minister's initial invocation of 'Global Britain', worried that 'Global Britain' was in danger of appearing a 'superficial branding exercise' that may actually damage the country's reputation abroad and undermine support for British foreign policy at home.

In the British case, such concerns are not unfounded. Since its initial articulation there has been a sense that 'Global Britain' has operated as a place holder and cover whilst the government has sought to figure out more precisely what to do. Yet, at the same time, 'Global Britain' was also a response to a palpable fear that Brexit would leave the UK diminished and the established British brand threatened. In this respect, the branding of 'Global Britain' has also been offered up as a solution with several interesting aspects to it. First, it offers a sense of reassurance to outsiders that, although the UK's relationship with the EU is fundamentally changing, it is not retreating in on itself and will remain active on the global scene, a responsible international actor. But the exercise also speaks to British citizens, especially to Remain voters, many of whom experienced Brexit as a parochial moment of little Englander nationalism, of closing in and withdrawing from the world (Browning 2018). Here, 'Global Britain' appears designed to offer reassurance by resonating with a more multicultural, cosmopolitan, and engaged vision of the country, not least captured in its most recent official branding programme, the 'GREAT Britain' campaign launched in the run up to London's hosting of the 2012 Olympic Games (https://www.greatbritaincampaign.com; Pamment 2015). However, it also appeals to a constituency of Leave voters for whom EU membership had kept Britain shackled. 'Global Britain', therefore, may also be about creating a *new* brand (Elliot 2018) by appealing to ideas of ontological fulfilment and becoming in which Britain's reputation and status as a leader and independent nation-state is enhanced (Browning 2019).

Understood as such, nation brands and nation branding may have more substance to them than critics claim. And it is certainly the case that, while states have always been concerned with matters of image and reputation (e.g., Lebow 2008; Paul et al. 2014; de Carvalho and Neumann 2015), this has intensified, with states increasingly focused on image management and brand cultivation, actively seeking to influence what various national and non-national audiences – be they other states, international investors, global public opinion – think about them. Consider, for instance, China's efforts to detoxify its image and play down concern about any possible expansionist ambitions by emphasising its 'peaceful rise' (Pathak 2015). Or consider how states compete to host major international sporting events like the Olympics and World Cup, with these events (and even the campaigns to host them) seen as opportunities for cultivating and repositioning states on the global stage as modern, developed, technological, engaged, and, not least, 'normal' (Grix and Houlihan 2014; Dembek and Włoch 2014).

More than this, however, positive nation brands are also seen to confer a competitive edge. We see this in the third quote taken from a speech by British prime minister David Cameron in the context of the 2014 referendum on Scottish independence, an example to which I return and further analyse in chapter 3. At root, however, Cameron was calling upon Scots to consider the hit to the UK's 'brand value' that a vote for independence would entail, a brand that is seen to exist, to have substance, and to matter because it gives the UK (including

Scotland) a competitive edge in global markets and contributes to the country's soft power. For Cameron, then, upholding brand value should be reason enough to stay together, while a vote for independence would not only damage the UK brand but was implicitly presented as a woeful act of Scottish self-harm and self-marginalisation from the global stage. In this respect, it should also be noted that Cameron delivered his intervention not in Scotland but at the Lee Valley Velo Park in London, the track cycling arena built for the 2012 Olympic Games, at which Britain outcompeted other nations to win a hatful of medals, and with Cameron immodestly signing off his speech invoking 'Team GB. The winning team in world history' (Cameron 2014). The performativity of such a staging was obviously intended to reignite the passions, enthusiasm, status, and sense of vicarious self-esteem many British people (including Scots) experienced during the Games.

If only impressionistically, then, what this opening UK-focused discussion highlights is not only how the language of nation branding has become a pervasive and naturalised part of everyday political and social discourse but also the extent to which the protection, cultivation, and management of nation brands is seen to matter politically. Indeed, while the discipline of international relations (IR) has so far had little to say about nation branding, essentially viewing it as epiphenomenal and superficial,[1] this book argues that to ignore the constitutive politics of nation branding is itself problematic. This is because nation branding intersects with international politics in complex ways. Thus, the above discussion includes allusions to issues of community, identity, status, and self-esteem; to competition in a world of globalised capital, markets, and trade flows; but also to geopolitics and security. One implication of this is that nation branding does not fit neatly into the sub-fields of the discipline, spanning issues central to the concerns of international relations, international political economy and development, security studies, and geopolitics. Moreover, as a phenomenon it also escapes a straightforward emplacement within established theories within the discipline. Thus, while its strategic and instrumentalist components sit uneasily with more constitutive approaches, in turn, its constitutive aspects sit uneasily with more rationalist approaches. Unpacking these aspects and providing some theoretical lenses through which to conceptualise and understand the role of nation brands and nation branding in international politics is a central task of this book.

OUTLINE OF THE BOOK

In the chapters that follow, the points raised above are unpacked more fully and further claims are analysed, but the central focus remains on understanding how nation branding affects international politics. The starting point for such an undertaking is therefore the assumption that nation branding, in its various forms and manifestations, matters. The book therefore warns against dismissing the proliferation of nation branding programmes in recent decades as epiphenomenal. Such a view treats nation branding as a superficial exercise lacking seriousness, little more than a form of snake oil salesmanship on the part of advertising and marketing consultants who have skilfully managed to convince gullible state leaders of the untapped potentials of nation branding. As Saunders (2017, 64) rightly notes, to dismiss nation branding as 'a trivial or even marginal aspect of contemporary statecraft' is foolhardy. Claims, though, that nation branding signals a fundamental transformation in the nature of international politics also need to be subjected to critical analysis.

The book treats nation branding as a broad phenomenon and set of practices that, depending on contextual factors, can be underpinned by different logics and manifest in varying forms. Specifically, nation branding is treated as politically significant for the conduct and practice of international politics. In particular, the following chapters engage with and analyse a number of emancipatory and progressive claims that have become central to the marketing assertions of nation branding consultants in recent decades but that have also made their way into some academic analyses, claims that suggest that nation branding raises fundamental questions about the underpinning logics of international politics. Such claims, it will be seen, activate discussions about globalisation and geopolitics, identity and community, norms and status seeking, security and peace, development and stigmatisation – all major themes within IR as a discipline.

Given this breadth, nation branding is more than simply an exercise in political communication and marketing. While all the chapters are theoretically oriented, chapters 1 through 3 lay out the broader theoretical framework and positioning of the book. In this respect, chapter 1 is tasked with definitional ground clearing and further outlining how nation branding is understood and approached in this book. It distinguishes nation branding from several related concepts, discusses its historical legacies and varying underpinning logics, and points to a steady expansion in the forms of nation branding that have become manifest over time. Chapter 2 picks up the discussion on the underpinning logics driving practices of nation branding but focuses specifically on prevailing claims of consultants and some academics that the economic logics of nation branding signals the end of traditional geopolitics, with the 'territorial state' transforming into the 'competition state'. The chapter charts the emergence of this discourse and the related emergence of a nation branding industry in the 1990s, with the key contribution of this industry being the claim that identity and culture now lie at the heart of states' competitiveness. Chapter 3 focuses in on this but suggests that the instrumentalist and strategic approach to national identity such a move entails needs unpacking. Here nation branding is refigured through the lens of recent theorising about ontological security within IR, with nation branding at one and the same time being seen as a response to, and generator of, extant anxieties about national identity and status in a changing world, with this also having an impact on the relationship between nation branding and nation building/national identity.

Having established a broader theoretical positioning for the book, the following chapters engage more specific claims about the emancipatory and normatively progressive potentials of nation branding. First, chapter 4 engages more recent claims that nation branding can foster a more normatively progressive politics by encouraging states to compete with each other by emphasising altruistic identities and status seeking through providing collective goods. It explores the role of consultants in pushing this agenda but argues for a more sceptical and critical view of such claims. It does so not only by considering what 'good state' nation branding entails for national identity construction and status seeking but also by reflecting on what the incorporation of altruism into nation branding entails for altruism in practice. The next two chapters have a more overtly geopolitical orientation, with chapter 5 analysing related claims that nation branding also fosters a more benign and peaceful international environment as well as having the potential to have a pacifying effect domestically, including within polarised and even war-torn societies. The chapter argues that positive examples need to be treated cautiously and should not leave us blind to the fact that nation branding does not actually signal the end of traditional geopolitics, as claimed by some, but is also often co-opted in its service. These geopolitical themes are extended in chapter 6, which explores widespread claims that nation branding can offer solutions to historically stigmatised states at the wrong end of global and geoeconomic hierarchies and is therefore a potentially valuable instrument for rectifying long-standing global injustices. Put slightly differently, to what extent does nation branding provide a tool for emancipatory geopolitics through tackling uneven global development? Last, the book's conclusion draws together key themes but also pushes the analysis further by considering claims that nation branding is facing various contemporary challenges that are raising questions about the possibility, legitimacy, and future direction of nation branding. At stake here are issues of its actual efficacy and whether nation branding is as inherently normatively progressive as is claimed by many of its advocates.

I

Brand(ing) States

To understand what nation branding may mean for international politics it is necessary to first clarify more precisely exactly how nation branding is understood in this book. The task of this chapter is therefore one of ground clearing and scene setting. This is important since, as becomes evident below and in subsequent chapters, the concept of nation brand(ing) is often used loosely and can be hard to pin down. For instance, references to a particular nation brand often suggest a tangible concreteness implying the existence of a clearly defined object of study, yet, in practice, scholars, consultants, and political operatives often seem to talk at cross purposes about what they understand a nation brand to be and what such a brand may include/exclude. In turn, nation branding may be associated with a set of communication, marketing, and policy practices, but it can also be understood – as it is here – as a discourse and a form of knowledge with constitutive effects. And, of course, how people understand and discuss nation brand(ing) is often related to their positionality and the more specific interests and concerns those positions entail. Yet, while there are often slight differences in focus and understanding, it is, all the same, possible to map out the broader linguistic and definitional contours around which debates about nation branding take place.

To do this, the chapter is divided into three sections organised around addressing three questions. The first question is definitional: 'What is nation branding?' The primary goal here is to set nation branding apart from, and to understand its relationship with, several closely related concepts, including national image, national identity, propaganda, public diplomacy, and soft power. However, this section also picks apart the distinction between nation brand as an object and nation branding as a practice. Section two then places nation branding within a broader historical perspective, addressing the question: 'To what extent is nation branding a recent phenomenon?' This question is important because, in contrast to many other analyses that see nation branding as a novel and emergent phenomenon, the argument developed in this book is that nation branding is better understood as conforming to different underpinning logics in different times and contexts. This, in turn, is central to developing a broader theorisation of the constitutive politics inherent within nation branding that are central themes for subsequent chapters. Last, section three addresses the question: 'Are there different forms of nation branding?' In other words, aside from different logics, the chapter also outlines different manifestations or forms of nation branding but where perhaps the most significant developments have taken place in recent decades.

CONCEPTUAL DISAGGREGATION

In this first section, then, we engage the question 'what is nation branding?', the aim being to distinguish nation brands and nation branding from several related concepts. In doing so, though, it is important to recognise that distinctions between different concepts are rarely categorical. For instance, it is not unusual for different concepts and associated practices to overlap and bleed into each other in various ways, and sometimes the relationships between concepts can be quite complex and even subject to change. Yet, despite this, important distinctions can usually be upheld, and whereas drawing distinctions is not an end, it is useful for analytical purposes to help better understand unfolding processes. In this section, we focus on five related concepts – national image, national identity, propaganda, public diplomacy, and soft power – while also unpacking the distinction between nation brand and nation branding in more depth. In debates about nation branding various other concepts are also frequently invoked, most notably reputation and status. These concepts are discussed at greater length in later chapters, though for now it is enough to note that they are neither equivalents for, nor interchangeable with, the concept of nation brand. For instance, most nation brands entail playing on states having a (good) reputation for something or other, while chapter 4 focuses on how reputations for 'being good' have more recently become a key nation branding strategy, yet a state's reputation will never capture the whole of its nation brand. Likewise, status – which can be understood in terms of positional standing or club membership (Clunan 2014) – can also contribute to a nation brand or even be a product of it. The relationship here is complex and is specifically taken up in chapter 3.

A good place to start, though, is with 'national image' since this is the concept that is most frequently treated as synonymous with 'nation brand'. However, while these concepts are sometimes used interchangeably – especially in popular discourse – doing so entails important conceptual slippages, whereas for analytical purposes they should be separated. Central to untangling these concepts is the role and presence/absence of agency, intent, and affect. In this respect, 'national images' are often complex and contradictory, but they relate to the mental pictures that spring to mind when people are prompted to think of a country or its people. Such images typically relate to stereotyped views about national character, reputation, environment, cuisine, and so forth and, as such, can be fluid, the images conjured depending very much on context (Saunders 2017, 13). National images may be benign or malign but are inevitably the result of the specific experiences people have of different places and people, or the snippets of information they have processed – often unconsciously – about them. 'National image' therefore relates to the unplanned and often random impressions people may have of different countries (including their own) that result from their specific associations and knowledge of a country and their personal values. The emotional inflection of national images, however, is usually weak. When national images come to mind, they do not (generally) pull on heart strings.

In contrast, the concept of 'nation brand' foregrounds the role of agency and intent, but it also speaks to issues of affect and emotional resonance by drawing attention to a sense of relationship between specific nation brands and target audiences (van Ham 2001, 2; 2005, 122). We can see the relational aspect if we strip out the national component and first focus on the concept of 'brand', which dates to the branding of cattle with a hot iron as a means of identifying and marking ownership of livestock. The similar branding of slaves and criminals likewise identified them as particular types of people, with slaves marked as possessions and objects of ownership. However, from marking ownership and as a means of preventing theft, brands later gained another function, as signifiers of quality that could be used to guide consumers' choices and, in doing so, establishing a sense of trust between consumers and producers (Cull 2019, 122–3). But contemporary brands do more than just activate trust and affect dynamics. For many people they have become central to making claims about who they are. Thus, people queueing outside Apple stores for the latest iPhone are not simply doing so because they trust Apple products but because association with the brand is felt as personally meaningful, as saying something about them, a marker of distinction that signifies adherence to a personal lifestyle choice/(political) philosophy (Banet-Weiser 2012; Klein 2000).

Nation brands are intended to have similar effects, and a successful nation brand will be one that stirs the imagination of an intended audience and that generates a sense of emotional connection with what that nation is presumed to stand for (Viktorin et al. 2018b, 4). Thus, just as product brands are the result of concerted action, nation brands are a result of active engagement by policy elites seeking to maintain or enhance their country's image (Saunders 2012, 51). This is precisely what invocations of 'Global Britain' outlined at the start of this book seek to do. Nation brands therefore seek to have an impact on – and selectively utilise – those national images that may be in circulation in different settings. However, while they may do this to some extent, nation brands are unlikely to fully colonise national images since the latter are typically more diverse, dispersed, fluid, and harder to pin down. For instance, the strapline 'Global Britain' is clearly intended to activate some images (cosmopolitan, active, engaged, responsible) while playing down others (parochial, isolationist) that debates over Brexit had generated. Yet alongside various positive resonances the 'Global Britain' brand also has the potential to unintentionally reanimate less positive images and impressions long in circulation (Empire, colonial, arrogant). Indeed, the worry of the Foreign Affairs Committee is that the Global Britain brand may backfire and become the basis for the emergence and circulation of less positive images of the country – for instance, when contrasted to the country's somewhat chaotic attempts to create new post-Brexit trading relationships or to manage its relationship with other global powers, not least China, the US, and the EU.

The emphasis on agency and intent also means it is important to distinguish between *having* a 'nation brand' and *practices* of 'nation branding'. As discussed in greater depth in chapter 6, it is sometimes argued that countries that fail to brand themselves may still discover that others have done this for them (Anholt 2005). A classic example is Sacha Baron Cohen's 2006 film *Borat: Cultural Learnings of America for Make Benefit Glorious Nation of Kazakhstan*, a film that portrays Kazakhstan and its people as bigoted and backward but that worked precisely because so few people at the time had any real notion of the country. Such a 'branding' resonated either by creating new images or because it activated already existing (racist) stereotypes about Central Asia amongst audiences (Saunders 2008). Africa provides another example, where it is argued that, to its considerable detriment, the continent has been negatively branded as plagued by disease, famine, war, and poverty, with this itself becoming a considerable impediment to development (Anholt 2007a; Browning 2016; Browning and de Oliveira 2017b). Such nations are therefore called upon to take control of their brands, even if the irony of the Borat example is that it highlights the extent to which, especially in an age of globalisation and new communications technologies, actors beyond the state (citizens, media, NGOs/corporations) can themselves engage in nation branding activities that governments may find difficult to control. Either way, be it undertaken by state functionaries or other actors, 'nation branding' *usually* refers to concerted and purposive efforts of brand creation, with nation branding therefore imbued with a sense of strategic action. I say usually, because 'nation branding' is a discursive as well as a technical practice. The point here, and as discussed in depth in chapter 3, is that in recent decades nation branding has also arguably emerged as a constitutive form of knowledge production, a way of apprehending and understanding the world.

However, the *scope* of nation branding also needs consideration. In this respect, nation branding is usually seen to differ from – or at least entail more than – simple tourist marketing or other more generalised forms of advertising that seek to entice visitors with images of nice places, friendly people, gastronomical excellence, and glorious weather, by emphasising the need to cultivate an emotional resonance and attachment to the country and what it is seen to stand for – even if such advertising may be part of a broader nation branding campaign (van Ham 2001, 2; 2005, 122). In other words, nation branding not only aspires to activate consumerist desires but also to establish a perceptual frame around which a story of the nation can be told that attracts positive feelings and lasting psychological attachments (Viktorin et al. 2018b, 4). In practice, though, and as lamented by Simon Anholt (2007b; 2020, 11), one of the pre-eminent consultants and thinkers in the field, many self-declared nation branding programmes often fall short in this regard and look more like standardised forms of tourist board marketing campaigns. To highlight the difference, Kaneva (2011, 118) therefore distinguishes between 'cosmetic' and 'institutionalised' approaches to nation branding. Cosmetic approaches are typically somewhat superficial, characterised by an emphasis on marketing and advertising, the coining of memorable straplines, and perhaps the creation of web-based interfaces and resources for national actors to help them project the brand. Institutionalised approaches entail a more concerted engagement, where nation branding becomes embedded much more centrally into national policy and becomes significant to how the country is run and organised, and considered more than just a matter of communication, presentation, and public affairs (Anholt 2008a, 23; Kaneva 2012b, 4). This may be manifest in significant infrastructural projects, the building of new capital cities (e.g., Astana in respect of Kazakhstan), new educational hubs (e.g., Education City in Qatar), the hosting of major sporting or cultural events, the creation of national airlines (Eggeling 2020). It may also entail bringing various policy sectors in line with broader claims made about a country in its nation branding actions, such as ensuring it really is as environmentally conscious as it claims to be.

Having discussed the difference between nation brand and national image, we can now draw a distinction with the concept of 'national identity'. The relationship between nation brands/nation branding and national identity/nation building forms the crux of chapter 3, but a brief discussion is warranted here as within the nation branding industry they are often seen as rhetorically and functionally equivalent (Aronczyk 2008, 49; Olins 2002, 242). Yet, even here nation branding typically treats national identity and culture as a resource *within which* the nation brand can be found, this suggesting that, even when they are seen as tightly linked, nation brands are a narrower or more simplified exposition of national identity. Moreover, such a view entails a primordial assumption that nations have identifiable essences that can be captured and distilled into marketable forms for both domestic and international audiences. For critics, nation branding therefore relies upon obfuscating or overlooking nuances in favour of simplified and hollowed out representations of national identity (Clegg and Kornberger 2010, 9). Indeed, as decades of academic research has amply demonstrated, the nature of national identity is much more complex, not least because national identities are historically embedded and inherently diverse and contested (Browning 2015a, 201).

In this respect, a focus on 'national identity' and 'nation building' draws attention much more to nations as *imagined communities* (Anderson 1991) forged through the politics of nationalist discourse with its appeals to kinship and history. In contrast, a focus on 'nation brands' and 'nation branding' places much more emphasis on nations as *imaged communities*, where such images are designed to appeal to international audiences at least as much, and usually more, than they are to domestic audiences.[1] A further difference, however, is that without constructing a national identity a nation cannot be said to exist, let alone act in the world. In contrast, national brands are much less intrinsic to subjectivity, something evident in that, while all states make identity claims, not all seek to market specific nation brands to the global audience. However, the fact that this is precisely what more and more states are increasingly doing, and understanding what the implications of this are for thinking about national identity, is one of the key motivations for this book.

Finally, several other practice-based distinctions can also be noted, specifically concerning the relationship between nation branding and 'propaganda', 'public diplomacy', and 'soft power', each of which is returned to in later chapters. Like nation branding, propaganda, public diplomacy, and soft power all refer to practices intended to influence audiences and affect their behaviour. Without denying the potential for overlap and certain compatibilities there are also identifiable differences. For instance, like propaganda, nation branding may be targeted both domestically and internationally and is also often targeted at non-state actors (corporations, investors, people). Propaganda, however, is characterised by its intention to manipulate political attitudes and potentially undermine foreign publics' support for their own governments, whereas nation branding is generally apolitical in presentation (if not effect), seeking to garner attention and cultivate emotional attachments (Saunders 2017, 49). Moreover, while propaganda is undertaken more or less exclusively by state agents, nation branding is something in which a much wider array of actors may engage. Indeed, contemporary official nation branding campaigns are often created and curated by foreign marketing and nation branding experts, something anathema to the very idea of propaganda (Viktorin et al. 2018b, 17).

Similarly with public diplomacy, where again the focus of activities is on the public relations functions of foreign ministries tasked with presenting and selling government policies to foreign publics, a function that itself is often tainted with accusations of propaganda (Cull 2008, 18; Mor 2012). In contrast, in principle at least, nation branding entails a more holistic and joined up approach to marketing the nation that unites a broader range of sectors and seeks to coordinate the diverse messages different agencies (e.g., cultural institutes, tourist boards, foreign ministries, exporter organizations) disseminate. Moreover, while public diplomacy focuses on explaining national policy positions to others with the aim being to maintain or smooth international relationships (Cull 2019, 21; Mordhorst 2015), in its more institutionalised form nation branding emphasises the need to develop coherent cross-sectoral national strategies from the start, thus embedding nation branding in the very policy-making process (Anholt 2007a, 74). Besides, while policy may be one of its elements, nation branding's principal focus is identity, with the question of whether nation branding is simply a reflection of national identity or also plays a role in actively constituting it is something that is taken up in chapter 3. Finally, while both practices are targeted at foreign audiences, this is not exclusively the case for nation branding, for which domestic constituencies are also important (Browning 2015a, 201–2).

This leaves the concept of 'soft power', which Joseph Nye (2004) introduced as a contrast to the coercive functions of hard power, arguing that the ability to entice, attract, and persuade such that others fall under your influence willingly is becoming an increasingly important aspect of international relations to which states should attend. Soft power is therefore the ability of one state to get others to do what it wants without ordering or forcing them to do so. According to Nye, a country's soft power will depend upon the attractiveness to others of its culture and political values and the perceived legitimacy of its foreign policy, with this conferring it with moral authority. However, and as discussed in chapter 2, while nation branding certainly plays to the politics of attraction and may contribute to soft power, it is not synonymous with it. Thus, unlike soft power, nation branding is not seeking to motivate other countries to make strategic, political, or economic choices they might otherwise not make; rather, it is seeking to influence people's (not just states') more general orientations towards the country, potentially predisposing them to visit or invest in it. As Saunders (2017, 51) notes, while a country endowed with soft power reserves 'is likely to have a marketable nation brand, the reverse – i.e., a country with a world-class brand possesses substantial soft power – is not necessarily true (a case in point: Switzerland)'. And just as with public diplomacy, it is also important to remember that, unlike soft power, external audiences are only one part of nation branding's foci.

NATION BRANDING IN HISTORICAL PERSPECTIVE

The above discussion seeks to specify nation brand(ing) by distinguishing it from several closely related concepts, but clarification is also needed in one further respect: its historical novelty. In this respect, commentary and analysis on nation branding is often split between those who see it as a wholly new and emergent phenomenon immutably bound up with capitalist logics in an era of globalisation (e.g., Aronczyk 2013) and those who suggest that such claims are overblown. The animating question of this section is therefore: 'To what extent is nation branding a recent phenomenon?' Developing a more nuanced position, this section argues that, although claims about historical novelty that link nation branding to capitalism and globalisation can be overplayed, the idea that nation branding constitutes nothing more than old wine in new bottles itself misses important developments and lacks analytical precision.

The latter position is characterised by the claim that, while the concept of 'nation branding' is new, to suggest that states have not been concerned with strategically cultivating national images before this point is palpably false. Thus, in their historical analysis of nation branding Viktorin et al. (2018b, 6) emphasise that states have been 'deliberately engaged in building nation brands long before there was such a term as "nation branding"'.[2] For the branding consultant Wally Olins (2005, 170–1), the marketing techniques of contemporary nation branding can be dated back at least as far as France's 'Sun King' (*le Roi Soleil*) Louis XIV's (1643–1715) building of Versailles as a symbolic embodiment of absolute power, followed by the French Revolution's (1789) overthrow of monarchism and 'rebranding' of the Republic with a new set of symbols/logos (e.g., the fleur-de-lis) and epithets/straplines (liberté, équalité, fraternité). Throughout history, he argues, other countries have engaged in very similar rebranding practices following political change and transformation. For him, nation branding is nation building, nothing more, nothing less, a view that – as noted above – is challenged in chapter 3.

In contrast, the former position holds that, while it is true that states have always cared about their image, the nation branding practices of today are fundamentally different. To conflate the past with the present is therefore to make a category error. In particular, it is argued that the end of the Cold War signalled the replacement of traditional geopolitical discourses with those of globalisation, emphasising the spread of neoliberal markets. The underlying logics of international politics are therefore seen to have transformed, with this fundamentally affecting the role and nature of the state and governments – the 'territorial state' being replaced by the 'competition state', a metaphor that depicts states as much less interested in war and geopolitical competition and, instead, as akin to companies competing for global investment and market share. Unpacking the underlying dynamics of such claims is the task of chapter 2; however, in its most lyrical framing it is claimed that 'power-oriented geopolitics' is being 'emasculated' by the emergence of a 'postmodern world of images and influence' (van Ham 2001, 4; 2002, 252). This claim, however, is overstated since even a cursory survey of global politics suggests classical geopolitical thinking is far from obsolete, while, as this book demonstrates, contemporary practices of nation branding are often heavily influenced by geopolitical concerns.

Rather than take sides in this debate, an alternative way of thinking about nation branding may be productive. Extrapolating and developing a suggestion made by Clerc and Glover (2015, 13–17), three different logics of nation branding can be identified. The first is a 'cultural' logics where the emphasis of state nation branding is on 'enlightening and educating foreigners about our national soul', with the specific aim of securing recognition for the country. Nation branding, therefore, can be understood as a mechanism for claiming subjectivity and the status of legitimate nationhood. This is particularly evident in periods of international structural transformation – like the end of the First and Second World Wars, the period of decolonisation, the end of the Cold War – when older states (and empires) break up or disappear to be replaced by new states seeking recognition and legitimacy. Such concerns are felt particularly keenly by small nations and micro-states, where a central problem for preserving their independence (or having it recognised) is the need to convince key constituencies that their nation meets the criteria for statehood. For instance, nation branding campaigns undertaken by the Palestinians can be understood at least in part in this way (Iriqat 2019). In other words, 'enlightening and educating' others through propagating cultural and other information is a way to enhance visibility and promote acceptance of a nation's right to exist for both domestic and international audiences. For instance, it is precisely on such grounds that Peterson (2006, 733) argues that, in the case of Qatar, nation branding has been nothing less than a strategy of state survival.

The second logics is one that emphasises 'diplomacy' and has a more overtly geopolitical dimension to it. Here, nation branding may appear 'as a tool in high politics' (Clerc and Glover 2015, 17) that can be utilised to pursue policy goals, such as securing acceptance for a claimed position or role in the international system. Examples include states that have sought to establish a role and position as a bridge builder or mediator in international politics, or to gain acceptance for their inclusion in a particular geopolitical club viewed as offering status and security benefits. For instance, at different points in time both Finland (Cold War – see Browning [2008, 194–202]) and Estonia (post–Cold War – see Ilves [1999]) have explicitly sought to brand themselves as 'Nordic' countries and thereby escape a 'Baltic' or 'East European' designation. In contrast, North Korea uses nation branding techniques to carve out a very different role in world politics, a defender against American imperialism (Cho 2017).

The third logics emphasises 'promoting commerce' and concerns 'selling the nation for the purpose of promoting economic growth' (Clerc and Glover 2015, 17). Here nation branding becomes part of the toolkit of economic competition nations may deploy as they seek to secure as large a slice as they can of investment and trade in increasingly globalised markets. It is on this logics that most academic analyses of nation branding have been focused. However, focusing on only this logics is empirically and theoretically limiting because it curtails our understanding of the different ways states have strategically mobilised their identities in nation branding practices and how they might invoke or draw on different logics at different times.

For instance, Varga (2013) neatly identifies how, over the last century, Germany shifted from an initial emphasis on 'cultural nationalism' (cultural logics) before the Second World War, the aim being to educate both citizens and foreigners about the nature of the newly formed state, to a focus on 'cultural diplomacy' (diplomatic logics) during the Cold War, driven by a desire to regain trust and understanding and secure political stability, through to an emphasis on 'commercial nationalism' (economic logics) in the 1990s, embracing discourses of economic competition and globalisation. Clerc and Glover (2015, 13–16) similarly suggest a gradual progression through cultural-diplomatic-economic logics of nation branding, tracing this progression from the interwar period, through the Cold War, to the 1990s and the era of globalisation and transnational markets. However, any sense of teleological progression should be guarded against. To the contrary, one thing the examples and thematic issues discussed in this book demonstrate is that states may not only prioritise different logics at different times but may also play with different logics at the same time. For instance, Russia uses nation branding both to reaffirm its desired status as a great power (diplomatic logics) and to present itself as a normal cosmopolitan state open for investment (economic logics), though as Szostek (2017) notes, these logics do not always align and at times evidently counteract each other.

However, while it is important to ward against claims of a definitive shift in favour of economic logics of nation branding, even if this is what drives many nation branding programmes today, we do need to note two developments that have significantly changed the context within which practices of nation branding now occur. First, it is evidently the case that, because of globalisation and new communications technologies, levels of interconnectedness have increased markedly, one outcome being that states are now exposed to a significantly expanded global audience. In a 'world of flows' (Castells 2000, 242) and global communications, an 'attention economy' has emerged that it is increasingly difficult to avoid. Today, states are undoubtedly seeking to target wider and larger audiences than ever before, both geographically and socially, with the techniques of nation branding viewed as a useful tool for engaging in such communications. Second, economic logics of nation branding differ from cultural and diplomatic logics in one crucial respect – by reconceptualising states as means rather than ends. In other words, under cultural and diplomatic logics, nation branding is directed towards upholding the very idea, existence, and success of the state. In contrast, under economic logics, the state and its various cultural assets are increasingly subordinated to market logics and assigned a key role in reproducing them. This is no more evident than in how, during the 1990s, nation branding shifted increasingly into the commercial sector with the emergence of a growing number of international and marketing consultancies promoting the idea of nations as marketable commodities (Volčič 2012, 150). Exploring this latter dynamic is a key task of chapter 2, where it also becomes evident that, under an economic logics, nation branding gains an increasingly ideological hue, whereby the 'tools' of nation branding practices also become constitutive of visions of how the world ought to be.

NATION BRANDING AND ITS FORMS

Nation branding, then, may operate according to different logics and these may be in play concurrently. However, if nation branding can manifest different logics, the question for this final section is: 'Is all nation branding alike or can it take different forms?' Unequivocally, the answer to this is that it can, with varying forms and manifestations being more or less compatible with the different logics of nation branding, though they do not map onto each other in any definitive way. Similarly, while it is tempting to think of a shift in emphasis between different forms of nation branding as a result of its having become an increasingly sophisticated activity, the suggestion here is that it is perhaps better to think of these forms as layered, with different forms of nation branding having different points of emphasis and targeted at slightly different audiences but usually operating alongside each other and often largely compatible. Indeed, coherent and effective nation branding programmes will likely draw on, but also seek to align, all these forms of nation branding, though the emphasis placed on them will be context specific and likely dependent on the dominant logics of nation branding in play. Four forms of nation branding can be highlighted.

Country of Origin

The first form of nation branding involves emphasising the proclaimed 'country-of-origin' effect. In this form, nation branding is understood in terms of encouraging consumers to purchase products because of the reputation associated with the country in which they were produced (Anholt 2002a, 232–3). An emphasis on 'country of origin' entails a form of co-branding in which values associated with one brand can be passed on to another brand. In other words, in 'country-of-origin' branding entities become linked together even though they essentially belong to different categories – that is, products and nations (Mordhorst 2019). Viktorin et al. (2018b, 6–7) note that such an effect was identified as early as 1896 in a pamphlet titled *Made in Germany* and written by the journalist Ernest Williams, with later studies demonstrating that consumers' images of a country could also have an impact on their perception of products made there. Later studies then suggested that this relationship could also be reversed, or indeed become mutually reinforcing, with consumers' perception of products influencing their image of the country in which they were made. For instance, the Audi strapline *Vorsprung durch Technik* has arguably played a significant role in shaping foreign consumers' images of Germany more generally since it was first used in an advertising campaign in 1971. People may not know what it means ('progress through technology'), but, all the same, it has become a shorthand for a German brand of engineering and technical excellence (Rice-Oxley 2012). Indeed, such is the presumed influence of the country-of-origin effect on consumers that companies often develop faux brands that seek to activate associations with countries other than their place of origin, parasitically trying to ride on their more valued nation brand – for example, 'Norwegian formula' hand cream (Cull 2019, 125–6).

However, the proclaimed 'country-of-origin' effect is not as causally robust as sometimes believed and inverse relationships also exist (see Fan 2006, 9). For instance, Western consumers still purchase vast quantities of Chinese products despite the prevalence of a generally negative image of the country and even though 'Made in China' does not carry the same resonances of quality or sophistication that some other country of origin brands do. Indeed, for many 'Made in China' is synonymous with being cheap, forged, or unethically produced (Chao et al., 2012). But this does not stop people buying Chinese goods.[3] By the same token, though, strong product brands do not always generate positive images of the country in which they are manufactured. Thus, the good standing of Lenovo in the technology market has not had much effect in shifting broader images of China. At the same time, in a world of increasingly dispersed transnational production chains it has also been argued that the 'country-of-origin' effect is losing its salience and ability to motivate consumers, with the branding consultant Wally Olins (2003, 131) arguing as early as 2003 that it is in terminal decline.

Place Branding

The second and most archetypal form of nation branding, and the central focus of most nation branding programmes in recent decades, is 'place branding'. Instead of seeking to sell products, the focus of place branding is on trying to attract resources to the nation, be that in the form of investments, investors, tourists, students, or (often highly skilled) labour. This can be undertaken in various ways but not least by selling appealing lifestyles or showcasing countries through vanity architecture (e.g., Dubai's Burj Khalifa), creating international education hubs (e.g., Qatar's 'Education City'), hosting major sporting events, and using opening ceremonies as opportunities for (re)branding through articulating an attractive national story, et cetera. Place branding has become the stock in trade of nation branding consultants, who argue that, with globalisation having turned the world into a single global marketplace in which everyone is competing with everyone else for market share, states need to engage in place branding to ensure they stand out from the crowd. In this 'supermarket of nations' (Landau 2021) countries that are unknown or that fail to generate a sufficiently attractive brand offering will be ignored and fall behind, it is claimed (Anholt cited in Aronczyk 2013, 70; van Ham 2008, 131).

While place branding should be seen as having a longer heritage, as evident for instance in the longer history of international cultural exhibitions and world fairs, it became a particular point of attention in the 1990s as the 'tiger' appellation became attached to several countries and regions undergoing economic expansion – the Asian tigers, Baltic tigers, and the Celtic tiger (the Republic of Ireland). Particular attention was also given to Spain's post-Franco transition to democracy, which Aronczyk (2013, 34) notes is often 'considered the original success story of nation branding' but where political transformation was accompanied by transformations in cultural production, architecture, economic reorientation, and with the country hosting the 1982 FIFA World Cup, the 1992 Barcelona Olympics, and the 1992 International Expo in Seville. Accompanying all this were tourist and country marketing campaigns, all encapsulated by Joan Miró's widely circulated sun logo (the 'Sol de Miró') (Aronczyk 2013, 34–5). Such developments were not missed in London, where Mark Leonard, a researcher at the *Demos* think tank, published *Britain TM: Renewing Our Identity*, a short booklet that actively calls on the government to take more interest in managing the country's identity, a call the incoming Labour government took up through its informal 'Cool Britannia' campaign, which sought to rebrand the country 'as a global hub for the media, design, music, film, and fashion industries' (van Ham 2001, 4; Cull 2019, 128). It was in the 1990s, therefore, that the contemporary nation branding consulting industry emerged, with London a central hub, and with place branding central to the offering.

However, and as becomes evident throughout this book, place branding is a contentious activity, and its claimed successes are often contested. Indeed, and as noted earlier, even consultants like Simon Anholt (2007b) have questioned its efficacy, his criticism being that in the name of place branding, nation branding often becomes little more than a glorified cosmetic advertising campaign. At the same time, Mordhorst (2019) argues that, while various sectors (tourism, education, business, agriculture, culture, etc.) may agree that nation branding through place branding is desirable, agreeing on the content of place branding is often difficult because different sectors have different interests that always have the potential to push place branding campaigns in different and potentially incompatible directions that deprive the brand of sufficient coherence.

Corporate Branding

Partly because of the aforementioned concerns, in recent years a third form of nation branding has emerged: 'corporate branding'. This reflects shifts in the business world where attention has to some extent moved from trying to appeal directly to consumers and investors to instead inculcating the brand throughout the internal organisation of the corporation. In other words, from the highest CEO to the lowliest employee, the emphasis is placed on getting all to 'become the brand', to 'live the brand' through emphasising their role as 'brand carriers' (Aronczyk 2008, 54). Think, for example, of Google's development of a particular branded work environment for its employees and the way in which employees are increasingly encouraged (expected?) to view themselves as representatives of the brand even when not on working hours. Such forms of corporate branding essentially seek to reinforce external branding messages communicated to consumers and investors by demonstrating that 'we really are who we say we are' (Mordhorst 2019).

Of course, when applied to nations certain problems may arise. As is discussed in chapter 3, corporate branding implies a considerable dose of governmentality as it signals to citizens which behaviours are considered sufficiently 'on brand' and which are therefore in some sense deemed 'unpatriotic' (Weidner 2011; Browning 2015a, 205). As Mordhorst (2019) notes, while that may be okay for corporations – who can reasonably get rid of employees who fail to share the company's vision – a nation cannot reasonably strip someone of their citizenship because of their perceived failure to sufficiently embody the nation's core brand values and identity. As we will see, when it takes this form nation branding can become a source of political tension and even resistance, perceived by many as a technocratic threat to democratic politics.

Policy Branding

The last form of nation branding is 'policy branding' and it is the most recent development in nation branding. As chapter 4 highlights, a growing emphasis is now being placed on policy transfer as a part of nation branding strategies. Thus, we see countries emphasising the possibility of exporting (amongst others) their educational, environmental, gender, criminological, and even administrative policies, models, and approaches. Instead of jealously guarding points of possible competitive advantage the message is instead apparently benevolent, a declaration that such countries may have something to offer that they are willing to share for the greater good. Policy branding entails a franchising element and is something that has become relatively widespread in the business sector, a way in which companies (the franchiser) can enhance profits while spreading the risks. However, it may also work for the franchisee, who benefits from knowledge, expertise, training, and the brand power of the franchiser, which they pay for through rents and a share of profits (Marsh and Fawcett 2011a; 2011b). When it forms a part of nation branding, however, the benefits of policy branding are less clearly economic. Policy branding may therefore be more attractive when driven by cultural or diplomatic logics of nation branding, where nation branding becomes about global positioning and status seeking, recognition and reputation building, and not least constructing and performing identity.

CONCLUSION

The aim of this opening chapter is to provide some broader context to debates about nation branding and thereby to more clearly identify the object of study and analysis. It does this in three ways. First, by engaging in some essential definitional ground clearing by distinguishing nation branding from several closely related concepts. These cognate concepts are inevitably invoked when talking about nation branding since they all capture aspects of what nation brands do, yet important points of distinction remain. This chapter also discusses the difference between nation brands and nation branding as a practice of brand cultivation and further notes that nation branding as a practice often breaks down into 'cosmetic' (i.e., relatively superficial) marketing campaigns and more 'institutionalised' (i.e., relatively extensive and embedded) approaches that entail varying degrees of social and political transformation. Yet it also points towards some of the broader concerns of this book by noting that 'nation branding' can also be understood as a discourse and claim to knowledge, with this foregrounding the way to chapter 2, where this idea is developed more fully. Second, this chapter provides a brief historical context for nation branding. Undoubtedly the story outlined here is oversimplified, but the principal aim is to emphasise that claims to novelty need to be treated cautiously. However, rather than reject such claims outright, this chapter argues that a historical sensitivity makes it possible to identify several underpinning logics that can provide nation branding practices with different orientations, goals, and points of emphasis. Moreover, while a general case can be made to suggest a transition of emphasis from cultural to diplomatic to economic logics there is nothing inevitable about this, with subsequent chapters showing that cultural and diplomatic logics remain very much in play. And third, nation branding is broken down in terms of different forms. In this respect, subsequent chapters engage mainly with 'place branding', 'corporate branding', and 'policy branding' forms of nation branding, devoting much less attention to 'country of origin', the reason being that the former have more direct political implications. However, distinguishing between different forms in practice is not always straightforward as, frequently, combinations (and sometimes all) are invoked at the same time.

What the above discussion suggests, therefore, is that, as an object of study, nation branding can be difficult to pin down. To end, then, a couple of clarifications are in order. The first concerns the aim of this book, which is not to take sides in a debate as to how nation branding as a practice 'should be' defined and then adjudicate as to whether or not different proclaimed nation branding programmes warrant the label. Nor is its aim to consider which modes and forms of nation branding may be most effective and to make recommendations about how they might be improved upon, something that is likely to be of more concern to scholars and practitioners from a business studies, marketing, or communication studies background. Instead, the point of interest lies in the discursive claims that underpin such campaigns and the constitutive effects they may entail. The focus, in other words, is on what makes nation branding politically significant.

Second, the focus of analysis is mainly on state-led nation branding programmes and actions. Some of these will be 'official' in the sense that, in recent decades, governments have increasingly made the very proclamation and creation of an official nation branding programme a central part of the nation branding exercise itself. Such programmes typically entail the constitution of nation branding committees, the hiring of consultants, the production of a handbook, and a proposed set of actions, all of which are well worthy of analysis, although often such texts are characterised by their aspirational nature. As a result, it is not always easy to determine which actions (if any) were a direct consequence of a nation branding programme and which would have been undertaken by state actors irrespective of such a programme. In practice, however, it is commonplace for such actions to be co-opted when it suits and where what counts more is how different actions, programmes, and proclamations have become incorporated within broader nation branding discourses in particular contexts. Indeed, to a large degree nation branding entails repackaging what is already there and representing it in distilled form. Meanwhile, if seen from an 'institutionalised' approach where the aim is to align all sectors of policy with the nation brand, the distinction between nation branding and other actions inevitably breaks down.

Last, this also extends more broadly in that the distinction between formal state-led nation branding and more informal modes of nation branding that might be undertaken by citizens, business actors, and other interests is also breaking down, with many states increasingly unable to monopolise the branding space. Needless to say, this can create tensions, particularly when non-state actors disagree with the nation brands officially purported in their name (see chapter 3). Indeed, the increasing emphasis on 'corporate' forms of nation branding that seek to encourage societal actors at large to internalise brand messages and 'live the brand' suggests clear recognition of this tension and an attempt to control it to some degree. In this respect, then, the distinction between 'formal' and 'informal' nation branding is also sometimes hard to draw. For the most part, however, this book focuses on state-led initiatives and programmes insofar as these have been seen by governments as offering responses to a varying set of national and international challenges.

2

Competition States

The nation brand is a clear and simple measure of a country's 'license to trade' in the global marketplace, and the acceptability of its people, hospitality, culture, policies, products and services to the rest of the world ... the only sort of government that can afford to ignore the impact of its national reputation is one which has no interest in participating in the global community, and no desire for its economy, its culture or its citizens to benefit from the rich influences and opportunities that the rest of the world offers them.
> *The Anholt Nation Brands Index Special Report: How Has Our World View Changed since 2005?* (Quoted in Aronczyk 2013, 70)

The previous chapter focuses on unpacking and specifying the object of study. This entailed a certain amount of conceptual ground clearing, distinguishing nation branding from related concepts and further excavating nation branding as a practice by identifying four different forms (or ways of doing) nation branding. That chapter also provides a broader historical perspective and argues that one benefit of a historical sensitivity is that it can help illuminate how nation branding can accord to several different underpinning logics. First, there is a 'cultural' logics in which the emphasis is on securing national recognition from key audiences. Second, there is a more overtly geopolitically oriented 'diplomatic' logics in which nation branding may help states pursue international policy agendas and secure acceptance for particular role identities. And third, there is an 'economic' logics that ties nation branding primarily to promoting economic rationales. A key argument is that, although it can be tempting to see these logics as temporally and historically sequential, there is nothing inevitable about this and, in practice, they often exist side by side.

However, as is also noted, as a concept and a discourse of international politics nation branding is relatively recent and can be dated to the 1990s, with this reflecting the emergence of economic logics underpinning nation branding practices. Thus, while recognising a longer history of practices of what we can term nation branding, chapter 2 focuses on accounting for the emergence of nation branding as a concept and discourse of international politics, which was initially framed predominately in terms of economic logics. In doing so, this chapter adopts a critical perspective in that it challenges what often appears as a sense of inevitability, even determinism, about the direction of travel leading to the emergence of 'brand states' from the 1990s onwards.

Specifically, chapter 2 considers how economic notions of nation branding have become increasingly taken for granted and naturalised, and it addresses the emergence of an industry and set of practices with which contemporary nation branding has become associated as both a consequence and cause of such a development. In making the argument it is important to note that this chapter is heavily indebted to the work of others. In particular, Melissa Aronczyk (2013) provides a much more developed book-length investigation and analysis of some of the themes discussed here. However, this chapter also makes several distinct points that provide an additional contribution to the excellent work of others. Moreover, it serves as a touchstone for those that follow in that, by outlining the core claims of the nation branding discourse as it emerged from the 1990s onwards, it sets out the terrain of later critique and critical reflection.

The discussion is organised into four sections, with the first pointing to significant changes in the underpinning constitutive discourses of international politics that began to emerge towards the end of the Cold War. These discourses were of a systemic nature and suggested that a fundamental transformation was underway that would have significant implications for the role of the state. Thus, if the underpinning structures and logics of international politics were changing, it was argued that states must respond in turn. Central to this was the idea of the necessary (even inevitable) transformation of 'territorial states' into 'competition states'. Framed as a question, the first section therefore asks, 'What are the key constitutive discourses underpinning many contemporary practices of nation branding?'

Today, claims about a transformation from geopolitical to economic logics towards the end of the Cold War have become so entrenched that they can sometimes appear to have been inexorable. The second section challenges this by highlighting the considerable role that various well-placed key actors and institutions played in constituting and cultivating a different geopolitical imagination, one that emphasised notions of transformative inevitability and the imperative that states adapt in turn. The second section is therefore concerned with 'how, and through what mechanisms, discourses of the competition state came to grab states' attention and become normalised'. Ultimately, it was these developments that paved the way for the emergence of nation branding as a concept later in the 1990s as well as the industry that has grown up around it.

Yet, while in part embedded within (and reproducing) these discourses and geopolitical imaginary, nation branding also possesses distinctive elements. To discuss these, the third section considers the question, 'What does it mean to speak of nation branding as a "knowledge brand"'? In this respect, the chapter discusses how nation branding (and the nation branding industry more particularly) has been dependent upon academics and consultants translating imaginaries of the competition state into policy paradigms concerned with how best to succeed in the world the economic imaginaries describe. In particular, the third section shows how such actors have been able to carve out space for a new economic field in which nation branding becomes a 'knowledge brand' that can be operationalised as a set of marketable policy ideas offering simple and user-friendly solutions to the problems it is presumed competition states now face.

The fourth and last section starts to consider what this has meant in practice, focusing on 'how and why culture and identity became central to understandings of competitiveness in nation branding discourse'. This gets to the crux of contemporary nation branding since nation branding ultimately assumes that culture and identity are now central to the ability of states to compete in a globalised economy. States, it is argued, need to be able to attract attention, and central to this is the development of an enticing 'competitive identity'. The full consequences of what this means for thinking about national culture and identity are discussed at length in chapter 3, whereas here it is simply noted how, in the process of subjecting them to market principles, national identity and culture inevitably become repackaged as products to be cultivated and deployed for instrumental and strategic purposes.

DISCOURSES

In this first section we consider how nation branding is often seen to raise questions about the underpinning constitutive discourses of international politics and their attendant logics and the extent to which nation branding entails a shift away from established geopolitical imaginaries. Before outlining such a development, embedded within this sentence are two concepts that bear unpacking: constitutive discourses and geopolitical imaginaries.

Regarding the first, a discursive orientation emphasises how knowledge about the world is always constituted through the language that we use to describe it. In other words, language does not passively reference a world out there but actively constructs and constitutes our experience of it, meaning that phenomena only become objects of knowledge through interpretative discursive practices (Guzzini 2000, 59; Searle 1995, 66–71). As Winch (1990, 15) puts it, 'Our idea of what belongs to the realm of reality is given for us in the language that we use. The concepts that we have settle for us the form of the experience that we have of the world'. Language, however, is always embedded within broader discursive structures and chains of meaning, and it is only in light of these that specific articulations become meaningful (Wæver 2002, 29; Tuathail and Agnew 1992, 193). It is these chains of meaning that constitute broader discourses about the nature of the world but where such discourses are, in turn, reliant on articulations to re-project them into the future. In this respect, discourses both organise and present us with our knowledge of the world; they shape the world that we see and animate our understanding of the key dynamics and processes that underpin it. Insofar as particular discourses come to structure meaning they can therefore have a delimiting effect on the sorts of claims that can be made in different contexts because they delimit what sorts of statements and actions will 'make sense' to those embedded within particular discursive contexts (Wæver 2002, 29–30).

At the same time, there is never only one discourse in play, although at points particular discourses may become hegemonic, crowding out other ways of apprehending the world and constituting what Foucault (1977) terms a 'regime of truth' that results in particular forms of knowledge and ways of seeing (and being in) the world becoming taken for granted (Lorenzini 2015; also Milliken 1999). For example, during the Cold War the hegemonic constitutive discourse of international relations entailed a realist emphasis on the international system as an anarchic and dangerous realm of self-help and zero-sum competition for resources and power, where conflict was an ever-present possibility. However, shifts in the discursive structure are always possible, particularly in the context of what Ringmar (1996, 83–5) terms 'formative moments', as a result of which established discourses and ways of thinking about the world may be challenged, with this creating space for the emergence of contending constitutive discourses. In particular, Finnemore and Sikkink (1998, 909; Barnett 1999, 10) suggest that 'world historical events' like wars or major depressions may lead to a search for new ideas and ways of understanding the world. In respect of nation branding, the end of the Cold War and the break-up of the Soviet Union can be seen as just such a formative moment.

The second concept that needs unpacking is geopolitical imaginaries, an idea that has close associations with critical geopolitics (Tuathail 1996; Agnew 2003). A geopolitical imaginary is here understood as a particular type of discourse that provides a more specific visual orientation for actors engaging with the world (Güney and Gökcan 2010, 23). In other words, geopolitical imaginaries entail translating a constitutive discourse into a particular spatial and temporal vision, one that typically incorporates an account of an actor's particular position in the world, the interests that derive from that, and that establishes expectations and a mental map for understanding the nature of one's environment that, in turn, provides a guide for how to read the current situation and act within it. To put it another way, constitutive discourses may potentially support a range of geopolitical imaginaries. For instance, the Cold War conception of a world divided into heavily armed implacable blocs locked in a precarious stand-off confronting the prospect of nuclear Armageddon is one geopolitical imaginary premised on a realist conception of international politics. However, Huntington's (1996) notion of the 'clash of civilizations' is also premised upon a realist-infused discourse about the underpinning logics of international politics but is inflected with a somewhat different geopolitical imagination, outlining as it does a different set of geopolitical actors and animating themes. Like constitutive discourses, geopolitical imaginaries are also likely to be contested and subject to transformation or replacement, particularly in the context of formative moments, at which point new imaginaries drawing upon different evocative metaphors will emerge.

As noted, then, the emergence of debates and practices of nation branding in the 1990s is typically associated with claims that the end of the Cold War crystallised a transformation in the underpinning constitutive discourses of international politics. In short, a geopolitical and realist-infused discourse and the attendant logics of great power confrontation it supported were increasingly challenged by an emergent constitutive discourse emphasising economic concerns and centred around the concept of globalisation. In particular, globalisation was presented as an irrepressible force transforming the contours of global politics and supporting a different set of geopolitical imaginaries. To quote Jansen (2012, 81):

> The end of the Cold War created a global geopolitical identity crisis, forcing nations on both sides of the historic divide to rethink their alliances and positioning in the world. The master narrative of 'globalization' was quickly instantiated in Western policy circles. Within this new narrative, 'market' was intended to replace 'war' as the foundational metaphor.

In the early 1990s, then, and with the break-up of the Soviet Union, a prevailing sense emerged that Western-centric conceptions of politics and economy were becoming predominant. Attendant with this was a growing sentiment that past conflicts and frames of reference could be left behind, with this most keenly encapsulated in Fukuyama's (1992) teleological claims about the 'End of History'. Framed in conceptual terms, the argument is essentially that 'Lockean' mind-sets and geopolitical imaginaries about the nature of international anarchy were increasingly superseding 'Hobbesian' preoccupations (Moisio 2008; Wendt 1999). Hobbesian imaginaries, for instance, characterise the world in terms of immutable geopolitical rivalries and conflict, where what counts is the need to defend borders and uphold, enhance, and expand sovereignty in the face of potentially threatening others. Indeed, in Hobbesian worlds national standing and status is typically connected to military capabilities and prowess and to one's relative position in the distribution of power (Larsen et al. 2014, 4–5). Indeed, in a Hobbesian world, military actions are typically seen as a test of a nation's virility, honour, and standing (Lebow 2008). By contrast, in a Lockean framing, the traditional concern with geopolitics and the martial spirit is downplayed, especially in relation to others also perceived to uphold Lockean values, which in the 1990s – aside from a few outliers – was assumed to be the general direction of travel. Instead of the Hobbesian emphasis on enmity, Lockean worlds are characterised by economic rivalries, with the claim being that the end of the Cold War signified how interstate competition was increasingly shifting away from an emphasis on war and the balance of power towards concerns over economic interdependence, trade, and market share, with states increasingly accepting a reconstitution of international order around globalisation and neoliberal modes of governance (Moisio 2008).

Given the focus, the aim here is not to assess the full extent to which such a transformation might be deemed as actually having occurred in any material sense (though see chapter 5) but, rather, to highlight the emergence and enabling effects of such a constitutive discourse. Particularly important in this regard is how such developments were (and still are) often presented as historically inevitable processes containing their own logics of success to which states must respond, distinct from those prevailing in the world of realist geopolitics (Fougner 2006, 179). For instance, one marker of such a transformation and how it has resulted in the normalisation of new modes of being is how the use of force within the club of OECD nations is now essentially rejected as outside the constitutive rules of the game and therefore only likely to undermine one's reputation and standing rather than to enhance it, as might be expected in a more Hobbesian setting.

However, in a context in which the underpinning rules of the game were perceived to be changing, and in which the emphasis was shifting towards economic globalisation with its promotion of deregulated markets, reduced barriers to trade, capital flows, and privatisation, the question then arose as to what this might mean for states. Specifically, a different geopolitical imaginary began to crystallise, one that now conceptualised world politics as a global marketplace within which states increasingly became viewed as akin to firms competing for investment and market share rather than for power, territory, and resources, and where what counts is the state's entrepreneurial capacities and attractiveness rather than its military strategic capabilities and acumen (Fougner 2006; Weidner 2011). The 'state as firm' metaphor therefore captured how, in a world of globalisation and the pervasive spread of neoliberal economics, states would now need to compete with each other on different grounds. In short, the imperatives of globalisation were now seen to be transforming the 'territorial state' of realist discourse into increasingly entrepreneurial 'competition states'. For instance, Cerny (1990) points out how states were no longer restricting their economic activities to promoting national champions in a bid to enhance exports but were increasingly becoming impelled to compete with each other to attract investments, in part because former national champions were increasingly transnationalising their operations and showing less loyalty to their nominal home states.

In this respect, Fougner (2006, 180) and Varga (2013, 449) chart a transformation of 'statesmen' into 'salesmen' and 'business actors', whose principal goal increasingly seemed to be that of selling 'the state as a location to globally footloose capital and firms', while Weidner (2011) highlights how states increasingly regard their component parts as assets and capital to be mobilised and maximised for the purpose of growing one's value. In a world of competition states, then, state leaders become reconceptualised as managers tasked with developing and deploying corporate strategies in the interests of facilitating industry and movements of global capital, as opposed to being political representatives leading peoples (Varga 2013, 448). Indeed, for Cerny (2010, 6) the underpinning logic of the competition state is now actually that of promoting further globalisation and global competition by 'prising open the nation-state to a globalising world', with the state increasingly operating in the service of the capitalist system, rather than any more traditional conception of the public good or *raison d'État*.

From the late 1980s onwards, this discourse became increasingly influential with a teleological tendency evident in claims that geopolitical calculation and the logic of conflict was being replaced by a new era of globalisation and a grammar of commerce (e.g., Luttwak 1990). However, as noted by Cowen and Smith (2009; also Agnew 2009), claims of a categorical shift from geopolitical to (geo)economic worlds can be overplayed. On the one hand, seen from a postcolonial perspective it entailed another case of 'geographical diffusionism' by assuming that developments in the capitalist core were equally applicable to the rest of the world (see Blaut 1993). But, as Cowen and Smith (2009, 24–5) note, even such a claim with respect to the capitalist core is oversimplified. In contrast, they suggest that (geo)economic forms are not replacing traditional geopolitical calculations in toto but are instead recasting them in light of market logics, the result being that 'geoeconomic calculation ... can never fully supplant geopolitics' (42). For instance, we see this in how traditional geopolitical practices like war and border control are increasingly permeated with neoliberal and market logics, not least evident in the growing role of private corporate actors in these spheres. However, this is also evident in the context of nation branding, with one of the core themes of later chapters being how many nation branding programmes remain deeply infused with significant geopolitical scripts. In this regard, nation branding does not so much transcend the field of geopolitics as become part of a (new) geopolitical imaginary fusing geopolitical and (geo)economic ways of understanding the world (see Browning and de Oliveira 2017a).

CONSTITUTIVE ACTORS

Oversimplified or not, claims about a transformation from geopolitical to economic logics became constitutively important, with nation branding ultimately just one part of the emergence of a broader hegemonic discourse that has sought to reshape states and international politics in terms of logics of capitalist competition. It is important to emphasise that there was nothing inevitable about this process, with the key question being how it was that discourses of the competition state came to grab the attention of states and other global elites and become normalised. Following Aronczyk (2013, 17), it is important to distinguish between globalisation as a set of material processes driving change and 'the power of globalization as a set of ideas and discourses used to *justify* national change' (emphasis added). In a similar vein, Sum and Jessop (2013, 268) emphasise how over the last thirty to forty years these economic imaginaries have come to have an important constitutive effect on how we perceive the nature of the world and the forms of subjectivity and behaviour that have come to be viewed as appropriate for acting within that world.

To account for this, they argue that these increasingly hegemonic discourses and imaginaries have been steadily normalised through the work of academics, consultants, politicians, and business leaders as part of their attempts to demarcate its core elements and distinguishing features (Sum and Jessop 2013, 279). Indeed, in a process reminiscent of Giddens's (1984, 20) conception of the 'double hermeneutic', in which scholarly concepts developed as a means of analysing the world can in turn come to have a constitutive impact on it, even critical academic reflections on the 'competition state' discourse can be seen as having further fed into such a reconceptualisation of the state. Aronczyk (2013, 38) outlines this process in more depth, in particular as it relates to nation branding. Specifically, she points to the emergence of a 'transnational promotional class' (TPC) that played a key role in promoting the idea of an inherent convergence of interests between private corporations and the nation-state, though it is important to recognise that the TPC was a 'loosely allied group of actors and institutions' sharing common goals rather than a clearly organised and self-constituted movement (see also Schwak 2018, 649).

As an example, Aronczyk (2013, 43–6) focuses in on the influential work of Michael Porter, a professor of business at Harvard University, who in 1990 published the book *The Competitive Advantage of Nations*, central to which was the argument that 'in a world of increasingly global competition, nations have become more, not less, important' (Porter 1990). Specifically, Porter argues that a nation's future prosperity would be dependent upon developing strategies at the level of the entire nation, rather than the corporation, and in particular by mobilising differences in national values, culture, economic structures, institutions, and histories, all of which, he suggested, can 'contribute to competitive success' but only if these are mobilised to facilitate continuous innovation. In other words, in a context of increasingly globalised markets and footloose capital Porter suggested that traditional economic notions of comparative advantage amongst nations, such as with regard to natural resource endowments, geography, labour, or physical capital, were becoming increasingly irrelevant, in part because the rise of knowledge-intensive over manufacturing work meant that the territorial specificity of such factors no longer held – that is, business could relocate almost anywhere. What mattered now were intellectual skills, know-how, mobility, and communications connected to new technologies (Aronczyk 2013, 44). Porter's conclusion was that, since most things could now be produced anywhere, it was not only companies that needed to continually innovate to compete but nations, too, needed to transform their approach to business. Rather than the traditional focus on using regulations to shape the actions of firms, the competitive advantage of nations would instead lie in 'adjusting the terms of the national environment to fit the key requirements of its key industries' (45). The role of government was therefore to make the country fit for business and industrial growth and to remove any impediments to this by creating an environment that would encourage firms to be innovative and dynamic. As Aronczyk (2013, 45–6) puts it, the state was to be reimagined as a

> facilitator of industry instead of a leader of populations …
> In this formulation, states were not subjects of governance but *objects of management*, and as such, required the expertise and

knowledge of management thinkers to function effectively. With competitiveness as the primary virtue, a virtue that governments had not previously considered in their active portfolios, the suggestion was that a new kind of knowledge and expertise was required for state administration, one that came from the worlds of marketing and management. (emphasis in original)

Amongst other aspects, Porter argued that national identity and character would also be important to success in this new competitive environment as it could help countries differentiate their offering and potentially be a marker of added value. The basic idea, of course, was highly resonant with established notions of the 'country-of-origin' effect. But, for this to work, identity and culture would need to be brought into the service of national production and made competitive. Identity and culture were therefore incorporated as *one part* of a broader emphasis on the need to make nations 'attractive' and 'competitive' (Aronczyk 2013, 47), something we come back to later in this chapter.

As this imaginary took hold, it is important to note that it was reproduced and further disseminated through other mechanisms. Particularly notable was the emergence and subsequent proliferation of benchmarking practices and indexes that sought to rank the relative competitiveness of countries and that, in doing so, (re)inscribed a competitive and hierarchical global imaginary. An early version of this may be found in the Global Competitiveness Reports of the European Management Fund (EMR), the first of which was published in 1979. These reports combined various statistical indicators of economic prosperity (e.g., GDP, balance of trade) with opinion polls conducted with business leaders and others about their willingness to invest in different countries (Aronczyk 2013, 49). Despite well-documented evidential flaws with benchmarking practices (e.g., Broome and Quirk 2015; Homolar 2015), such rankings nonetheless masquerade as offering a technocratic, scientific, and objective measure of the relative economic competitiveness/attractiveness of those countries ranked. Insofar as such rankings have a constitutive effect, they come not only to influence the investment decisions of different economic actors but also to create incentives for states to try to improve their ranking in the next report by undertaking reforms that respond to the selective criteria utilised in compiling such reports in the first place. In this way, benchmarking practices have great potential to normalise the discourses and imaginaries on which they are premised and, in this case, have played an important role in proliferating and normalising the very idea and rationale of the 'competition state'.

Come the late 1980s, the EMR had transformed into the World Economic Forum (WEF), whose annual Global Competitiveness Reports now rank countries globally, are eagerly reported by the press, and are referenced in government publications and statements, all of which further enhances their legitimacy and the influence of the constitutive discourses that underpin them. As Aronczyk (2013, 49, 52) puts it, the reports and the workshops, symposia, and media attention surrounding them are 'performatives, constituting the competitiveness they claim to measure'. Moreover, over the years they have become more complex in seeking to measure, evaluate, and rank different aspects of 'competitiveness' aside from brute economic indicators. This has included a growing emphasis on cultural factors like education, attitudes, values, motivation, with the aim being to turn each of these into a marker of economic value. In turn, other organisations have begun to develop their own competing benchmarks ranking competitiveness. These include the IMD World Competitiveness Centre, the Council on Competitiveness, and the Harvard Business School, along with numerous others produced by various consultancies and public relations firms specialising in developing services to help countries improve their competitiveness and standing. In other words, the very benchmarking of competitiveness has itself become a new opportunity for business (Schwak 2018, 649).

Overall, then, for those within the transnational promotional class identified by Aronczyk, the competition state offers a technocratic solution to the problem of economic globalisation, yet this is a 'problem' and way of looking at the world that these actors have themselves played a central role in constituting and popularising. Insofar as such an economic imaginary has become embedded, it has become the basis for targeted forms of action. In this respect, Sum and Jessop (2013) argue that the constitutive actors of Aronczyk's TPC have not only been crucial in producing such global economic imaginaries but also in transforming them into various policy paradigms concerned with how best to succeed in the world the imaginaries describe. Hence, we see various consultancies and public relations firms identifying business opportunities connected to helping states compete in this new market-oriented world in which competitiveness and attractiveness matter more than power and force. In short, apparent descriptions about the nature of the world have been 'translated into management/consultancy knowledge about how to "get the competitiveness right"' (299). The emergence of the nation branding industry and attendant consultancies specialising in this field from the 1990s onwards is one particular manifestation of such a development, and it is to this that we now turn.

NATION BRANDING AS 'KNOWLEDGE BRAND'

The emergence of nation branding as a concept is evidently connected to the proliferation of discourses of the competition state. However, while the concept and the industry that has developed around it is heavily indebted to this discourse, the two are not synonyms. Rather, when viewed through the lens of economic logics, nation branding can be understood as one particular way of responding to the proclaimed imperative of states to enhance their competitiveness. In other words, in seeking to make themselves more attractive states have various options available to them. For instance, they might place emphasis on gaining a competitive edge through initiating more enticing economic policies and conditions and engaging in various forms of structural adjustment. In contrast, nation branding foregrounds issues of culture and identity and, in particular, the need to rearticulate national identity in marketing and advertising terms (Kaneva 2012c, 115). Like most marketing scholarship, the nation branding industry 'accepts markets and competition as basic realities' and then 'seeks to identify modes of action that would improve the strategic positions of specific agents' (i.e., states). However, nation branding as it emerged as a discourse and object of consultancy practice from the late 1990s holds that it is not merely a luxury or potentially beneficial addition to other strategies; rather, it is a *necessity* for nations as they 'compete against each other in the global marketplace for scarce resources, such as tourists, investments, qualified workers, or political goodwill' (Kaneva 2016, 179; Anholt 2003; 2007b, 72; Dinnie 2008).

In other words, to even be able to compete in the global marketplace it is argued that nations need to cultivate nation brands that make their goods and services and the nation itself stand out. Underpinning this is the idea extrapolated from the literature on product branding that successful nation brands will add emotion and trust to national products insofar as they come to signify 'reliability', 'customer service', 'high technology', 'environmentalism', et cetera, thereby making the choices of potential consumers/customers/investors/migrants/tourists easier and potentially establishing brand loyalty (Anholt 2002a, 232–3; Olins 2002, 246). In turn, they may also contribute to the nation's soft power and political influence (van Ham 2008, 126, 129–30). The sense of imperative that underpins this discourse is evident in claims that any failure to successfully project a sense of national cultural specificity will likely entail a lack of visibility and recognition, which in turn is likely to translate into a loss of economic competitiveness. To lack a nation brand is therefore to risk remaining unseen and unknown and is considered by advocates to be fundamentally irresponsible. As van Ham (2008, 131) puts it, why would anyone invest in or visit an unknown country or pay any attention to its political or strategic demands? In short, 'if we have no clue what the country is about ... why should we care?' For this reason, Anholt (2009, 217) argues that, in a globalised world, the fundamental responsibility of any government must be to protect and pass on the nation's image and reputation intact – and preferably enhanced (see also Freire 2005). As noted by Anholt in the epigraph to this chapter, in the context of the contemporary 'attention economy' (Davenport and Beck 2001, 3), nation brands provide a 'license to trade'.

As outlined in chapter 1, amongst its advocates differences can be identified between more 'cosmetic' approaches to nation branding that prioritise marketing and communication strategies and more 'institutionalised' approaches that encourage a more systematic reorientation of national policy across sectors to reinforce nation branding messages, thereby integrating nation branding into the policy formulation process. However, irrespective of whichever approach is adopted (and many fall between the poles), advocates emphasise the need to educate and train state leaders in the need to think in terms of brand strategy, the idea being that nation branding needs to become an instinctual reflex of government. As such, Kaneva (2016, 179–80) argues that nation branding needs to be seen as being more than simply a practice of 'recommending pragmatic programs of image management' and is better understood as offering 'a philosophy of statecraft' informed by the scientific principles of marketing. As is pointed to below and in chapter 3, this philosophy in turn encourages a 'post-political' conception of nationhood because of how, in a nation branding world, national identity becomes increasingly subject to the 'expert knowledge' of highly paid branding consultants and less a matter of political contestation. However, insofar as the claims of nation branding consultants and experts have proliferated, they have also increasingly become accepted as common sense for nations making their way in the world.

In this respect, nation branding looks like a good example of what Sum and Jessop (2013) describe as a marketable 'knowledge brand', where claims about the nature of the world have become the basis for marketable consultancy interventions (for a similar point see Surowiec 2012, 125–6). They define a knowledge brand as

> a resonant hegemonic meaning-making device advanced in various ways by 'world-class' gurus-academics-consultants who claim unique knowledge of a relevant or strategic policy field and pragmatically translate this into (trans-)national policy symbols, recipes and toolkits that address policy problems and dilemmas and also appeal to pride, threats and anxieties about socio-economic restructuring and changes. (Sum and Jessop 2013, 305)

A knowledge brand therefore operates as a set of marketable policy ideas that are understood as offering 'simple, user-friendly, problem-oriented' solutions to common problems, anxieties, and dilemmas and that are assumed to be 'readily useable, saleable and transferable' largely irrespective of context. Much consultancy work, Sum and Jessop (2013, 301) note, essentially involves leveraging and trading in 'knowledge brands'.

As noted, nation branding itself looks like a particularly good example of a knowledge brand. For example, the archetypal guru-cum-academic consultant of nation branding is Simon Anholt, who first coined the concept in 1998 (Anholt 1998) and helped institutionalise it through writing a raft of policy papers and books,[1] and gave it enhanced academic credibility and endorsement through setting up the journal *Place Branding and Public Diplomacy*, with the first issue published in 2004. His subsequent client list soon extended to over fifty countries. In turn, other academics/consultants joined the fray, similarly re-theorising the nature of international politics and the role of the state precisely by drawing on economic imaginaries related to globalisation and the competition state, and academising and scientising this through publishing articles and handbooks. These included Wally Olins, former chairman of Wolff Olins branding consultancy and later of Saffron Brand Consultants; Keith Dinnie, the founder of Brand Horizons (www.brandhorizons.com) who also wrote a best-selling textbook on nation branding (Dinnie 2008); and Robert Govers, a co-editor of *Place Branding and Public Diplomacy*, an independent adviser to countries, and chairman of the International Place Branding Association (IPBA) (Saunders 2017, 51–2). Indeed, associations like the IPBA, research centres like 'Nation Branding' at the Hochschule Rheinmain in Wiesbaden, and online research/knowledge portals like *The Place Brand Observer* (https://placebrandobserver.com) have further supported the normalisation of a new industry into which a growing number of consultancies, beyond those already noted, have moved (Viktorin et al. 2018a, 9). The result of this has been the creation, institutionalisation, and legitimisation of an industry in which consultants propose largely generic solutions to governments that they proclaim will help them solve the problems their countries face as a result of globalisation.

The point here is that the need for the services provided by nation branding consultants needs to be actively cultivated. For this reason, 'branding experts and marketing gurus ... have a vested interest in telling peripheral and unbranded countries how obsolete they appear without a state brand of their own' (Metahaven 2008, 6). Or, as Ståhlberg and Bolin (2015) caustically note, nation branding consultants often need

> to work hard to convince people of the core ideas in the nation branding discourse; that we live in a world in which each nation has to take command of its own reputation; that tourists and investors have to be tricked into coming; that the domestic industry can only export if their products come from an attractive place; that the country is associated with 'wrong' things internationally, that is, that international media only report negative news or nothing at all; and – last but not least – that every other country does it.

And to be fair, nation branding consultants have been very persuasive in making the pitch. However, to make the case/sell, and further cement the establishment of nation branding as a knowledge brand, nation branding consultants have used a number of 'scientific' techniques, the most notable of which is comparative indexes, with this paralleling the benchmarking practices that have been central to promoting the broader underpinning discourse of the competition state. The best known of these is the Anholt Ipsos Nation Brands Index (formerly the Anholt-GFK Roper Nation Brands Index), which Simon Anholt initially set up in 2005 in collaboration with the German market research company GFK and the Roper Center for Public Opinion Research in the US (Saunders 2017, 51). The index itself seeks to measure and rank the reputation of fifty nations in respect of six areas of national competence: exports, governance, culture, people, tourism, and immigration and investment. It does this by conducting online interviews of one thousand people in each of twenty panel countries and, in this respect, is a survey of public opinion. For each country, the six assessed dimensions are captured within a 'Nation Brand Hexagon', with this designed to provide a clear visualisation of the relative strength of different aspects of the overall brand and, in turn, to suggest those areas in which more work needs to be done (see https://www.ipsos.com/sites/default/files/anholt-ipsos-nation-brands-index.pdf). The suggestion, therefore, is that strong and successful brands need to elicit considerable consistency across all six areas (see figure 2.1) (Anholt 2009, 215). Anholt's hexagonal model has become prominent and persuasive and has come to influence not only how many countries view their 'brand' but also first getting them to take matters of brand performance and standing seriously. It is therefore not unusual to find policy-makers invoking the framings of the hexagonal model and to see countries including them as reference points in their nation branding programme documents. For instance, as stated by Zimbabwe's deputy prime minister Arthur Mutambara, it is important to get the 'hexagon of branding' right, 'you must be known well in those six areas of branding, and they must interact and feed into one another' (quoted in Brand Africa 2011, 15).

However, following Anholt's intervention other companies soon began producing their own indexes. Amongst others, these include the FutureBrand Country Brand Index, which uses the input of industry professionals with respect to their perception of the image management of different countries, and EastWest Communications Global Index 200, which, although short-lived (2008–11), ranked two hundred countries and territories based on how they are described in major media (https://eastwestcoms.com/global-indexes) (Beaumont and Towns 2021; Cull 2019, 131). Another is Bloom Consulting's Country Brand Ranking, which seeks to measure the impact of international perceptions and reputation on a country brand over time but which

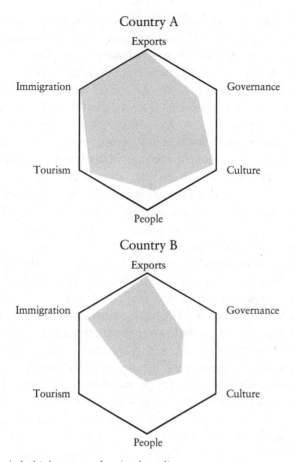

Figure 2.1 Anholt's hexagon of nation branding

also produces a Digital Country Index that measures the total number of searches performed by people globally towards different countries and which it is assumed is an indicator of a country's 'brand appeal' (https://www.bloom-consulting.com/en/country-brand-ranking).

Several things might be noted about such indexes. The first is the assumption that the annual accumulation of data will both increase their reliability and make it possible to measure the impact of nation branding campaigns over time (Jansen 2012, 94n2). In this respect, the production of indexes provides another way of legitimising the development of the nation branding industry by incentivising states to stay in the game. A second point, however, is that one of the more interesting things about Anholt's index is that, while he initially expected to find a lot of volatility year on year, with some states rising and others falling in response to coordinated branding campaigns, or through hosting major sporting events, or (more negatively) as a result of scandals, wars, et cetera, in practice little movement was discernible and national reputations seemed rather stable (Araratyan 2015). For instance, as Cull (2019, 130) notes, despite hosting the Olympics in 2012 and investing heavily in the GREAT campaign, the United Kingdom's ranking barely changed, with Anholt instead concluding that already well-known countries like the UK may actually need to occasionally host such events precisely in order to maintain their high ranking. However, in this regard it is notable that the methodologies behind some of the other nation branding indexes introduce scope for much more volatility, particularly, for instance, when they focus on internet searches, media treatment, or professionals' perceptions of image management as opposed to peoples' more general perceptions of different countries' reputations and brands. Indeed, as Aronczyk (2013, 71) notes, one thing that marks out most nation branding indexes from those like the Global Competitiveness Reports of the World Economic Forum is that, while the latter started out by drawing mainly on quantitative economic and statistical data (so-called 'hard facts') and have only more recently come to include qualitative indicators, nation branding indexes are overwhelming constructed through surveys and other mechanisms designed to assess international opinion (so-called 'soft facts). Of course, from an industry perspective more volatile measures may help sell the value of nation branding by supporting the idea that concerted nation branding programmes can have a discernible effect (Cull 2019, 131–2).

A third point is to reiterate the constitutive process at play, with indexes creating league tables that claim to assess the brand value and attractiveness of each country relative to each other (but also existing as a proxy for judging the success of nation branding programmes). By looking at the tables, states can see how well they are doing in the global branding competition. Such benchmarks therefore establish the criteria upon which national reputations are to be calculated and judged, and which, in turn, create incentives for states to respond by targeting precisely these criteria in order to enhance their position. That these indexes are taken seriously is evident in how different countries' nation branding programmes and discussion papers almost invariably include reference to and reproduce these branding tables as a basis upon which the nation's international image, reputation, and overall competitiveness is to be judged.

Fourth, though, it is also important to note that nation branding indexes do not simply provide relative assessments of the strength of different nation brands but have also become co-opted as part of the branding process itself, especially by those nations that perform well in them. In other words, a strong ranking is not just taken as a sign of a competitive brand but can itself be mobilised to reinforce just such an impression amongst target audiences through emphasising high benchmarking performance in branding messages. A good example of this was provided by South Korea when, in 2009, the Presidential Council on Nation Branding of South Korea introduced its very own nation branding index that ranked the country higher than did any other indexes, with its performance improving in subsequent years (Cull 2019, 133).

Finally, it is also important to recognise that the constitution of nation branding as a knowledge brand has also been supported by historical circumstances and where the consequences of the end of the Cold War also provide a context for seeing such knowledge branding in action. In this respect, the usual way of outlining the recent history of nation branding is to reflect on the growing influence of neoliberal economics in key Western countries in the 1980s and how these resulted in some early efforts of state rebranding (not least in post-Franco Spain). Key mention, however, is normally reserved for Mark Leonard's (1997) influential booklet, *Britain TM: Renewing Our Identity*, which was published shortly after the election of the New Labour government under Tony Blair – a party that had itself undergone a significant rebrand through emphasising its embrace of free market principles and downgrading of socialist commitments – and which called for the government to actively overhaul Britain's flagging and staid identity (Cull 2019, 128). In turn, this became the basis for the 'Cool Britannia' campaign that focused on British accomplishments in the realms of music, media, and the arts as a means of appealing to foreign audiences while simultaneously rejuvenating a sense of national pride. Although not the first, the significance of the British campaign is precisely that it was a concerted campaign undertaken by a major Western country and that, as such, garnered a lot of international attention, in turn helping to spread the discourse of nation branding (Viktorin et al. 2018a, 7–8).

However, the experience of countries in Eastern Europe in the early 2000s is also illustrative insofar as the collapse of the Soviet Union created an environment ripe for new knowledge and an opportunity for a new industry that helped further sediment nation branding as a legitimate and necessary practice of statehood. Specifically, as an emergent knowledge brand, nation branding resonated with a historical moment for countries undergoing a process labelled at the time as 'transition', where transition was understood as a linear process of 'transformation from state command economies to free market ones, and from authoritarian one-party systems to liberal democracies' (Kaneva 2012b, 6). As Kaneva notes, within the region the state of 'transition' carried emotional and psychological resonance in that it came to signify a state not only of 'indeterminacy between the communist past and the post-communist future' but also of 'inadequacy' and the need to escape a 'shameful' identity and past for something more desirable (6–7). In the context of such instability and anxieties, Kaneva (2012b, 7–8, 15) argues that nation branding arrived with the promise of offering a way out of the identity crisis through its ability to provide a different 'discursive technology' for rethinking the nation and the future, while simultaneously enabling post-communist elites to reclaim legitimacy by fusing a resurgent nationalism with market ideology (see also Surowiec 2012, 129–30). Throughout the early 2000s almost all East European countries initiated nation branding programmes, with this also reflecting a more general deference to the West's 'superior knowledge', which, at the time, was pervasive.

On the other side, of course, for Western elites, Eastern Europe was seen as both a problem and an opportunity, with governments and Western-backed international organisations like the International Monetary Fund and World Bank deploying consultants to the region to offer (typically neoliberal) economic and political cures. Amongst these were nation branding consultants with a pre-packaged knowledge brand on offer for 'new' and unknown nations who were not only facing the challenge of transitioning into the neoliberal global market but 'also needed to be re-introduced to the world' now that they had emerged out of the shadow of the Soviet Union (Jansen 2012, 81; Kaneva 2012b, 8). Indeed, in a context in which local knowledge and ways of being had been largely delegitimised, Jansen (2012, 93) argues that it is unsurprising that the 'totalizing logic, and fear tactics of nation branders have successfully pressured nations of the former Soviet

Union – who did not want to be left behind – to succumb to Anholt's immutable law' about the imperatives of nation branding in a globalised economy.

In this respect, Eastern Europe became something of a proving ground for Western-based nation branding consultants, with this also being promoted by Western governments. For example, in Bulgaria the British Council funded a project titled Branding Bulgaria (2001–04), with such initiatives replicated by other NGOs, and where funds were used to introduce Western branding consultants to potential customers with this driven by the idea of sharing Western experience, expertise, and knowledge with respect to nation branding (Kaneva 2012c, 103–4). In Poland, for instance, Surowiec (2012, 135–6) points to how between 2003 and 2007 a team from the London-based Saffron branding consultancy, led by Wally Olins, first undertook what can only be described as an unsatisfactory 'audit' of national and international perceptions/stereotypes about Poland that was essentially set up to sell a problem about the country's nation brand to Polish leaders: 'the lack of recognition of Poland overseas'. This was then translated into a report titled *A Brand for Poland – Advancing Poland's National Identity*, which offered a nation branding-focused solution. This is an archetypal illustration of how Sum and Jessop suggest knowledge brands work, but it is the stock-in-trade practice of nation branding consultants in almost every case.

COMPETITIVE IDENTITY

Central to nation branding as a knowledge brand, and what differentiates it from broader discourses of globalisation and the competition state, is, of course, its focus on matters of identity and culture as the key to national competitiveness. In other words, while benchmarks like that of the World Economic Forum's Global Competitiveness Index have increasingly come to incorporate a cultural/identity component, thereby recognising the benefits of cultivating an appealing image of the nation-state in order to entice investment, the policy advice and recommendations of the WEF and other key international organisations (e.g., World Bank, IMF, OECD, WTO, etc.) also continues to emphasise the importance of other variables of competitiveness and comparative advantage. Identity/culture therefore appears as just one variable amongst others that affect a state's ability to make it in a globalised market-oriented world. In contrast, prevailing discourses of nation branding, propagated especially from within the industry, suggest identity/culture is *the* core underpinning variable of national competitiveness. As Aronczyk (2013, 53, 72) puts it, the difference can be seen in that, while organisations like the WEF emphasise the competitive *advantage* of nations, the nation branding industry is more interested in emphasising the competitive *identity* of nations.[2]

As indicated earlier in this chapter, underpinning this is the belief that, in a world of globalised markets, without a strong brand, states are 'doomed to fail'. As Anholt (quoted in Sussman 2012, 30) puts it, again invoking the state-as-firm metaphor, 'Countries have to play the market rules just as companies do, like it or not'. For consultants like Anholt – who also claims that branding accounts for up to a third of all global wealth (cited in Jansen 2008, 125; Sussman 2012, 31) – in a context of global capitalism in which brands rule, the need for states to cultivate competitive national brands is no longer an option but a fundamental requirement (Jansen 2012, 92–3). To the extent to which state leaders have come to accept this market-framed imaginary of the international system, and thereby to see a need to operate in terms of market logics, practices of nation branding are not only normalised but deemed essential in that a strong brand becomes tied to improving the economy and therefore also essential for addressing other social problems (Kaneva 2012c, 114–15; Volčič 2012, 147). Indicative of the pervasive influence of this discourse is that, today, there are very few states that do not engage in some kind of 'structured national-image promotion on the global stage', even if this is not always framed explicitly through official nation branding programmes (Saunders 2017, 46).

However, where such programmes do exist the pervasiveness of viewing national identity and culture as conferring a possible competitive edge is evident in the processes through which nation brands are curated and where these typically rely on a number of largely set mechanisms (or tools of the trade). For instance, while the precise formulation may vary in each individual case, typically domestic (and often also international) nation branding and marketing consultants are hired and committees created comprised of government ministers, business leaders, and cultural representatives, which together are tasked with formulating and implementing the brand. To engage stakeholders in various fields, at the more 'cosmetic' end of the spectrum slogans, symbols/logos, and straplines are created to identify the nation in different contexts, while 'toolkits' or sets of online and digital resources are developed, which stakeholders are encouraged to use and adapt for their purposes (for an overview of the process see Saunders 2017, 56–60). More particularly, it has become common to refer to branding committees as 'teams', while on occasion nation branding programmes can result in the nation itself being framed in this way, as in 'Team Finland', a metaphor that further reaffirms the reconceptualisation of national identity in terms of competitive identity (Prime Minister's Office 2012).

Of course, the brand itself needs to stand out and be competitive, and while more is said about this in chapter 3, the emphasis is inevitably on trying to package national identity in a way that is transnationally appealing, valuable, and attractive to others (and potentially also to citizens). As Anholt (2007b, 73) notes, 'Most countries, if they look hard enough, will find something that is theirs, and inherently competitive'. There are two things we might note about this. The first is how, when driven by underpinning economic logics and discourses of the competition state, the 'something' that is to be found cannot be just anything but needs to be an aspect of national identity and culture that can be framed in such a way that it corresponds to market logics (see chapter 3). To this extent, Turner (2016, 21–2) sees nation branding precisely as a process of subjecting nationalism to market dynamics in a form of what Volčič and Andrejevic (2011; 2016b) call 'commercial nationalism', where 'the nation, the brand, and the market all merge into each other'. To be clear, it is important to reaffirm that this claim can be overplayed, especially since nation branding, as highlighted in subsequent chapters, is not in each and every case driven solely (or even mainly) by economic logics and can also, for example, be valued for its potential contribution to a state's 'soft power' ability to shape political agendas, although this itself still also rests on the idea that broader systemic changes have entailed significant consequences for how states might best pursue their strategic goals. Yet, when economic logics is at play – as it typically is in the presentational framings of consultants – market-driven rationales do feature prominently.

This leads to the second point, which is that insofar as nation branding values national identity and culture for their ability to be mobilised in the service of turning a profit, they are inevitably at risk of being treated in a wholly instrumentalised fashion, as something that can be manipulated and packaged in whichever way is deemed most profitable. In this respect, branding consultants typically depict national identity and culture as 'fixed assets' (e.g., Anholt 2008b, 34) to be deployed in gaining economic and status benefits. Thus, Gary Harwood of the marketing services company HKLM argues that 'nation branding ... is no different from any other kind of branding' (quoted in Markessinis 2009). Here, identity and culture are viewed as little different to any other product or form of intellectual property (Jansen 2008, 121). For instance, according to the World Intellectual Property Organisation, 'every country has a culture, a heritage, resources, natural beauty, and internal qualities that can be identified and defined, highlighted and captured, in a nation-branding initiative which is both pleasing and economically effective' (quoted in Aronczyk 2008, 45).

In chapter 3 the consequences of thinking about national identity and culture in this way are unpacked and critically reflected upon; suffice it to note for now that the commodification and instrumentalisation of identity/culture and its management and curation through committee is not always welcomed and can foster a sense of alienation and disenfranchisement amongst citizens. As Saunders (2017, 46) rightly suggests, it is worth reflecting on what might be lost when national identity and culture are 'sacrifice[d] ... on the altar of marketization' and, in particular, the extent to which it might diminish and devalue 'what it actually means to be a nation'. What is evident in this discussion, though, is that while nation branding consultants are apt to see nation branding as simply a (necessary) (apolitical) tool to be mastered by experts and states seeking to survive in a globalised market-driven world (Kaneva 2012c, 113–14), when framed through economic logics and discourses of the competition state, nation branding actually becomes part of a broader ideological fetishisation of market logics (Surowiec 2012, 137).

CONCLUSION

The focus of this chapter is on accounting for the emergence of nation branding as a concept and discourse of international politics. It argues that this has been fundamentally tied to the emergence of new constitutive discourses from the end of the Cold War reframing the underpinning dynamics of international politics in terms of economic logics of globalisation centred on the inevitable spread of market capitalism to all corners of the world. Insofar as this constitutive discourse has become pervasive and dominant it has had a delimiting effect on how the world is understood, in terms of both the key dynamics animating such a world and the types of claims and subject positions that can be legitimately conceived or even articulated. In turn, this discursive shift has supported the emergence of new geopolitical imaginaries. Specifically, this chapter highlights how globalisation came to be seen to entail fundamental implications for the role of the state, with the traditional Hobbesian 'territorial state' now recast as an emergent Lockean 'competition state'. Instead of states being locked in a realm of inevitable war and conflict, they were increasingly re-envisioned as akin to firms competing for market share.

However, the chapter also argues that there was nothing inevitable about this. Although globalisation can appear to be an irrepressible force, the point is to recognise the role of particular actors (consultants, well-placed academics, key international organisations) in presenting it as such and convincing states and other global elites of the necessity for states to transform themselves in response. In this respect, notions of the 'competition state' were performative, serving to *justify* national changes, as much as they were descriptive (Aronczyk 2013, 17), something clearly evident in the mobilisation of benchmarking indexes explicitly designed to identify those performing well and those performing less well, thereby marking out the 'fit' (winners) from the 'weak' (losers). Evidently, one of the attractions for state leaders was that, at a time when others were arguing globalisation signalled the impending irrelevance or even death of the state (Ohmae 1995), geopolitical imaginaries of the competition state placed the state at the heart of national competitiveness. But to do this, states needed to transform and rethink their role and function, primarily in terms of making the state fit for business in a context of unbridled capitalist competition for footloose capital and increasingly transnational firms. States, it is argued, needed to become attractive and competitive to command attention and entice investors, and where identity/culture was seen as a possible marker of added value to be emphasised.

Nation branding as a concept and practice can be seen as one response to these developments. Specifically, nation branding has been presented as a (necessary) solution to the challenges faced by states confronted by the 'realities' of globalisation, with the argument being that to make their goods and services stand out, states need to cultivate attractive nation brands. In this respect, nation branding is highly resonant of a 'knowledge brand' (Sum and Jessop 2013), where claims about the nature of the world have become the basis for marketable consultancy interventions. This chapter therefore highlights the emergence and role of self-styled nation branding consultants in developing and propagating this knowledge brand and mobilising 'scientific' techniques (benchmarks, journals, research centres, etc.) to foreground the role of nation brands as a marker of international competitiveness. The success of such practices is evident in the normalisation and proliferation of nation branding around the world such that Kaneva (2016, 179–80) argues it has become nothing short of a 'philosophy of statecraft'. However, the discussion also notes that the successful emergence of nation branding as a marketable knowledge brand, and the industry that has grown up around it, also owes much to historical circumstance and the formative moment of the end of the Cold War, which, in Eastern Europe and the former Soviet Union, had the effect of delegitimising local knowledge and providing a unique opportunity for nation branding consultants with a pre-packaged knowledge brand for states undergoing 'transition'.

Last, this chapter reiterates that what distinguishes much contemporary nation branding (and certainly the nation branding industry) from broader conceptions of the competition state is its foregrounding of identity and culture as the key to competitiveness. In other words, for its advocates nation branding is not just a useful supplement but, in a globalised, media-, and image-saturated world, it is also a fundamental necessity of contemporary statecraft. As seen, the choice is presented in typically stark terms as one of 'brand or fail'. In this process, though, identity and culture become prized for their competitive potential rather than for any other intrinsic value they may hold. From a nation branding perspective, identity/culture is therefore to be crystallised into a brand that corresponds to market logics and as a result of which it is treated in highly instrumentalised terms. However, as Banet-Weiser (2012, 4–5) points out, branding entails more than simply a process of commodification or an economic strategy that seeks to commercialise 'something that was not previously thought of as a product'. Branding, she notes, also 'impacts the way we understand who we are, how we organize ourselves in the world, what stories we tell ourselves about ourselves'. In other words, branding has an emotional and affective component that makes it a cultural as much as an economic/commercial activity. This paves the way to the next chapter, in which the relationship between nation branding and identity/community is explored in more detail.

3

Anxious States

There is in reality nothing new about national branding, except the word 'brand' and the techniques that are now used, which derive from mainstream marketing and branding techniques.

Nation branding consultant Wally Olins (2005, 170)

For many, nation branding represents a profaning of the sacred idea of national identity. Its use is premised on the identification of a country by calculations of its most competitive image, not what its own people regard as the useful pursuits of their state.

Gerald Sussman (2012, 42)

It will feel really good to be a Finn.

Country Brand Report (2010, 37)

As suggested in chapter 2, quotidian understandings of nation branding are prone to emphasise its economic dimensions, the focus being on the extent to which in a world of competition states an attractive nation brand framed around the cultivation of a sufficiently 'competitive identity' is increasingly fundamental if states are to secure and entice international investment, (skilled) workers, international students, tourists, et cetera. There are two things to note about this. The first is the justification and evaluation of nation branding in terms of its ability to respond to emerging economic imperatives associated with globalisation. The second is the implied instrumentalist and strategic approach to national identity and culture that developing a nation brand seems to imply. Insofar as it entails subordinating the state to logics of capitalism while simultaneously depicting national identity as little more than a strategic resource, nation branding often raises hackles. However, such a framing is also limiting. For instance, it fails to recognise how, in practice, nation branding is not solely subservient to, or undertaken solely in line with, economic imperatives. As explored in later chapters, nation branding is also often linked to concerns of geopolitics and soft power. Yet nation branding's relationship with (national) identity is also much more complicated than is often recognised. The issue for this chapter is therefore to explore the complex ways in which nation branding is bound up with ideational issues, central to which are questions of identity and community. Thus, whereas the previous chapter emphasises nation branding as an externally oriented activity, this chapter focuses on its implications at the level of the nation.

The chapter addresses four issues, with the first two sections re-theorising nation branding by drawing on and developing links between literatures on ontological security, status seeking, and recognition dynamics. The value of these literatures for thinking about nation branding lies in how they direct attention towards the centrality of coping with anxiety as a driver of action. For instance, in chapter 2 it is already noted how the end of the Cold War was experienced throughout much of Eastern Europe and the post-Soviet space as a source of anxiety, with such anxiety connected not only to feelings of stigmatisation, low status, and lack of recognition but also to the denigration of local forms of knowledge. In this context, nation branding was perceived as offering a way out of the pervading sense of identity crisis and anxiety through the promise of a new ontological grounding. Yet, to sell their wares, nation branding consultants actively played on extant anxieties through the pitch of 'brand or die'. These sections therefore consider the relationship between nation branding, anxiety, and ontological security and ask the question: 'To what extent is nation branding a response to ontological anxieties and a form of ontological security seeking?' In addressing this question we consider the needs both of the nation-state and of its citizens.

Building from this, section three interrogates the relationship between nation branding and nation building. The distinction between nation branding and national identity/nation building is addressed briefly in chapter 1, where it is argued that, while they are sometimes viewed by advocates (not least by consultants like Wally Olins – see epigraph above) as rhetorically and functionally equivalent, there are good reasons to treat them as distinct, not least because, while nation building is concerned with nations as *imagined* communities, nation branding is more interested in them as *imaged* communities (Clerc and

Glover 2015). Yet, while critics are often excoriating about the nation building claims of nation branding consultants,[1] it is also the case that, while they are not synonymous with each other, nation branding does sometimes become explicitly integrated as part of nation building projects, while at other times it operates in opposition to them. Moreover, when nation branding and nation building do align it is important to consider whether nation branding may actually be transforming the bases upon which national identities are constituted. For instance, contemporary practices of nation branding may be shifting the grounds on which nations become a source of ontological security for their citizens, while many contemporary practices of nation branding also pose interesting questions about the role traditionally assigned to difference and (radicalised) otherness in the constitution of national identity.

Section four pushes this discussion further by considering what nation branding does to national identity and, more specifically, what it might mean for the constitution of national community, subjectivity, and politics. In this respect, the commodification and instrumentalism embedded in nation branding's treatment of identity and culture is something that particularly concerns critics. However, while these concerns are real and will be explored, it is important to consider whether such a process also entails implications for the constitution of subjectivity by affecting the relationship between citizenship and national identity at the domestic level. Drawing on work on 'consumer nationalism' it therefore considers how, in some contexts, nation branding may challenge claims about the inherently alienating effects of capitalism that are often levelled against it. A key aspect of this is how much contemporary nation branding seeks to reframe national identities in line with market preferences, with a particular emphasis on nations (and their citizens) as entrepreneurial subjects. In turn, it is argued that questions also emerge with respect to how inclusive and democratic the treatment of national identity is when subject to practices of nation branding.

The last section explores what nation branding may mean for the actual practice of citizenship. It is often argued that nation branding operates as a form of governmentality that seeks to discipline citizens to abide by the performative behavioural requirements of the brand, that is, to view themselves as 'brand carriers' and 'live the brand'. In this respect, nation branding sometimes operates as a form of banal nationalism (Billig 1995), though such claims can be overplayed. In particular, it is important to consider not only how nation branding may generate dissent but also the potentials that exist within nation branding to co-opt and/or tame such dissent for nation branding purposes. The question driving this section is, therefore: 'To what extent is nation branding a form of governmentality disciplining acceptable forms of citizenship through practices of banal nationalism?'

NATION BRANDING, ANXIETY, AND ONTOLOGICAL SECURITY

As indicated, as a discourse and as a 'knowledge brand' of consultancy practice nation branding is intriguingly bound up with a politics of anxiety, seeking to cultivate anxiety while simultaneously offering a response to it. It cultivates anxiety in several ways. First, insofar as it is embedded in discourses of globalisation and competitiveness it suggests that states are always in danger of losing their competitive edge and of failing and being neglected/surpassed. Consultants therefore suggest that states lacking a brand (or with a weak brand) will lack visibility, will remain unknown, and therefore will fail to secure the attention needed to succeed (van Ham 2008, 131). In contrast, a (strong) nation brand is depicted as a 'license to trade' (Anholt quoted in Aronczyk 2013, 70). This is a key point of chapter 2, where nation branding discourse plays to and cultivates anxieties that the state will not be (or is insufficiently) competitive. Second, it also plays on desires for status and recognition, that states be recognised as distinct (successful, worthy) subjects, playing particular roles. Thus, we have also seen how across Eastern Europe and the post-Soviet space the period of post-Cold War 'transition' was marked by feelings of shame and inadequacy with respect to self-identity, but where such anxieties were also actively fostered by nation branding consultants (Kaneva 2012b, 7; Surowiec 2012). And third, anxieties are also fostered by the tools of the craft, most notably the use of benchmarking indexes that add a sense of precarity and warn against complacency insofar as states are seen to be rising/falling on an annual basis. However, on the other hand, nation branding also offers a response through the adoption of nation branding strategies to salve such anxieties and secure the visibility, recognition, and status desired, with this, in turn, potentially bolstering collective self-esteem. Of course, as a discourse nation branding suggests that this is necessarily an ongoing process; nations that rest on their laurels, that fail to cultivate their reputations, images, and identities, will always be at risk of becoming uncompetitive and being ignored. Nation branding therefore requires constant and sustained attention.

Evidently, then, and despite how it is often presented, nation branding is not a purely strategic, rational, or instrumental activity but is bound up with psychological and affective dynamics. To understand the activating mechanisms at play therefore requires drawing on theoretical perspectives specifically attuned to analysing the role anxiety plays in the constitution of subjectivity. This section therefore engages the developing literature on ontological security in international relations, with the next section linking this to debates about status-seeking and recognition dynamics.

Originally coined by the psychiatrist R.D. Laing (1959/2010), in more recent years, ontological security – which can broadly be understood as the 'security of being' – has drawn increasing attention across the humanities and social sciences where it has been most influentially popularised by the sociologist Anthony Giddens (1991). Although it can be understood and theorised in different ways (see Kinnvall and Mitzen 2018 for an overview), at the heart of work on ontological security is a concern with subjects' ability to 'go on' with their everyday lives in the face of potentially debilitating anxieties inherent to everyday life (Giddens 1991, 35). Of course, anxiety can come in different forms and manifest different levels of intensity, but it also needs to be understood as a fundamental condition of existence. For instance, for Kierkegaard anxiety is the flipside to human freedom, where anxiety always attends to our ability to choose one path or another. Indeed, in this sense, anxiety is often a productive force driving us on (May 1977, 34–6; Kierkegaard 1980).

Sometimes, though, anxieties can be experienced as overwhelming, with psychologists distinguishing between 'normal' and more 'neurotic' forms or experiences of anxiety, and where the latter can be a highly pathological and debilitating condition (Gustafsson and Krickel-Choi 2020; May 1977, 193–200). In many respects, this corresponds to the distinction drawn by Laing between *ontologically secure* and *ontologically insecure* subjects. For Laing (1959/2010, 41–2), ontologically secure subjects experience their being 'as real, alive, whole; as differentiated from the rest of the world ... so clearly that his [sic] identity and autonomy are never in question'. In contrast, ontologically insecure subjects will experience their 'identity as always in question', may lack a sense of their own temporal continuity and cohesiveness, and may experience a genuine feeling of dread at the prospect of 'losing the self' that can leave them petrified and feeling overwhelmed, fractured, and unable to act (Laing 1959/2010, 41–9; Rossdale 2015, 371).

As a psychiatrist, Laing was primarily interested in patients suffering from deeply pathological psychological conditions like schizophrenia, suggesting that feelings of ontological insecurity are relatively rare. However, as the concept has been rendered across disciplines it has also been recognised that experiences of ontological insecurity are more widespread. This is particularly the case with respect to Giddens's more sociological reading of the concept,[2] where he depicts subjects as inhabiting a tenuous social world of day-to-day interaction and discourse on the other side of which 'chaos lurks', a chaos 'not just of disorganisation, but the loss of a sense of the very reality of things and of other persons' (Giddens 1991, 36). Such anxieties, though, can take different forms. For instance, the theologian Paul Tillich (2014, 39–49) distinguishes between *anxieties of fate and death*, which are connected to our inherent awareness of the terminal fragility of our lives; *anxieties of emptiness and meaninglessness*, which relate to our ability to provide our lives with a sense of purpose, direction, and cosmological meaning; and *anxieties of guilt and condemnation*, which emerge whenever subjects question whether they are living up to their own self-concepts or when they feel they may have gone astray, at which point feelings of shame may emerge (see also Rumelili 2015b, 12)

As discussed shortly, such anxieties are not just limited to individuals but can also be experienced by collective subjects, including states and nations. Before this, though, it is important to note that the animating question for ontological security scholars is how it is that subjects manage such anxieties, with this enabling them to 'go on' with everyday life. Various strategies are available, though central to all of them is how they help subjects establish a sense of stability and order about the nature of their world and, in doing so, 'bracket out' and set aside existential questions about the nature of existence. Most significant, however, is the need of subjects to develop routinised biographical narratives of self-identity. Such narratives not only establish a sense of self-being but also, in doing so, map out the nature of the subject's salient environment, locate the subject in relation to significant others, and thereby provide a way of ordering and understanding everyday events, interactions, and activities (Giddens 1991, 39, 54; Kinnvall 2004, 746; Steele 2008, 10–12). Insofar as subjects feel a sense of ontological security, it is often argued that this is because they are able to maintain a sense of integrity and biographical continuity, with this often being dependent on their ability to develop routines reaffirming such biographical claims. In contrast, it is argued that ontological anxieties are liable to kick in whenever subjects' feel that their sense of self-identity is being questioned or in trouble (Mitzen 2006; Rumelili 2015b).

The suggestion, therefore, is that once established subjects will often feel impelled to defend claims to self-identity to keep them going. For instance, within international relations ontological security has been used to provide alternative explanations to several key phenomena. For example, rather than seeing security dilemmas as resulting from the inherent uncertainties about others' intentions generated by the nature of international anarchy, Mitzen (2006) argues they are better explained in terms of how their endurance also perpetuates and reinforces mutually exclusive claims to identity. The challenge of overcoming security dilemmas is therefore less a concern with 'physical security' – which would actually be enhanced – than it is with how ending them requires addressing key ontological questions about self-identity, the identity of the other, and cosmological questions about the (unfolding) nature of global politics. Thus, while physical security obviously matters in international politics, various studies show that often the desire to 'maintain consistent self-concepts' matters more (Steele 2008, 2–3; see also Rumelili 2015a). Indeed, this tendency of states to try to uphold established biographical narratives of self-identity, and therefore also a sense of cognitive ordering, is alluded to at the very beginning of this book in respect of the UK government's post-Brexit referendum attempts to (re)brand the country as 'Global Britain', a slogan clearly conjuring up and playing on established conceptions of self-identity but that can be seen as precisely an attempt to respond to deeply felt anxieties then manifest within government (as well as throughout much of society) that Brexit would leave Britain not only diminished but also no longer the country that many Britons have grown up thinking it is (see Browning 2018).[3]

As highlighted by these examples, in the face of emerging anxieties and in their attempts to secure their sense of ontological security subjects can end up adopting an overly rigid approach to their identities, seeking to protect them at all costs (May 1977, 43), something that Giddens (1991, 40–1) argues can also leave the subject feeling fearful, anxious, and paralysed. Theoretically, there is therefore a danger of 'securitising subjectivity', whereby subjectivity is closed down around a particular identity, and which is sometimes seen as signifying an unhealthy and maladaptive sense of attachment to established and routinised forms of being (Kinnvall 2004; Mälksoo; Mitzen 2006). In this respect, while biographical continuity is often important, ontological security is not reducible to this. Instead, ontological security also requires a certain amount of reflexive awareness to claims about self-identity, this suggesting that, in light of changing circumstances, subjects also need to consider whether their biographical narratives remain relevant or need modifying (Craib 1998, 72; Browning and Joenniemi 2017).

As becomes evident below and in later chapters the relationship between nation branding and ontological security is complex. One thing to note at this point, though, is that insofar as dealing with anxiety and upholding a sense of ontological security requires a sense of reflexive awareness and an ability to cope with (and even embrace) change by adapting narratives of self-identity to changing circumstances, then in some respects nation branding can speak to this. It does so insofar as it suggests states need to be flexible, entrepreneurial, and adaptive in terms of how they relate to their identities given proclaimed significant changes in the nature of international politics – something clearly evident in the pitch nation branding consultants made to East European and post-Soviet states after the end of the Cold War. In this respect, as a discourse nation branding speaks to the broader neoliberal promotion of the adaptable and flexible entrepreneurial subject. The flipside of this, of course, is that insofar as such a discourse supports the instrumentalisation of identity it may also have the potential to generate ontological insecurity by further fracturing the subject's embedded and collective sense of selfhood – something to which this chapter later returns.

ONTOLOGICAL SECURITY, SELF-ESTEEM, AND STATUS

Extant debates and applications of ontological security in IR have generally focused precisely on this issue of subjects' need to establish a sense of order and stability through upholding (and adapting) routinised biographical narratives of self-identity and the processes they go through whenever this is challenged and anxieties about self-identity intrude. However, this emphasis on cognitive ordering and stability only captures one aspect of ontological security. As the socio-psychological literatures on status, self-esteem, and recognition point out, subjects are also driven by desires for self-worth. Indeed, Tillich's (2014, 50–1) emphasis on how existential anxieties can emerge whenever subjects feel they are not living up to their own self-concepts, what he terms 'anxieties of guilt and condemnation', speaks directly to the moral component of being and clearly suggests that merely 'going on' is insufficient alone – people also want to live lives that are meaningful and valued (Browning et al. 2021, 22). In this respect, although a sense of purpose and self-esteem can be generated internally, subjects are also invariably concerned with the perceptions and valuations of others. In other words, claims about self-identity typically need to be recognised by others if they are to be satisfying since recognition confers acceptance, status, and standing (Larson et al. 2014), which, in turn, means that claims about self-identity also need to be enacted and performed for the benefit of both the self and salient others (Laffey 2000). What this means is that a subject's sense of ontological security is also dependent upon the extent to which their claims to self-identity are recognised, esteemed, and seen to bestow upon them status, where such status may take the form of being recognised either as a legitimate member of a particular group to which the subject aspires (club status) or where their claims about themselves are seen to positively stand out in some way (positional status) (Beaumont 2017). In turn, however, the absence of such recognition can be a source of considerable anxiety.

Of course, IR has not been completely silent on these dynamics. For example, Larson et al. (2014, 18) highlight how states do not simply desire enhanced status because of its perceived instrumental benefits in inducing deference to one's interests and views from others (as rationalist accounts of status-seeking emphasise) but because status seeking is also a central requirement by which groups generate a sense of self-esteem (see also Clunan 2014, 279). Similarly, Lebow (2008, 63) argues that the realist emphasis on fear and reason and the liberal emphasis on appetite and material interests can only provide partial explanations of state action because they fail to take account of the actor's sense of spirit, honour, and standing, all of which are also central to building self-esteem (see also Welch 2010, 448). Self-esteem, he argues, is 'achieved by excelling in activities valued by one's peer group or society and gaining the respect of actors whose opinions matter' and is a fundamental driver of action (Lebow 2008, 61).[4] A similar point has been made in nationalism studies, with Greenfeld (1995, 491) arguing that 'national identity is, fundamentally, a matter of dignity', her point being that nationalism is ultimately motivated by a community's desire to justify and legitimise itself while also enhancing its position and standing.

Seen from this perspective, self-esteem is not simply a question of self-perception but of self-perception as mediated through the eyes of others – that is, whether others are felt to hold the subject in high regard or not. This makes gaining recognition for the claims the subject makes about itself fundamental to securing a healthy sense of subjectivity and for upholding ontological security (Lindemann 2010, 2, 9). In the absence of such recognition subjects are liable to experience heightened feelings of anxiety, stigmatisation, and shame. For example, Zarakol (2011) shows how such dynamics, resulting from their non-recognition as full and equal partners by the West, has generated significant and enduring ontological insecurities that have had notable effects on domestic and international politics in Turkey, Japan, and Russia. Taken to an extreme, non-recognition may even challenge the symbolic existence of the group/nation. Faced with non-recognition by salient others, subjects have various options that might range from redoubling their efforts to secure future acceptance through to re-negotiating a new self-narrative for which recognition is forthcoming (see Ringmar 2002; Adler-Nissen 2014).

Interestingly, though, and particularly given its emphasis on attracting the attention of foreign audiences, the role that nation branding might play in contributing to a nation's status, self-esteem, and ontological security has been little discussed (although see Browning 2015a). In this respect, it is worth considering that, while a desire for status and self-esteem may reflect fundamental imperatives of the human condition, the norms through which these might be sought are socially constructed. The point is that, from this 'psychological constructivist' position, it is not given that self-esteem and international standing should be derived through war and power politics as implied in more traditional (realist) conceptions of international politics (Hymans 2010, 463). In situations in which war and power politics have been downgraded and lost their attraction, the question is therefore whether they might be achieved in different ways (Wohlforth 2010, 470–1). Of course, in a context in which the veneration of the armed forces remains widespread in many societies and in which preparation for and participation in war still often remains a signifier of courage and international citizenship, it would be naïve to suggest that such traditional framings have become entirely irrelevant. Yet, as discussed in chapter 2, insofar as discourses heralding a fundamental transformation of the nature of the international system have become prevalent, and insofar as these call for a fundamental reconceptualisation of the nature and role of the state, then historically contingent norms of international subjectivity and statehood have changed.

In this respect, the emergence of nation branding as a concept and discourse of international politics since the 1990s arguably also reflects broader changes in how national self-esteem, status, and dignity are understood and can be achieved. Increasingly, it seems, these are as likely to be generated through attracting multinational corporations and investments, hosting international conferences and sporting events, or winning and hosting events like the Eurovision Song Contest as they are through troop deployments and military actions (Browning 2015b, 290–1). In this context, then, nation branding has arguably emerged as one mechanism through which recognition, status, self-esteem, and ontological security can be generated, with this, in turn, having an impact on the types of identities constituted. For instance, and to give just one example, the report that launched Finland's nation branding programme back in 2010 explicitly included amongst its six objectives 'Promoting the International Status of the Finnish State' and 'Raising the national self-esteem of Finns'. The new nation brand, it was argued, would ultimately tackle the Finns' perceived endemic awkwardness, modesty, and low self-esteem such that, in future, 'It will feel really good to be a Finn' (Country Brand Report 2010, 23, 37, 343, 355, 361).[5] And, as we saw earlier, the idea that it might offer one way of tackling feelings of inferiority, shame, and stigmatisation was also a key motivator for the adoption of nation branding programmes by many Eastern European and post-Soviet states.

Finally, these examples also direct us to the issue of whose ontological security and sense of status and self-esteem is actually at stake in practices of nation branding and whose sense of ontological security might nation branding speak to. The argument here is that nation branding is often operative in regard to ontological security in two respects. First, it can be seen as operating at the collective level of the nation and/or state.[6] Within debates on ontological security this is sometimes a controversial move since it is argued that collective actors like states do not experience psychological and affective processes in the same way as do individuals (Krolikowski 2008). On the other hand, the growing work on group psychology suggests otherwise in that it points to processes of emotional or affective contagion across population groups (e.g., Barsade 2002).[7] In this respect, it is also worth noting how it is common to ascribe psychological and emotional concepts to states, such as when they are described as humiliated, shamed, anxious, or eliciting pride. More particularly, though, it is certainly the case that state representatives often feel a sense of responsibility for upholding the standing, reputation, identity, and ontological security of their state (Steele 2008, 15–20).[8]

Second, though, nation branding may also be relevant for thinking about ontological security at the level of individual citizens, not least since citizens often generate a sense of ontological security through vicariously identifying with the nation – that is, living through the nation and its experiences and achievements, not least through internalising claims about national identity in self-identity narratives enacted at the level of the everyday (Browning et al. 2021, 55–9). In this respect, national identification can help individuals cope with a range of potential ontological anxieties. For example, it can help manage anxieties of fate and death by offering the illusion of being able to live on through the nation's continued existence (Berenskoetter 2010). And it can help them cope with anxieties of emptiness and meaninglessness insofar as the nation's achievements can become a personal source of self-esteem, as evident, for instance, in the sense of reflected glory many citizens experience at the successes of their national sportsmen and -women. In this respect, they may even draw a sense of self-esteem from their nation's more general international standing and status, something nation branding practices speak to directly. More generally, though, national identification can also help citizens feel historically anchored and thereby provide them with a sense of continuity, stability, and meaning, with Marlow (2002, 247) pointing to how citizens typically expect their national leaders to provide an overarching, reassuring, and coherent narrative of society that outlines a sense of national purpose and direction.

The argument here, and as is explored below, is that, to varying degrees, nation branding can speak to these different dynamics of ontological security-seeking at both a collective and an individual level – by potentially responding to the desire for consistent biographical narratives of self-identity and the desire for recognition and status. Indeed, insofar as citizens 'live through' the imagined community of their nationhood (Anderson 1991), then invocations for them to 'live the (nation) brand' are on the face of it not too dissimilar, with nation branding actively promoting citizens' emotional investment with the nation. This is particularly so in an age in which people are increasingly living and crafting their identities through their branded consumer purchases (Banet-Weiser 2012). However, whether nation branding *necessarily* operates as a form of ontological security enhancement and whether it is a *good* mechanism for generating a sense of ontological security is a different question – and one that requires us to explore in greater depth the relationship between nation branding and nation building.

NATION BRANDING AND NATION BUILDING

The nature of the relationship between nation branding and nation building is complex. As noted previously, amongst consultants the terms are sometimes treated as synonyms, with nation branding appearing as little more than a more modern and updated terminological framing – albeit one that reflects the advent of new digital and marketing techniques – of what are essentially historically ingrained practices. As Olins (2005, 170) claims: 'There is in reality nothing new about national branding, except the word "brand" and the techniques that are now used, which derive from mainstream marketing and branding techniques' (see also Olins 2003, 152; Saunders 2017, 4).

At face value there is much that supports this view. For instance, the logos, images, and slogans that are often embedded in contemporary nation branding programmes do bear resemblance to various key practices central to nation building, not least the design and flying of flags, the development of a national currency, and the composing and performance of national anthems, et cetera (Ståhlberg and Bolin 2015). For Billig (1995, 49–50), these are all representative of the routinised and often mundane and overlooked everyday 'flagging of nationhood' that he sees as central to what he terms 'banal nationalism' – where the nation is symbolically and almost unconsciously reproduced and normalised for its citizens as the basis of their sense of moral community and identity. In this respect, both practices of nation branding and nation building are also designed to stimulate desire and seek to activate affective attachments (Kaneva 2012b, 10–11; Viktorin et al. 2018a, 4). However, despite the similarities the relationship between the concepts (and between a national identity and a national brand identity [Volčič 2012, 148]) is inherently complex since they are neither synonymous nor necessarily mutually compatible and reinforcing. In this respect, at least three points of distinction can be noted.

First, although the argument of this chapter is that nation branding entails implications at the national level, and while this is sometimes explicitly recognised as one of its rationales, it is important to remember that fundamentally it is predominantly directed at (or at least legitimised in terms of) external audiences. As Ståhlberg and Bolin (2015) point out, its aim is therefore to encourage outsiders to *identify with* the nation such that they recognise the nation and might want to visit and/or invest their capital there. In general, the aim is not to encourage external actors to view themselves *as members* of the nation and build a sense of national community, which is the principal goal of nation building and practices of banal nationalism. The 'in general' is relevant here as it is also important to recognise the more recent emergence of a niche form of nation branding undertaken by states who have sought to commercialise their citizenship by offering citizenship to wealthy foreigners in return for investment in the country, something that is, of course, dependent upon their perceived attractiveness (Parker 2017). However, such practices are an outlier within the broader context of nation branding, which, in general, when directed externally, is not seeking to erase the distinction between the identities of self and other, even if these do get framed in new ways (see below).

The significance of this distinction can be seen in contexts in which the imperatives of nation branding and nation building become misaligned. For example, Marat (2009, 1125–6) notes how Uzbekistan's government has been notably inconsistent in its messaging of internal and external audiences, recognising that what might resonate internally might not sell externally as part of its nation branding activities – and vice versa. As Marat notes, while appealing to global markets may make sense as a strategy of nation branding, she suggests that, for newly emergent nations in particular, what might count more is activating and recovering particular national histories that may be 'of little relevance to investors or tourists' who might be more interested in 'products, people or places'. Saunders (2017, 226) makes a similar point about Estonia, citing one of the Interbrand consultants who worked on the country's nation branding campaigns of the early 2000s who noted that one of the sticking points between the Interbrand team and the Estonians was the latter's 'dogged obsession with the past' and their desire to emphasise the country's deep roots and 'to go back nine centuries in explaining their country to Western European investors and tourists'.

This highlights a second point of distinction, which is that national identities are fundamentally much broader than nation brands and the brand identities they convey. As noted in chapter 1, nation branding is typically conceptualised in terms of distilling and refining national identity into a more simplified exposition. In this respect, even though it is an inherently constitutive practice it can be seen to entail primordial assumptions, at least insofar as consultants typically see themselves as seeking to identify, capture, and market the nation's most marketable and eye-catching essences (Aronczyk 2008, 52; Jansen 2008, 122). Of course, irrespective of now several decades of academic research emphasising the socially constructed nature of nations, the politics of nation building is also frequently replete with similar (competing) essentialising claims. However, as Kulcsár and Yum (2012, 194) note, there is a fundamental difference between the 'totalizing logic of branding and the complexity of national identity formation'. As noted, nation branding requires elaborating a set of core messages derived through borrowing only those aspects of national identity that are seen to resonate (Volčič 2012, 148). Complexity is to be avoided. In contrast, national identities are typically multi-layered and often socially contested in how they may activate debates about social norms and relations with respect to things like race, religion, gender – all things nation branding generally steers clear of (though see chapter 4 with respect to gender). As further discussed below, what this also highlights is how nation branding differs from national identity insofar as the former generally takes the form of a time-constrained managerial and marketing exercise whereas national identity is emergent from an ever ongoing process of social contestation across the nation.

A third point to note, therefore, is that it is not only that dominant discourses of national identity might not always align with representations in national branding programmes, at times they may even signify considerable points of tension, with nation branding becoming exclusionary and potentially at odds with building the national community. For example, Jordan (2015) shows how Estonia, like many other countries, used its hosting of the 2002 Eurovision Song Contest as an opportunity for a concerted effort of national promotion, in this case designed to signal the country's 'return to Europe'. The branding campaign itself, despite making a nod in the direction of multiculturalism, ultimately presented the nation in ethno-linguistic terms by explicitly excluding the country's sizeable Russian-speaking population and their heritage from the national image projected. The explanation for this presumably lay in how, until that point, the Estonian government had spent much of the post-Cold War period trying to establish a sense of difference and distance from Russia in the minds of foreigners (Browning and Oliveira 2017a, 492–3); however, as argued by Budnitskiy (2012), such a continuing ethnicised approach to its brand has actually undermined the process of building a national community embracing the country's resident Russian population – a population who are not going anywhere (Saunders 2017, 226). Indeed, Kulcsár and Yum (2012, 196–7) point to how such tensions have been notable for many countries in Eastern Europe, who in rediscovering their sense of self after the end of the Cold War often drew upon embedded ethnic conceptions of national identity yet, in turn, also felt a need to embrace norms of multiculturalism and minority rights then prevalent in Western Europe and the EU as part of their claims to Europeanness. It is in this respect that we therefore also see tensions between the nation as an *imagined community* and the nation as an *imaged community*, with nation branding typically more concerned with the latter (Clerc and Glover 2015).

And yet, while the relationship between nation branding and nation building can have its tensions, it is also true that states have sometimes actively deployed nation branding practices in the service of nation building. In this respect, it has sometimes been argued that the concept of 'nation branding' is a misnomer since in many cases what is actually at stake is 'state branding'. For example, Eggeling (2018) suggests this is the case in respect of so-called 'artificial' states that are inherently multinational in their make-up, with her focus being on Kazakhstan and Qatar and where she points to how 'the institution of the state was superimposed on territories occupied by different nations and/or tribes'. Here, she argues that 'the idea of the state is used as an identity anchor to tie a heterogeneous society together in an overarching, politically unifying identity narrative' (68). In such cases, however, 'state branding' is evidently operating in the service of nation building, and insofar as it is successful then it arguably segues into a form of nation branding. In other words, insofar as such efforts are intended to create a unifying sense of supranational identity that binds together other national/tribal identities, then state branding may appear as a particular form of nation branding, especially to the extent to which notions of Kazakhstani and Qatari national identities become inextricably tied to and invested in the idea and standing of their respective states.[9] For instance, in each case she highlights the emphasis that has been placed on city development (e.g., iconic architecture, and a new capital city in the case of Kazakhstan), building global-facing education hubs, and not least investing in sports (including bidding to host major tournaments). However, underpinning such activities are arguably two drivers. One relates to outward-facing 'cultural' and 'diplomatic' logics of nation branding centred on securing international recognition and positioning the state internationally (chapter 1), while the other operates to encourage citizens' vicarious identification with and investment in the state – that is, they are encouraged to draw pride, status, self-esteem, and a sense of ontological security through their relationship with the state, thereby tying the nation to the state (or even to the regime – see chapter 5).

In such cases, nation branding therefore operates as part of an effort to try to generate a sense of solidarity and loyalty to the state amongst citizens. Of course, and as indicated earlier, how effective utilising techniques of nation branding in the service of nation building is, is another matter and may vary between cases. The danger, however, is that, insofar as such efforts are inherently top-down rather than part of a more organic bottom-up process, they may be susceptible to vulnerabilities. For instance, reflecting on the post–Cold War experience in Eastern Europe and on Bulgaria more particularly, Kulcsár and Yum (2012, 198–9, 202–3) note how such efforts often failed to take account of divergent and conflicting narratives and identities and imposed a homogenising view that favoured particular elements over others, which was often politically contentious and perceived by some as an attempt to capture the idea of the nation by specific interest groups. The danger, therefore, is that, when placed in the service of nation building, nation branding is far from guaranteed to promote a cohesive national identity or sense of social solidarity, especially insofar as particular constituents perceive their own local and group identities as excluded and marginalised.

However, insofar as nation branding does enhance nation building then it is important to recognise that, at least when underpinned by economic logics, arguably it may also shift the basis upon which nations become a source of ontological security for their citizens. This is because nation branding ultimately entails building a sense of national identity and ontological security around status dynamics (i.e., what *they* think of *us*) rather than in terms of kinship ties (i.e., what *we* think binds *us* together). As Aronczyk (2013, 16) notes, ultimately the hope of national leaders is that the brand will 'generate positive foreign public opinion that will "boomerang" back home, fostering both domestic consensus and approbation of their actions as well as pride and patriotism within the nation's borders'. In other words, at least in respect of discourses of the competition state, national self-esteem becomes (at least to some extent) reliant on having an attractive brand desired by others.[10]

A good example of this is highlighted in this book's introduction in respect of British prime minister David Cameron's speech at the Olympic Park in London in 2014 concerning the then imminent referendum on Scottish independence. As noted, Cameron's (2014) motivating argument presented the UK 'as a brand' – and 'a powerful brand' at that – but one that could only be dramatically diminished if Scotland voted to leave the Union. Evidently, Cameron believed that Scots, too, should be invested in the UK brand. Yet the notable thing about such an argument is how the appeal is not framed in terms of what the constituent nations of the United Kingdom might think of each other (i.e., an appeal to kinship ties) but, rather, in terms of what others think of them (i.e., an appeal to international standing and status). It is suggested that this itself should be a source of such pride and self-esteem as to both enhance the sense of collective national belonging and illustrate the folly of going it alone. In such a framing, kinship, history, and narratives of shared identity – those elements that lie at the heart of the nation as an imagined community – are therefore subordinated to the needs of the brand and ultimately matter only insofar as they can be mobilised as brand enhancers. In Cameron's terms, then, the Scottish independence vote was therefore at least as much about questions of brand value as it was about questions of identity, but where the brand was valued not simply because of the instrumental or material benefits a strong brand is seen to enable but also because a strong brand is seen to enhance the national standing, status, self-esteem, and sense of self of the nation as a whole as well as of its individual citizens.[11]

However, while Cameron's appeal to the nation brand can be criticised, it should not be derided outright. This is because, in the contemporary age at least, globalisation has posed significant challenges for how nations establish a sense of subjectivity. Indeed, van Ham (2005, 123) goes so far as to suggest that, in a context in which ideological battles are no longer the activating dynamic of global politics and are therefore losing much of their relevance in political programmes, nation branding might be offering an alternative replacement for people's loyalties. Indeed, this is something clearly demonstrated by Banet-Weiser (2012, 3) in respect of the broader emergence of brand culture, not least insofar as brands have become a surrogate through which people now invest their desires to recapture a lost sense of authenticity. However, insofar as this is happening, then the argument of this discussion is that it has begun to shift the bases upon which nations establish a sense of ontological security and self-esteem.

Finally, the emphasis in nation branding on the affirmation and recognition of others and on trying to entice such others to 'identity with' (though not become) the nation also suggests a significant challenge to established assumptions about identity in international relations. Whether in realist or poststructuralist mode, IR theorising generally emphasises how national identities are constituted through the identification of radicalised and threatening otherness (Campbell 1992; Mouffe 1994). However, at least when nation branding is underpinned by economic logics, enmity largely drops out of the picture, with chapter 2 highlighting the transition away from Hobbesian to more Lockean conceptions of others as rivals in competition state discourses. In such a discourse, an emphasis on absolute difference in constituting subjectivity is replaced by an emphasis on one's desirability and attractiveness. This entails two slightly contradictory elements. The first points towards a positive valuation of one's difference in that to be attractive, enticing, and to get noticed there is a need to stand out. Yet, necessarily, such difference will also be bounded, since the nation brand should not identify the nation as being so different that it loses its attraction. This is the second element. In this respect, Aronczyk (2013, 31) notes that the marketing of difference in nation branding campaigns is little more than a 'fantasy of diversity', where such diversity that is evident is 'defanged' insofar as it exists only for the purposes of global trade. Difference cannot be such that the nation puts itself beyond what is likely to be positively received (or sold) internationally, with this ultimately limiting the national imaginaries activated in nation branding processes (Kaneva and Popescu 2011, 202). It is precisely for this reason that the nation branding campaigns of many countries end up proclaiming their difference by predictably drawing on the same sorts of motifs and emphasising the same sorts of attributes as most other countries (Philo and Kearns 1993, 20–1). In other words, insofar as nation branding supports ontological security and self-esteem enhancement, it generally does so by fostering emulation in respect of national identity rather than differentiation.

COMMODIFYING CULTURE AND IDENTITY AND THE RISE OF CONSUMER NATIONALISM

Aspects of the above discussion can be taken further, not least because, for its critics, nation branding is seen to entail two particularly negative effects at the level of the nation. The first is that the process of nation branding is seen as *an act of dispossession alienating citizens* from their national identity. Central to this critique is how contemporary practices of nation branding underpinned by economic logics and discourses of globalisation and the competition state are premised on instrumentalising and commodifying national identity and culture. Thus, the emphasis is not on developing or defending claims about the nation's authentic or intrinsic nature but is instead conceived in terms of bringing together often highly decontextualised claims about the nation that it is felt might best appeal to outsiders' desires, thereby enticing investors, visitors, global capital, and drawing positive attention. National identity and culture are therefore treated as 'fixed assets' (e.g., Anholt 2008b, 34; Moilanen and Rainisto 2009, 3) to be appropriated (or discarded), moulded, and reassembled in whatever way is deemed might best suit the nation internationally. The result, of course, is that national imaginaries are liable to be limited by the commercial considerations driving the branding process, thereby eschewing any deeper engagement with contending ideas about the nation's history and identity. In this respect, Kaneva and Popescu (2011, 201) see nation branding as promoting a form of 'national identity lite' in which culture and history are decontextualised, depoliticised, and valued only insofar as they are seen to have economic utility, which essentially means privileging the desires, preferences, and norms of outsiders over those of the nation's citizens (Meade 2012).

This can have several interesting outcomes. One is an emphasis on being as neutral and inoffensive as possible, as illustrated by the suggestion of the inaugural chairman of South Korea's nation branding council that a key goal of the country's nation branding programme should be to 'initiate programmes aimed at helping Koreans learn about globally accepted norms and etiquette and become more acceptable to other cultures' (Euh Yoon-dae quoted in Jeong-ju 2009). Or which can be seen in how, as part of its push to develop a national brand, the Royal Government of Bhutan (2010, 6) emphasised the need to tone down 'the brightness of our textiles' and use more 'sober colours that the affluent Western markets prefer'. In other words, national identity and culture are to be moulded and packaged with the preferences and tastes of outsiders foregrounded. Another has been a predilection for self-stereotyping as nations seek to carve out a particular niche identity for themselves (Jansen 2008, 133).[12] This has been particularly notable in cases where developing or marginalised communities seek to target Western consumers by appealing to their orientalist desires to experience the 'exotic' other (Comaroff and Comaroff 2009; Volčič 2012, 159).

Sometimes, though, one's own national culture might be deemed to be insufficient to convey the message desired, the belief being that traditional and national cultural artefacts may be meaningless to global audiences, particularly in respect of lesser-known nations whose historical paths and 'points of reference are significantly different from other nations' (Kulcsár and Yum 2012, 197). For instance, in the early 2010s an attempt was made in Finland to establish a new Guggenheim Museum in Helsinki as a means of bolstering the city's reputation as a place where international culture could be consumed and thereby raise Helsinki into the elite level of cultural capitals. For critics, though, the plan signalled a blatant rejection of indigenous culture in favour of importing foreign brands that it was believed would be more appealing to the global cultural elite (*Helsingin Sanomat International Edition* 2012). Moreover, the case is also instructive in how it contrasts with the period at the end of the nineteenth century when, as an aspirational nation-state, the then Grand Duchy of Finland (then a part of Tsarist Russia) was internationally active in promoting those cultural products deemed to be the most distinctively and authentically Finnish, with this conforming more to cultural logics of nation branding (chapter 1), the emphasis then being on gaining recognition as a (potential and legitimate) independent nation-state, as opposed to appealing to the consumerist desires of foreigners (Browning 2015b, 291).

The second issue, though, is that nation branding can also be seen as being inherently *anti-democratic in orientation*. The main concern in this respect is how contemporary nation branding programmes are typically outsourced to a mixture of domestic and foreign-based branding consultancies as well as appointing business leaders to key positions on branding commissions. Not only does this further support the prioritisation of commercial logics in debates about the framing and presentation of national identity, but it also privatises and depoliticises the process of determining what is deemed worthy to include in any nation branding campaign (Kaneva 2012b, 16; Sussman 2012, 32). Indeed, while the views of citizens are sometimes sought, not least via focus groups, polling, and internet portals, the belief being that this will encourage citizens to invest in and feel empowered by the brand, critics argue that such mechanisms typically function as an illusory legitimation exercise in which nation branding becomes, at best, limited to a form of pseudo 'democratic co-creation' (Volčič and Andrejevic 2011, 598–602; Volčič 2012, 155). It is limited, on the one hand, because focus groups and polling data are 'not a substitute for, or even a supplement to, deliberative democratic discourse' about how – or even whether – citizens wish to sell the nation through branding exercises to outsiders (Sussman 2012, 42–3). And, on the other hand, it is limited because while (some) citizens may be asked to input into the process, ultimately it is the branding consultants and commissions that determine what counts and whether the inputs received are deemed to be in line with the framing logics in play as to the type of brand identity that is to be crafted.[13]

And these logics are evidently important for how national identities are constituted in many contemporary nation branding programmes. For instance, under the influence of discourses of globalisation and the competition state it is significant how national identity is typically framed in ways deemed to generate a competitive identity fit for global capitalism and market exchange. For example, Varga (2013, 451–3) describes how German national identity was 'simply re-described within the vocabulary of neo-liberalism'. The driving concept of the brand was that of Germany and Germans as *spielmacher* ('playmakers'), a concept that conjures up notions of the country as orchestrating and leading a game, with the brand further emphasising the Germans' coolness, flexibility, and playfulness. The brand therefore appears to have been mainly about promoting Germany and its citizens as exemplary entrepreneurial neoliberal subjects, as opposed to celebrating anything particular about the country's national identity or culture. As Varga notes, 'the problem "what should Germany export as her identity?" is prevented from even occurring. Germany is risk-taking, flexible, and willing to permanently re-work and change itself – what more could markets ask?' (453). But Germany is not alone, and similar appeals to the nation as an entrepreneurial subject can also be seen in iterations of other countries' branding programmes. For example, amongst its near neighbours Poland has previously branded itself as a country of 'Creative Tension' (Surowiec 2012, 137; Aroncyk 2013, ch. 4), a concept that was coined by the marketing consultant Wally Olins and that was – amongst other things – seen to point to the country's individualism, perpetual motion, passion, idealism, and resourcefulness (Trawińska n.d.). Meanwhile, Estonia has made great play of framing itself as a computer-literate E-nation that is an 'adaptable self-starter' offering 'innovative solutions' (Jansen 2012, 86). Indeed, today, few nations would risk drifting too far from a narrative that typically emphasises flexibility and dynamism in a business-friendly environment.

Yet criticisms of the inherently alienating and anti-democratic effects of nation branding should also be treated cautiously and may also need to be disentangled insofar as they are not necessarily mutually reinforcing. While we extend this discussion in the final section below, it is worth recalling that it has already been noted how analysts (and advocates) have pointed to how, in some contexts, nation branding (and certain forms of product branding) can become points of attachment for generating a (renewed) sense of belonging that responds to the ontological security and self-esteem needs of individual and collective subjects through emotionally investing in the brand (Banet-Weiser 2012; van Ham 2005, 123; York 2011; Freire 2005). Such an observation resonates with the idea of 'consumer/commercial nationalism', central to which is the reframing and production of citizens not simply as consumers but as *nationalist(ic)* consumers', where national belonging becomes manifest through practices of consumption (Volčič and Andrejevic 2016b, 6, emphasis in original) and where the 'market rather than the state has become the reference point for national identification' (Edensor 2002, 111; Kania-Lundholm 2016, 106–7). Consumer nationalism, though, is not just about the promotion of patriotic consumption as part of encouragements to help boost the national economy (something somewhat resonant of internally directed 'country of origin' branding) but often also entails consciously branding the self and performing citizenship, such as through the purchase of *nationally branded* products. For instance, Sarín (2016, 55, 58) notes how in the Colombian context the widely popular 'Pasión es Colombia/Colombia is Passion' nation branding campaign saw a movement of citizen participation towards the marketplace. As he notes, by 2008 around 220 companies had paid for the right to use the 'Pasión es Colombia' logo, and anything marketed in terms of 'passion' soon carried allusions to patriotism, be that table salt, cars, chips, razors, and, of course, coffee. Yet, as noted by Turner (2016, 18, 22), the growing emphasis on the citizen as a (nationalistic) consumer is often at the expense – or in place – of an enhanced role for the citizen as a political subject and actor. As he notes, there is nothing intrinsically democratic about the process of marketization, yet, for all that, investing in branded products and merchandising increasingly seems to be one way through which citizens generate a sense of ontological security and self-esteem because, and as Banet-Weiser (2012, 9) puts it, it reflects how brands in general have become cultural spaces through 'which individuals feel safe, secure, relevant and authentic'.

CITIZENSHIP, GOVERNMENTALITY, AND BANAL NATIONALISM

However, the critique of the anti-democratic nature of contemporary nation branding can also be extended. The argument is not simply that genuine democratic engagement is fudged in favour of a form of pseudo democratic co-creation but that nation branding increasingly comes to support disciplinary forms of governance. Jansen (2012, 91–2), for instance, goes as far as to declare the methodology of nation branding 'ur-fascist' owing to the fact that it 'is a monologic, hierarchical, reductive form of communication that is intended to (a) privilege one message; (b) require, insofar as possible, that all voices of authority speak in unison; and (c) silence or marginalize dissenting voices'. Indeed, at its most robust the desire to cleanse the brand and present only positive images of the nation can take overt and sometimes brutal form, as evident, for instance, in attempts to create sanitised brand-friendly spaces by hiding undesirable elements and images from view. For instance, this is evident whenever countries bid to host major international conferences and then create exclusion zones to control the global optics by keeping protestors and recalcitrant citizens at a distance. And it is evident in the context of sporting mega-events, like the Rio Olympics, which saw the bulldozing of 'unsightly' slums and the eviction of their populations as part of an effort to present only a modern and aesthetically pleasing image of the city and of Brazil (Watts 2016). Such actions raise the question about who nation branding is ultimately for in such contexts, and we return to it in chapter 6.

Often, though, such efforts are subtler, with other critiques noting how nation branding has increasingly come to operate as a form of governmentality or 'technique of governance' (Browning 2015a,

205–6, 212; Volčič and Andrejevic 2011, 598; Schwak 2018, 652) that seeks to reconstitute the responsibilities of citizenship in terms of 'living the brand' (Aronczyk 2008, 54), something that in turn comes to implicate citizens as agents of foreign policy (Browning 2015a, 205). For instance, consultants frequently emphasise that success is dependent also upon citizens internalising and taking responsibility for brand implementation by only engaging in 'on brand' forms of behaviour (Weidner 2011). As Simon Anholt (2007a, 80) puts it, success requires 'getting everybody in the country to speak with one voice'. And such claims are in turn repeated in branding programmes, as evident, for example, in the declaration of the *Handbook of Brand Slovenia* that 'the power of the brand lies in the content and motivation of the Slovene citizens to live the brand' (quoted in Volčič 2012, 161).

Indeed, at times practitioners and state representatives can be quite explicit about these dynamics. For instance, and to cite three African examples – though this is a more general point – Zimbabwe's deputy prime minister, Artur Mutambara, called on his country's citizens to assume the role of 'brand ambassadors' (cited in Brand Africa 2011, 15) while Miller Matola (2012), the chief executive officer of what was then the International Marketing Council of South Africa, emphasised the 'need to unite with one strong voice, committed to thinking, acting and speaking positively about the many things that South Africa is getting right, instead of constantly focusing on the negative and stimulating global negative sentiment'. And last, but in a similar vein, Mathias Akotia (2010) of the Brand Ghana Office called for 'conscious citizenship programmes' that would help internalise the country's brand values and promote 'the appropriate citizenship behaviour'. Evidently, such invocations signal to citizens which forms of behaviour are to be encouraged and deemed patriotic – because of their brand resonance – while implicitly setting boundaries as to what constitutes unpatriotic behaviour (Weidner 2011). Given such interventions, it is therefore understandable why critics argue nation branding may pose a threat to fostering a vibrant participatory democracy. Indeed, in this respect, as van Ham (2002, 267) and Jansen (2008, 135; 2012, 92) note, the fact that Singapore, with its emphasis on media censorship and authoritative government, is often championed as a successful example of nation branding, should provide pause for thought.

At the same time, though, such criticisms can be overplayed since (most) governments' ability to decisively orchestrate branding campaigns and manipulate their citizens to its needs usually has limits (e.g., Jiménez-Martínez 2017). Indeed, at least in more democratic contexts it is difficult to enforce brand conformity. Thus, while encouragements for citizens to 'live the brand' and reconceptualise themselves as 'brand ambassadors' reflects attempts to transfer across to states more recent developments in the commercial sector focused on the emergence of 'Corporate Branding' (see chapter 1), the 'state as firm' metaphor ultimately has limits in this regard. As noted by Mordhorst (2019), at the end of the day, while firms can part company with obdurate employees, states are generally stuck with their citizens and need to rely on moral suasion instead.

Several points might be noted in this respect. First, Glover (2015) highlights how certain forms of dissent can be tamed by co-opting them into the nation brand and, in turn, strengthening it. In this respect, he distinguishes between 'authorised' and 'unauthorised' dissension and draws on Swedish image policy of the 1960s by way of example. During this period, he notes, Swedish politics was polarised between, on the one hand, those calling 'for more active and effective promotion of Swedish capitalism' and who supported the projection of a 'total image' of Sweden in line with the marketing ideals of brand coherence favoured by contemporary nation branding consultants and, on the other, those on the left who were more anti-nationalist in orientation, who emphasised solidarity and democratic socialism instead, and who found such attempts to 'sell Sweden' abhorrent. The official response was to try to make a virtue out of such diverging positions by encouraging critics to discuss their reservations in the Ministry for Foreign Affairs' official publication dealing with promoting Sweden abroad. Authorising, and thereby co-opting, such dissent became a way of pursuing the goal of total image projection by highlighting how such debates reaffirmed established images of the country's consensus culture. Poland's strapline of 'Creative Tension' was coined with precisely the same idea in mind. By contrast, Glover (2015, 137–9) notes how other forms of criticism and dissent were deemed beyond the pale, acted against, and therefore left 'unauthorised'.[14]

Second, in a context of digitalisation and the proliferation of social media, though, the scope for citizen (critical) engagement with nation branding processes has expanded enormously. This itself makes controlling (and/or co-opting) dissent increasingly difficult, and there are numerous examples of official nation branding campaigns being lampooned by the state's own citizens because they were perceived as problematic, disingenuous, or embarrassing in some way. For instance,

Bardan and Imre (2012, 182) note the proliferation of Romanian blogs denigrating the country's 2009 'Come to Romania, the Land of Choice' campaign as deceitful and divisive, with citizens also producing their own videos to set the record straight, with titles including 'The Truth about Romania' and 'We Are the End of Choice'.

Third, though, what examples like this also show is how digitalisation and social media have created spaces through which citizens can themselves actively participate in nation branding practices beyond the scope of the state. One result of this is that the advent of new technologies and communication platforms has also shifted the emphasis increasingly towards expanded efforts of 'co-creation' beyond the limited engagement with focus groups, polling, and surveys noted above. This, itself, also reflects more recent developments in the marketing of product brands where increasingly the aim is to cement relations between producers and consumers and ultimately enrol consumers in product branding by fostering their feeling of authentic engagement with the brand to the extent to which they become willing brand activists and ambassadors (Banet-Weiser 2012, 38–43). In terms of nation branding this is evident in how vicarious identification with the nation may combine with the turn towards consumer nationalism noted above, such that citizens literally become living embodiments/exhibits of banal nationalism who adorn themselves with nationally branded products. But it is also evident in how nation branding internet portals increasingly feature resources that national citizens and businesses can utilise in ways that encourage them to wrap themselves and their products in the national brand. While we also see it in the unofficial (and often humorous) online interventions of citizens that are often framed in nation branding terms, a good example being the proliferation online of satirical 'America first but [x country] second' videos following the US presidential election of Donald Trump in 2016 (Irshaid 2017). These videos were interesting in various ways but were notable in how they almost all comprised three elements: (1) genuine boasts about the nation's selling points typically found in nation branding campaigns (e.g., with respect to cuisine, culture, nature, science, architecture etc.), (2) an interesting use of self-stigmatisation highlighting more negative aspects (e.g., racism, sexism, drunkenness, bad architecture...), but (3) where this was done through directly parodying the pre-eminent global power (and, for many of these countries, a military ally). They therefore raise interesting questions about the subversive/redemptive use of humour that has become an increasing feature of nation branding. To give just one example to illustrate the intertextuality between official/formal and informal/citizen-led forms of nation branding, the Slovenian intervention actively referenced the country's official nation branding strapline in noting: 'We even have the word "love" in the name of our country' ('America First ... Slovenia Second (OFFICIAL)' 2017).

CONCLUSION

This chapter considers the implications of nation branding at the level of the nation, with particular attention paid to how nation branding intersects with issues of identity, community, and subjectivity for both the collective and for citizens. In this respect, the chapter begins by exploring the relationship between nation branding and the ontological security and status needs of subjects. It shows how nation branding both preys upon and cultivates pervading anxieties about status and being but is also often positioned as offering a response to such needs. This, it is argued, is particularly the case in a context in which underpinning constitutive discourses of international politics connected to war and conquest have been replaced by discourses emphasising globalisation and market competition and that, to some degree, privilege the power of attraction over brute force. In this context, states often see nation branding not only as a means of enhancing the status and standing of the state through its potential to generate positive recognition from salient peers and global audiences but also as able to bolster the sense of self-esteem and ontological security of national citizens, with this being a consequence of how citizens are prone to vicariously identify with and intermesh their own self-biographies with that of the nation.

However, the relationship between nation branding and nation building is far from straightforward. Despite certain similarities, this chapter argues that nation branding and nation building are conceptually distinct. In part, this is because, although nation branding is, to varying degrees, targeted at citizens, its primary audience exists beyond the nation, the result being that while nation branding can align with – and has sometimes been explicitly utilised in the cause of – nation building, often they pull in different directions. Indeed, sometimes nation branding can be notably at odds with nation building and a cause of significant tension for groups who perceive themselves as marginalised or excluded from nation branding messages. Moreover, when nation branding is aligned with nation building one significant consequence is that – when it is underpinned by economic logics – it arguably also shifts the basis upon which nations become a source of ontological security and self-esteem for citizens. Instead of being derived through kinship ties and a search for authentic narratives of selfhood central to the nation as an *imagined* community, the emphasis instead shifts towards the nation as an *imaged* community by securing recognition and status from global audiences for possessing a desirable brand. Central to this becomes an emphasis on emulation rather than differentiation, the point being that while, in principle, nation branding is about standing out from one's competitors, difference necessarily needs to be bounded such that the nation does not appear too distinct/foreign and thereby lose attraction.

Nation branding, however, is also often criticised as being both alienating and anti-democratic in orientation. Insofar as it is alienating, this is because of how it commodifies and instrumentalises identity and culture, treating them as 'fixed assets' to be selected, moulded, and manipulated in whatever way it is felt will best resonate with external audiences. One particular result is an increasing tendency to reconceptualise and present the nation (and its citizens) as a flexible, dynamic, and entrepreneurial subject fit for global economic competition. However, it is also noted that such criticisms should be tempered given how branding has increasingly become a cultural context for everyday life and for the constitution of individual and collective identities and the building of affective relationships (Banet-Weiser 2012, 4). This is evident in the emergence of consumer nationalism, through which citizens may generate a sense of belonging, authenticity, status, and ontological security by engaging in demonstrative nationalistic modes of consumption.

However, while the alienating aspects of nation branding are complex, its anti-democratic elements are evident in the limited role assigned to citizens in the development of nation brands. For the most part, nation brands are designed by commissions with an emphasis typically placed on the role of consultants and business interests. Citizens, though, cannot be cut from the process entirely. On the one hand, and in line with practices of Corporate Branding, citizens are also increasingly seen as a resource, with there being a desire to responsibilise citizens as promotional brand ambassadors who 'live the brand'. Such practices have led to criticisms that nation branding increasingly appears as a form of governmentality that subtly seeks to discipline citizens by implicitly marking out patriotic from unpatriotic modes of being. Yet in most contexts the state's ability to do this has limits. This is particularly the case in an age of digitalisation and social media that has increased opportunities for citizens' own active interventions, with a key task for states today being that of trying to co-opt and thereby unconsciously/informally recruit citizens into the branding process.

In the following chapter, the concerns of the above discussion are writ large, particularly in respect of further illustrating the links between nation branding, ontological security, and status-seeking. However, the discussion also shifts to explore one of the more interesting moves in respect of nation branding in recent years, one that not only emphasises how status and ontological security are not simply to be derived through making the state appear as attractive as possible in terms of the perceived requirements of economic globalisation but that also introduces a more altruistic dimension. Today, states are also competing to out-brand each other in terms of their contribution to the collective good.

4

Good States

But the basic principle is a simple one: if you want people to admire you, it's not enough to be successful, you have to do something for them. So the question to ask is not 'which sectors can we excel in and therefore use to boost the country's image?' The correct question is 'What could be Armenia's gift to the world?' ... If Armenia wants to improve its image, it has to do something for humanity – do it well, do it prominently, do it imaginatively, courageously and consistently for a very long time. It's as simple as that.

Simon Anholt quoted in Araratyan (2015)

A key component of the Good Country Equation is the discovery that nothing improves a country's prosperity more than a powerful and positive national image, and nothing improves a country's image more than working internationally and contributing to the international community, tackling the 'grand challenges' in partnership with other nations and organizations.

Simon Anholt (2020, 228)

Recent years have seen an interesting development in debates about, and practices of, nation branding. Specifically, normative dimensions have been foregrounded where the aim is no longer to appeal only (or even primarily) to the material and aesthetic desires for conspicuous consumption of targeted consumers, tourists, and investors but to appeal to their consciences and humanity instead. Spurred on by developments in consultancy advice, states have increasingly begun to emphasise altruistic components in their nation branding strategies. Here, an attractive image and positive brand is to be cultivated by positioning the nation as a moral actor, selflessly addressing commonly held problems of international concern for the good of all. This is the world of the 'good state' and of nation branding as conspicuous do-goodism.

The shift towards 'good state' nation branding entails several dimensions. On the one hand, and like the emphasis on the competition state, it further attempts to shift (or at least expand) the criteria through which status, self-esteem, and ontological security can be claimed within international politics away from the traditional emphasis on material power. Here, competition is reframed in terms of emphasising altruistic identities and status seeking through providing collective goods. In turn, this also entails a shift in the form of nation branding prioritised in nation branding strategies. In other words, 'country of origin', 'place branding', and 'corporate branding' are to some extent sidelined in favour of an emphasis on 'policy branding' and policy transfer. Rather than jealously protecting their assets of competitive advantage, good state nation branding entails emphasising the possibility of exporting successful policies, models, and approaches, potentially across a wide range of issue areas, be that in the fields of education, science, environment, gender, criminal justice, administration, health, et cetera.

Given the inherently competitive ethos underpinning contemporary discourses of nation branding such a development may appear counter-intuitive and raises the obvious question as to why, over the last decade, states have increasingly begun to shift their nation branding programmes and messaging in this direction. This question is addressed in the opening two sections of this chapter. Specifically, section one provides a broader background by suggesting that the conceptual origins of good state nation branding can be seen in a couple of realms. Perhaps most obviously, it can be seen in the emergence of discourses about ethical consumption and Corporate Social Responsibility within the business sector from the 1990s onwards. However, it can also be seen as a linked extension to developing debates about status seeking, especially within the small states' literature, that, while having a longer heritage, have also become crystallised in more recent years. Section two, however, returns to the constitutive role of consultants in being able to influence nation branding agendas, strategies, and practices. In this respect, the emergence of good state nation branding reflects growing awareness amongst some consultants that mainstream approaches to nation branding rarely seem to have the impact promised. The result has been a reframing of the industry model and a normative shift in orientation, but one that has been notably supported by the mobilisation of a new set of statistical indicators and indexes.

Having addressed the issue of why this is happening, section three considers the question of what states seek to gain through embracing a politics of policy branding/transfer and cultivating a good state image. Several motivations are identified. These include indirect economic cost-benefit calculations and potential domestic political and strategic dividends that may be gained through wrapping up particular policy orientations in the sentiments of patriotism and thereby protecting them from assault by political opponents. Principally, however, the third section mobilises Bourdieu's theory of 'distinction' to demonstrate how good state nation branding in particular appeals to states' (their governments and populations) desires to establish a sense of 'virtuous difference'. In this respect, good state nation branding resonates with subjects' desires for positive recognition, with this seen as enhancing ontological security, status, and self-esteem.

Section four subjects good state nation branding to a more critical assessment. In particular, it considers the implied assumptions and implications that underpin existing benchmarking criteria of international 'goodness' and asks what happens to altruism and morality when 'goodness' becomes reconceptualised as a commodity to be competed over and ranked. Fundamentally, of course, in a nation branding world doing good is insufficient in and of itself: what really counts is *being seen to be doing good*. This raises questions as to what gets missed when the emphasis is placed on 'conspicuous' do-gooding and how such benevolence is itself being directed towards whatever can be calculated and represented in good state benchmarks and indexes. This chapter therefore warns against taking the ostensibly beneficent nature of good state nation branding at face value. Indeed, while recognising that there are potentially positive and pro-social motivations at play,[1] good state nation branding ultimately struggles to escape reaffirming geopolitical imaginaries that remain premised on a politics of leveraging perceived competitive advantage.

Chapter 4 ends with an evaluative case study of recent regional promotion efforts by the Nordic countries, with this providing an empirical context through which to illustrate the themes discussed in the earlier sections. The case is chosen for two reasons. First, because the Nordic states have a long-standing reputation as benevolent, yet exceptional, and in some sense superior, actors in international politics. Central to this has been the idea that they possess policy expertise, a knowledge brand and way of doing things – often framed as the Nordic model(s) – across a range of issue areas that mark them out from others but that they have also sought to offer to the world. Second, because in recent years not only have they engaged in explicit processes of region branding, but central to such exercises has been an emphasis on fostering a brand of the Nordic good state. While the chapter shows how this has various dimensions, for illustrative purposes it focuses on the branding of 'Nordic peace' and highlights how in these branding processes notions of Nordic distinction and virtuous difference remain largely intact.

TOWARDS CONSPICUOUS DO-GOODISM AND THE 'MARKET FOR VIRTUE'

The emergence of good state nation branding is not as surprising as it might initially seem. Indeed, it can be seen as the logical effect of several precursors. In particular, it manifests striking similarities with developments in consumer marketing strategies and corporate branding that have been building over decades but that have become increasingly prominent since the 1990s. In this respect, Banet-Weiser (2012) highlights two linked processes.

The first of these processes is the clever co-optation of social activism by consumerist brand culture. In the face of the emergence of counter-cultural movements in the 1960s and 1970s that reacted to the perceived 'stifling conformity of mass production and consumption' and that saw the emergence of social activist movements around issues like civil rights and second wave feminism, Banet-Weiser (2012, 32–4) notes how counter-culture itself became subjected to the logics of consumption. In other words, perceptive advertisers recognised in this development the opportunity to foster new markets rather than seeing it as a threat to consumerism as such. Key to this was understanding and embracing a new and more interactive relationship between marketers and consumers. Instead of viewing the marketing process as unidirectional, in which consumers are simply to be convinced and have their desires shaped by the marketing message, it was instead recognised that companies might start by recognising the desires and identities of potential consumers and seek to appeal to them instead. In this way, Cross (2000, 167) argues, ultimately counter-culturalists 'became rebels through consumption', that is, through purchasing 'tie-dyed dresses, as opposed to cashmere sweaters and pleated skirts … The "counter" in the culture was very much within the confines of consumerism' (quoted in Banet-Weiser 2012, 32). Rather than the death of it, consumerism was refigured as the path to authenticity via the process of branding lifestyles. As Banet-Weiser notes, 'Like other identities, such as race and gender, the social activist in its current manifestation is managed, organized, and exchanged not simply as a commodity but as a brand' (48).

The second process marks an extension of this and concerns companies seeking to align themselves with the social and ethical concerns of consumers, something that has become captured in the notion of corporate social responsibility (CSR). At root, the CSR agenda entails aligning political and social causes with the logics of business and exploiting what David Vogel (2005) terms 'the market for virtue'. Despite appealing to notions of justice and morality, CSR is primarily driven by corporations' realisation that their visible support for social issues can be good for the company's brand and therefore also good for business. As put by Banet-Weiser (2012, 144), 'saving the world, in the language of the corporation, can be profitable'.

The existence of such a market is evident, for instance, in how consumers are often willing to pay a premium for products marketed as ethical because, for example, of their environmentally sustainable credentials or claims about non-exploitative production processes. And consumers may even align themselves and identify with companies they have come to perceive positively in this light. In this respect, CSR agendas encourage consumers to view their engagement with products and companies as a form of political and social activism. Through ethically branded purchases consumers are offered the possibility of performing claims about self-identity that may serve to maintain idealisations of 'a politically virtuous self' and, in so doing, contributing to the individual's sense of ontological security. Ethical consumption assists consumers in feeling good about themselves, while no doubt personal branding around such purchases can also facilitate a certain amount of virtue signalling and personal status enhancement (Banet-Weiser 2012, 146–8).

There are, or course, no shortage of criticisms of CSR, as evident, for instance, in accusations of 'greenwashing', 'pinkwashing', et cetera, and where the suggestion is that CSR operates as a diversionary tactic that improves the brand image and profits of corporations while ultimately doing little to change things on the ground. In particular, CSR agendas absolutely are not focused on tackling or questioning the inherently exploitative nature of advanced capitalism. Yet, despite these criticisms, it is also the case that many consumers do engage with particular CSR-derived brand cultures because they want to believe that, in doing so, they are also contributing to something positive and good (Banet-Weiser 2012, 144–5).

At least in part, the advent of good state nation branding can be seen as a form of translating CSR from the corporate to the state level, and one early manifestation of this has been the emergence of ethical tourism and its associated marketing campaigns. A good illustrative example is discussed by Carah and Louw (2016), who focus on an Australian tourism marketing campaign that linked the 2008 epic film *Australia* to a series of *Come Walkabout* television advertisements that directly referenced the film, its themes, and characters, and both of which were directed by Baz Luhrmann. For Carah and Louw, the significance of the branding campaign lies in how it directly engages otherwise problematic aspects of Australia's colonial past – especially its treatment of the Aboriginal population – and rescripts them to facilitate a commercially viable form of 'ethical' tourism. Specifically, they note how the advertising campaign taps into feelings of postcolonial guilt assumed to reside within the white settler community within Australia and amongst potential middle-class tourists located abroad – depicted as 'lost, defeated, and in crisis' – and frames 'going on holiday', embarking on one's own walkabout of the country in order to experience the redeeming power of the land, as an ethical and redemptive response (36). The *Come Walkabout* advertisements, they note, are not simply targeted at appealing to pleasure and consumption but, instead, reimagine tourism as a form of apology.

> The film invites audiences and travellers to identify, or misrecognize, their journey as acknowledging indigenous connection to country and apologizing for colonial exploitation. Westerners implicitly uncomfortable with tourism in a colonial sense – consuming exotic cultures, exploiting the underdeveloped world, using culture as a resource for individual pleasure and enjoyment – feel more comfortable with tourism in the postcolonial sense as a transformative journey. (Carah and Louw 2016, 40)

Of course, much the same can be said of the burgeoning industry in eco-tourism, the ecologically beneficial aspects of which are questionable at best, particularly once the carbon footprints of eco-tourists are considered. Perhaps unsurprisingly, Carah and Louw (2016, 43, 40) remain critical of such campaigns, noting how once again Aboriginal peoples remain objectified, 'presented only as resources for our own self-reflection and self-expression as ethical consumers' or assigned agency only insofar as they are perceived as possessing 'value for the branding of the nation state'. Yet there is also a bigger point to be made here, which is that the implied apology evident in such campaigns is one in which the idealised sense of self (of Australia and the prospective tourist) remains sanctified and intact, ready to be rediscovered, recognised, and enacted through a commercial transaction of tourist adventure.[2] In this respect, be it through ethical tourism or the branding campaigns of CSR, the aim is ultimately to enable tourists/customers to (re-)experience their own ethical claims of selfhood through investment in and engagement with the product/nation.

Another precursor to good state nation branding, however, has a somewhat different, less economic and more geopolitical, derivation, one that lies in developing debates about status seeking in international relations. As highlighted by Wohlforth et al. (2018), the status literature in international relations has long been limited by a restrictive realist conflation of status with material power and its use and display within realpolitik competitions between the great powers. It is understood this way because great powers status has generally been understood in terms of establishing a reputation for being a state to be reckoned with. Yet status is not something that preoccupies the great powers alone. Indeed, Neumann and de Carvalho (2015, 1, 16) suggest that status concerns activate small powers at least as much as great powers. Indeed, in their view small powers are likely to suffer more from 'status insecurity', with this making status games much more important to them.

The problem for small powers, of course, is that for the most part they are unable to seek status in the same ways as great powers. Unable to compete on the terrain of power, they will instead emphasise alternative arenas 'on which status can be measured' and recognition secured (Wohlforth et al. 2018, 527, 532–3; Neumann and de Carvalho 2015, 10–11, 16; Beaumont 2020). Specifically, it is argued that smaller powers are liable to seek status through establishing a reputation for being 'good powers'. For instance, this might take the form of establishing a reputation for being 'useful allies, impartial arbiters, or contributors to [the] system's maintenance' (Wohlforth et al. 2018, 530; Neumann and de Carvalho 2015, 2, 9–10; de Carvalho and Lie 2015).

This emphasis on getting noticed and 'being seen' resonates with the cultural and diplomatic logics of nation branding discussed in chapter 1, where the aim is either to secure recognition for one's very existence and subjectivity or where the aim may be to carve out a particular geopolitical role or identity in international politics. This latter resonates with a longer literature analysing the role that small and middle powers have sometimes been able to play as 'norm entrepreneurs' in international politics and the strategic dividends they may gain from that (e.g., Ingebritsen 2002). Of course, in ontological security terms such forms of status seeking may also be pursued because of their own inherent worth as contributing to self-esteem and reaffirming notions of self-identity (something returned to below). The argument, therefore, is not that such developments are new as such, although considering systemic changes in the international system and the opportunities and problems associated with globalisation it may be that the scope for such interventions has expanded. Indeed, it is precisely to this that notions of good state nation branding have increasingly begun to appeal.

CONSULTANTS AND THE GOOD STATE

While the developments and processes just noted are important, arguably the crucial role in the emergence of contemporary practices of good state nation branding has been played by certain industry consultants and, most significantly, by Simon Anholt. Important, in this respect, has been growing awareness within parts of the industry that mainstream – and typically more 'cosmetic' – approaches to nation branding rarely have the impact promised, either in terms of improving national images and reputations or contributing to economic investment (Anholt 2007a, 74; Browning 2016, 57; Schwak 2018, 5). Instead of 'cosmetic' approaches, it is argued that nation branding requires more sustained and 'institutionalised' actions (Kaneva 2011, 118). 'Institutionalised' forms of nation branding, however, have generally been understood in terms of undertaking fundamental domestic political, social, and economic restructuring and reforms, a process of remaking the nation and bringing it into alignment with the claims the state makes about itself in official nation branding programmes and messaging. By contrast, while still emphasising concrete actions and sustained forms of engagement, good state nation branding pushes in a slightly different direction. Specifically, the focus is less on an inward process of renewal and regeneration (though that might conceivably be one consequence) and more on reaching out and directing actions externally and to the direct benefit of others.

Some nation branding consultants have therefore begun to suggest that states should stop focusing on what others can do for them in their nation branding programmes (i.e., buying products, investing, visiting) and focus on a more altruistic message by emphasising what 'they can do for the world'. In particular, nations are increasingly encouraged to identify global problems and to establish a competitive identity based on marketing their ability to solve those problems (e.g., Anholt 2012; 2020). Interestingly, this formulation has now become increasingly common in certain states' nation branding campaigns. For instance, Colombia, South Africa, and Turkey have all used their nation branding programmes to emphasise their ability to contribute to peace and conflict resolution, while other countries emphasise their ability to help solve other global problems, be they related to health, the environment, education, et cetera. An early mover in this regard was Finland, which subtitled its nation branding report of 2010: 'How Finland will solve the world's most intractable problems' (Country Brand Report 2010). It is no coincidence that the lead consultant in formulating this nation branding programme was Simon Anholt.

One of the interesting things about the emergence of good state nation branding, of course, is that it directs the focus of competition onto a moral and ethical plane, refiguring nation branding in terms of a competition between states as international citizens. In a recent intervention, Anholt (2020, 1) argues that states need to think carefully about questions such as: 'What is your country *for*? What is its gift to the world? How can it make a difference to the whole of humanity, not just its own citizens? How should a country *make itself useful* in the twenty-first century and so earn its place in the world?' (emphasis in original). In this respect, Anholt's thinking has developed over time and manifests a distinctive perspective, his claim being that he is now less concerned with branding nations as such and more concerned with trying to find ways to solve the gravest global challenges currently facing humanity – challenges that he sees as having been caused by the competitive behaviours of countries and people in a context of global interdependence. For him, the task is therefore one of trying to direct inter-state competition in more pro-social and benevolent directions. Yet he also argues that a concern with national brand image ultimately holds the key and will 'prove to be a new and powerful incentive for governments to join the fight against climate change, disease, poverty, inequality, conflict, and other global challenges' (7).

Essentially, Anholt argues that countries need to reconceptualise altruism and collaborative pro-social behaviours as a competitive advantage. In this respect, he appeals to notions of enlightened self-interest, explicitly arguing that such forms of behaviour do not entail national or political sacrifice – as governments are prone to fear – but instead boost national standing and promote growth and innovation (Anholt 2020, 3). Indeed, he even goes so far as to suggest that such behaviours also happen 'to be the *only way* countries can improve their image, and consequently attract more tourists and investment, as well as sell their products and services at a higher margin' (193, emphasis added). Serendipitously, then, doing good and cultivating a good state image is also good for business. Thus, despite claiming no longer to care about nation branding as such, the fundamental nation branding claim that a cultivated identity is the key to economic competitiveness remains firmly intact (see chapter 2).

An emphasis on 'doing' good, however, has other implications for nation branding, not least by affecting how it is conceived in more material terms. In particular, the previous focus on place branding, country of origin, and corporate branding is now to be accompanied by a growing emphasis on 'policy branding'. Encouraged to consider how they can be useful and make a positive difference in the world, states are therefore prompted to identify those policy areas and sectors in which they might be able to claim special knowledge or expertise and, in so doing, cultivate the idea that they possess what Sum and Jessop (2013) refer to as sector-specific 'knowledge brands' (policies). As indicated, in their nation branding programmes countries are increasingly making a virtue of claims to possess neatly packaged policy-focused brands suitable for export. In particular, Anholt (2020, 31) encourages governments to embrace 'symbolic actions', that is, 'real projects and real policies that prove to the world that a country deserves the reputation it desires; that are imaginative and unusual enough to "do their own marketing"; that are coherent with a clear, long-term strategy relating to the country's desired role in the world'. Insofar as such actions help countries find 'a helpful and productive role ... in the community of nations', then this will enhance the nation's reputation, image, and standing.

To support his claim for the enlightened self-interest benefits of such actions, Anholt (2020, 116–17) undertook an analysis to determine, once and for all, 'the true drivers of a positive national image'. To do this, he drew on the resources of the Nation Brands Index he had established previously, crunching the mass of data points of seventeen surveys of international perceptions accumulated between 2005 and 2011 with respect to sixty-four countries. The result is what he terms the MARSS model of the key drivers of overall national standing. In other words, Anholt suggests that national standing is a result of a country's reputation with respect to *morality, aesthetics, relevance, sophistication*, and *strength* (MARSS). However, from his analysis Anholt concludes that the different drivers are not equally weighted. Least important, he argues, are 'relevance' (whether a 'country has the power to impact one's life in some direct way') and 'aesthetics' (whether a 'country – its people, its cities and landscapes, even its products and cultural productions – are regarded as pleasing to the eye'). 'Strength' (the perception of a country's hard power understood as its ability to 'wield direct influence over us or others') is next, followed by 'sophistication' ('a measure of how advanced a country is perceived to be'). However, Anholt claims that, out front 'by a wide margin, and correlated most strongly with each country's overall NBI [Nation Brands Index] score', is 'morality' (a measure of 'whether people approve of the country and its behavior in the international domain: is the country perceived to exert a positive and principled influence on humanity and the planet?') (117).

> The message from the analysis was clear: The countries that people prefer aren't necessarily the biggest, strongest, richest, or most beautiful, although these are important considerations. The most likely reason why somebody would admire a country is that they believe it contributes something of value to the world we live in, that it is motivated by positive values and principles. In other words, *people admire good countries*. (Anholt 2020, 118, emphasis in original)

On reflection, Anholt suggests that this should not surprise us: after all, isn't this precisely the lesson of the corporate social responsibility agenda, that 'consumers admire good companies' – or at least those that are seen to be good? Why would the same not also be true for states? Understood this way, 'doing good' is not a distraction but a necessity for a country wishing to improve its reputation, national image, and wanting to succeed economically (Anholt 2020, 118–9).

Anholt, however, went further and set about seeking to quantify the relative 'good' that different states contribute. One aspect of this was to develop a model outlining six stages demonstrating differential levels of commitment to doing good. The lower stages entail things like basing one's practices on knowledge derived from others, possibly imitating them, but remaining largely passive in terms of policy development oneself. By contrast, the higher stages entail enhanced willingness to share experiences, cooperate, and ultimately cede sovereign power to collaborative governance structures (Anholt 2020, 173–4). Most significant, however, has been his development of a new benchmarking mechanism, the Good Country Index (https://www.goodcountry.org), the first iteration of which was collated in 2014 (see table 4.1).

The Good Country Index seeks to provide a simplified measure 'of what each country on earth contributes to the common good of humanity, and what it takes away, relative to its size' (https://www.goodcountry.org/index/about-the-index). Countries are ranked across seven fields, each of which comprises five separate indicators. The seven fields concern contributions to: science and technology; culture; international peace and security; world order; planet and climate; prosperity and equality; health and wellbeing. To account for the relative wealth of each country, scores are in turn divided against the respective country's GDP on the assumption that for several indicators the size of a country's economy will have an impact, positively or negatively, on its ability to contribute (Anholt 2020, 209–10; Cull 2019, 138–9).

The thirty-five indicators used to compile the Index are themselves drawn from other benchmarking indexes. For instance, the field of 'science and technology' uses measures such as UNESCO data on the number of foreign students studying in a country, SCImago statistics on the number of articles published in international journals, the accumulated number of Nobel prizes assigned to countries based on laureates' country of birth as well as institutional affiliation, and the number of international patent cooperation treaty applications as recorded by the World Intellectual Property Organization. Contributions to 'world order', meanwhile, include indicators such as UNHCR records of numbers of refugees hosted and the number of refugees abroad, World Bank data on birth rates, and information held by the Charities Aid Foundation on the percentage of the population that gives to charity (https://www.goodcountry.org/index/source-data).

The combining of such an array of statistics is clearly understood as an attempt at generating as objective an index as possible, although

Table 4.1
The Good Country Index*

Rank	Country	Science and technology	Culture	International peace and security	World order	Planet and climate	Prosperity and equality	Health and wellbeing
1	Sweden	15th	13th	39th	9th	2nd	1st	2nd
2	Denmark	8th	9th	57th	8th	7th	3rd	4th
3	Germany	27th	26th	33rd	10th	13th	12th	1st
4	Netherlands	11th	7th	41st	5th	42nd	9th	7th
5	Finland	17th	11th	63rd	31st	1st	5th	18th
165	Sudan	120th	135th	167th	144th	162nd	122nd	161st
166	Libya	139th	148th	164th	114th	169th	150th	132nd
167	CAR	127th	163rd	169th	149th	165th	116th	131st
168	Mauritania	165th	126th	145th	147th	157th	139th	153rd
169	Syria	134th	155th	154th	167th	161st	168th	165th

* Compiled using data from the Good Country Index version 1.5, which uses data mainly from 2020 (https://index.goodcountry.org).

there are problems with this. To note just two (more are discussed shortly) the positive/negative valence of some indicators may not be as self-evident as they initially seem. For instance, whether high or low birth rates represent a contribution to world order and the global good is arguably a matter of perspective and circumstance. Second, the combination of multiple other indexes measuring a range of factors as a proxy for a singular measurement of the 'good country' is also problematic. For instance, in a different context, Homolar (2015) shows how similar attempts to combine a range of already existing benchmarks (such as a country's GDP) as a proxy metric for 'human (in)security' ultimately have had the effect of producing only a narrow understanding of what it means to live a 'secure' life, in this case, one premised on market dynamics and purchasing power. Yet even here it is important to remember that GDP is a measure of the overall performance of the state's economy, not a measure of wealth distribution or of the actual impact of GDP on people's lives. The problem, therefore, is that metrics used to measure one thing inevitably introduce normative assumptions and distortions when used as a proxy for assessing something else.

Irrespective of this, the Good Country Index is clearly designed as a device through which to influence and motivate state behaviours. Ranking states by their 'goodness' once again targets the competitive instinct. In this respect, while it may be tempting to dismiss the Good Country Index as another cynical theoretical innovation calculated to reignite governments' interest in nation branding, thereby rejuvenating the consultancy business model once more, it is important not to ignore the constitutive effects of such practices. As Schwak (2018, 652) notes, rankings like this can be powerful in establishing 'standards for acceptable state identity'. As with nation branding in general, the Good Country Index therefore appears as another form of marketable consultancy 'knowledge brand' claiming to know the relevant techniques and strategies countries should adopt in their pursuit of success.

DISTINCTION, VIRTUOUS DIFFERENCE, AND THE APPEAL OF 'GOOD STATE' NATION BRANDING

Having discussed some of the drivers behind the emergence of good state nation branding, it is important to consider in more depth why such apparently altruistic forms of policy branding may appeal to states. What exactly is it that states seek to gain through embracing a politics of policy branding/transfer and cultivating a good state image? At least four suggestions can be made.

First, of course, are the indirect economic cost-benefit calculations to which Anholt himself alludes: the idea that, ultimately, economic success is driven by cultivating competitive identities and that the most competitive identities in the contemporary world are those evidencing a good state orientation. In more direct economic cost-benefit calculations, though, such an approach is not self-evident in and of itself. This point has been made by Marsh and Fawcett (2011a) who draw a comparison with practices of policy branding at the level of the corporation via the practice of franchising. Franchising, they note, has a clear economic rationale (profit motive) for companies on both ends of the relationship. In a business model, franchising enables the franchiser to spread their business model at limited cost, while it is also argued that, because they have explicitly bought into the brand, the franchisee has greater incentives than normal employees to make the brand work (247). The risk, of course, is that the franchiser loses a certain amount of control over the process since franchising grants the franchisee more leeway than a normal employee would have. For franchisees the attractions lie in being able to draw upon the knowledge, expertise, training, and brand power of the franchiser, which they pay for through rents and a share of the profits.

However, when it comes to policy branding and policy transfer as a form of nation branding it is less obvious that the profit motive would be the key underpinning factor, particularly for governments who generally want to see a direct economic return on their investment. Put differently, despite Anholt's claims about the economic benefits of good state nation branding and behaviour the links are at best correlational rather than causal. Of course, one should not discount the fact that (state-backed) consultancies specialising in particular policy areas might not also emerge that are able to ride on and exploit these processes – for instance, developing a business model premised on offering services helping to implement 'the country x approach to y'. In general, though, when a country like Finland, for instance, advertises itself at the World Economic Forum as having one of the best education systems in the world, it is not clear that the aim is to capitalise on this economically (World Economic Forum 2018). Offering up 'Finnish lessons' in education rather seems to be about image and reputation building.

To this extent, Marsh and Fawcett (2011a, 253–4) suggest a second reason, arguing that there may be reputational reasons for making policy branding a central part of nation branding. Specifically, they argue that countries may increasingly be driven towards adopting a branding and franchising approach to policy export to ensure that policy transfer is done in a consistent and comprehensive manner. They will do this to protect the brand by attempting to prevent failures arising from poor implementation that might otherwise reflect badly on the country brand and reputation. In other words, if others are going to adopt your approach to education, criminal justice, et cetera – or at least claim to be doing so – then branding those approaches (and providing follow-on advice and training) can be one way of ensuring they do it properly and do not sully the country's reputation through poor or selective implementation. For instance, the so-called 'Nordic prostitution model' is often held up and promoted by campaigners in other countries,[3] even though the very existence of a common 'Nordic prostitution model' is questionable and attempts to implement it elsewhere often problematic (Skilbrei and Holmstrom 2014). This can create a perceived need to protect the nature of the policy brand, even in instances (such as this) when the reality of the brand is contested.

A third argument, by contrast, suggests that nation branding through policy export may also be a way of fighting political battles at home by wrapping up specific policy orientations in the sentiments of patriotism and national values and thereby protecting them from assault by political opponents. Understood this way, policy branding also has the potential to function as a means for disciplining citizens towards accepting particular approaches to the provision of public goods, thereby delimiting the level of ideological diversity (Marsh and Fawcett 2011b, 517). For instance, Marklund (2017, 634) analyses how 'promoting the reputation of the Nordic countries as social pioneers abroad also serves as a powerful incentive to live up to this expectation in domestic policies'. Much the same might be said of the branding and policy export of other socio-economic models, not least the notion that the United States is so indelibly linked to ideas of free-market capitalism that anyone arguing for higher levels of social welfare provision is easily marginalised as a 'socialist' and de facto 'un-American'. Returning to the Nordic case, though, Marklund also interestingly notes that, in the 2010s, the Swedish Social Democratic Party sought to register the 'Nordic model' as a protected trademark, thereby 'identifying this concept as an intangible asset belonging to the rights holder' (629). It did this to protect the social democratic and welfarist characteristics associated with the idea of the 'Nordic model' from becoming diluted by the more neoliberal policies of parties on the centre and right of Swedish politics who had recently started to appropriate the concept for themselves, aware of its powerful brand resonance amongst the electorate.

However, from an ontological security perspective a fourth suggestion can also be made as to why good state nation branding via the cultivation of policy-focused knowledge brands for export may appeal – an explanation in which Bourdieu's (1984) theory of 'distinction' is instructive. Bourdieu uses the concept of distinction to refer to the temptations people feel to establish a sense of virtuous difference towards others and that, when they are doing so, can help them generate positive self-concepts, pride, status, and self-esteem. Here, then, the valuing of difference takes a different form to the constitutive othering and enemy imaging emphasised in poststructuralist thinking in international relations (e.g., Campbell 1992). Instead, the other is a subject to be attracted and whose admiration is sought yet is simultaneously to be kept at an (inferior) distance in the very same process. For example, much of Bourdieu's analysis focuses on class politics and where he notes that the appeal of class attributes lies precisely in their exclusivity and (sometimes) rarity. One example of this is how the upper classes gravitated away from some initially upper-class sports (like football and rugby) once they were perceived to have become too popular with the masses (and therefore sullied), instead switching to other more exclusive sports (Bourdieu 1984, 212). Similarly, we might consider why people enjoy belonging to exclusive clubs or why we place high monetary value on rare gemstones, even when they have limited utility. For Bourdieu, therefore, difference is potentially a source of enjoyment to be cultivated, especially when difference takes the form of being exclusive or rare and is valued by others. By extrapolation, the conspicuous do-goodism of good state nation branding can be seen as establishing similar feelings of virtuous difference.

Of course, the enjoyment of distinction is itself dependent upon others recognising, admiring, and valuing one's difference – a proxy and indicator of which for good state nation branding would be benchmarks like the Good Country Index. Insofar as they do, status is attributed, with this helping affirm one's own sense of self-esteem and a positive view of selfhood. Such a sense of virtuous difference therefore requires that the subject perform their distinction in front of others – such as through things like admirable and pro-social marketable knowledge brands – which can often stimulate others to attempt to imitate one's distinction. Indeed, the enjoyment of distinction may even require encouraging others precisely to engage in such actions, since doing so reaffirms those hierarchies upon which virtuous difference depends (Bourdieu 1984, 50).

Arguably, then, the shift towards cultivating policy-based knowledge brands in nation branding practices can be understood to appeal to similar desires to cultivate a sense of virtuous difference by emphasising one's distinction, especially when this is premised on being pioneers (i.e., rare) in at least some areas of activity. For instance, the previously mentioned Finnish nation branding programme that was launched in 2010 not only sought to position the country as the 'problem solver of the world' (Country Brand Report 2010, 3) but also, by emphasising the country's ability to assist with problems, including international conflicts, water shortages, and education, hoped thereby to earn the country international distinction and help build self-esteem (Ministry for Foreign Affairs 2010).

In a context in which nations are increasingly being urged to brand themselves and compete in terms of their sense of international civic duty – of how 'good' they are – offering up policy solutions to global problems becomes one way of standing out and climbing those benchmarks whose very purpose is to mark out those worthy of accolades in the first place. Offering up solutions to global problems may therefore be one way through which states may be able to (re)assert a sense of their distinction as 'good', humane, and beneficent actors, in turn fostering a sense of self-esteem and pride at what this is presumed to mean for the nation's international standing – a standing that can, of course, be evidenced through performance in benchmarking tables of good citizenship.

UNPACKING GOOD STATE BENEVOLENCE

With its explicit encouragement for states to adopt a more other-regarding and pro-social perspective and to generate a sense of status and self-esteem through competing at a moral level, rather than (only) in terms of economic attractiveness or power, 'good state' nation branding obviously has intuitive appeal. However, while at face value it suggests that states are becoming increasingly altruistic and benevolent, the shift towards 'good state' nation branding also needs critical reflection.

First, it is important to remember that when operating under 'economic logics' (see chapters 1 and 2) nation branding is fundamentally underpinned by a discourse of how states might best compete in a globalising world of international markets and deregulated capitalism. This raises questions as to the limits of its transformative potential. In other words, how much 'good' is good state nation branding likely to produce? At the end of the day, insofar as its proponents accept such a world as given, then good state nation branding is likely to remain implicated in a set of socially, politically, and environmentally exploitative practices that have been a significant driver of many of the global problems that those states branding themselves as 'good states' are now claiming to be able to solve. As noted above, Anholt's (2020, 3, 193) sales pitch for the 'good state' is that it should appeal to enlightened self-interest. His 'good country equation' essentially breaks down as follows:

1 Doing good will improve the national image.
2 This will attract tourists and investment.
3 Ergo, doing good is good for business.

It is unlikely, therefore, that good state nation branding will provide a fundamental challenge to the extraction, consumption, and exploitation (of people and environments) at the heart of global capitalism. To the contrary, good state nation branding remains embedded within the logics of market capitalism and, as such, may well function to mask rather than to alleviate the problems it claims to address (Banet-Weiser 2012, 49). One effect of this, of course, may be that instead of *doing* good, good state nation branding provides a comforting feeling or *illusion* of do-gooding that enables citizens, tourists, and investors to assuage anxieties about the state of the world and to feel empowered through their consumption of and identification with 'good state' brands. As Banet-Weiser notes with respect to CSR and businesses' embracing of their environmentalist credentials, 'even when greenwashing does occur, consumers still may feel as if they are "doing good" and operating as virtuous selves by participating in green brand cultures' (152–4).

This indicates a couple of bigger issues: the interlinked questions of what constitutes the parameters of do-gooding in good state nation branding and who gets to decide. Again, the business world provides some useful insights. With respect to the first, companies are unlikely to place issues at the heart of their CSR agendas and branding campaigns that are controversial or deemed potentially alienating or offensive to their customers. To the contrary, they are most likely to embrace issues that have become socially accepted as important and are therefore politically safe and ontologically affirming of their consumers' political convictions and sense of moral virtue (Banet-Weiser 2012, 148–9). The same arguably applies to good state nation branding. Here, the focus has typically been on emphasising states' contributions with respect to issues like the environment, poverty reduction, education, peace and conflict resolution – issues that few people are likely to find controversial or problematic at face value. By contrast, more contested issues are generally avoided. For instance, nation branding campaigns rarely emphasise things like being for/against gay rights or being for/against pro-choice regimes on abortion. They also tend to steer clear of anything that does not comply with hegemonic discourses of democratisation, free trade, and postcolonialism – criteria that have become central to ideas of the 'good state'. Indeed, in this respect it is notable that the proliferation of nation branding in the 2000s has been most marked amongst those states (for example in Eastern Europe, Central Asia, and Africa) seeking to align themselves with broadly 'Western' conceptions of political economy and democratisation (Carah and Louw 2016, 42). In other words, in general (though see chapter 6) there is little space for reconceptualising the fundamentals of the globalised capitalist order. Thus, while one political and economic model is foregrounded and promoted, alternative modes of being and conceptions of the 'good state' remain sidelined. Good state nation branding therefore remains largely a reflection of the established normative social, political, economic, and international order, arguably reinforcing rather than questioning it.

Second, it is also important to reflect on what happens to altruism and morality when 'goodness' becomes reconceptualised as a commodity to be competed over and ranked via benchmarking practices claiming to be able to order states in terms of their relative contribution to the overall global good. At this point it becomes relevant to distinguish between 'doing good' and 'being seen to be doing good'. States may, of course, be interested in the former; however, insofar as states have become interested in developing a reputation and brand for altruism, and increasingly see their performance on global benchmarks – like the Good Country Index – as both a proxy for this *and* as a central part of their brand strategy, the importance of 'conspicuous do-goodism', of being seen to be doing good, is likely to be emphasised. This is likely to have practical consequences. For instance, one of the known problems with benchmarking practices is that they come to shape behaviours by encouraging actors to engage in activities that are recognised and recorded in the benchmarks, while diverting attention and resource away from other activities that might be equally (or even more) important but that remain uncounted. Of course, as the number of international public policy performance indicators and rankings has expanded over the last few decades into areas such as education, health care, gender equality, et cetera, this has also expanded the scope of areas around which states might seek to demonstrate their exemplary performance (Beaumont 2020; Gilady 2018). At root, though, the logic of benchmarking is that if states want to be seen to be 'good' then they are more likely to engage in 'symbolic actions' that will be reflected and have visibility or impact in the benchmarks. In this respect, Anholt (2020, 217) reports how he receives 'a steady trickle of emails from governments around the world asking [him] to explain their country's results in the *Good Country Index*, or asking what they would need to do to improve them next time', and of course the criteria and datasets through which the Good Country Index is compiled itself provides some significant clues.

A third point is that the inherently competitive logic underpinning benchmarking practices suggests that good state nation branding is unlikely to escape from reaffirming geopolitical imaginaries premised on leveraging perceived competitive advantage for primarily status gains – indeed, in part this seems to be largely the point. In other words, there is always the possibility that winning the status competition through demonstrating one's conspicuous goodness becomes the primary end, with the danger being that the perception of performance – the brand – may become more important than the performance itself (Marklund 2017, 625; Leira 2021, 209). This can have a couple of interesting implications that arguably sit at odds with the assumptions of those promoting good state nation branding. First, while Anholt (2020, 119) suggests that an emphasis on doing good should lead states to become increasingly collaborative, the opposite sometimes seems to be the case. For instance, and as is developed shortly, while all the Nordic countries emphasise peace promotion as part of their good state nation branding efforts, they also sometimes fail to collaborate in this area because they fear that to do so will reduce the level of individual recognition received (Hagemann and Bramsen

2019). Ultimately, the need to be recognised for one's distinction that (good state) nation branding plays to at least sometimes seems to suggest that the competitive instinct will override the potential benefits of collaboration.

A second implication, and an extension of a previous point, is that states may ultimately be tempted to prioritise being seen to be doing good to the detriment of the effectiveness of the actions they are seeking to undertake. For instance, and to pick a different Nordic example, Moss (2021, 67–8) notes that, despite Norway and Sweden having similar positions on promoting gender equality, Swedish officials seem to be much more concerned than their Norwegian counterparts with how such policies are branded. Concerned primarily with the effectiveness of their actions, Moss argues that Norway is often willing to let other countries take the lead on Norwegian gender-equality initiatives on the grounds that 'it is often more powerful if the message is fronted by South Africa or Colombia rather than the Nordic countries' (Norwegian diplomat quoted in Moss 2021, 67). By contrast, Sweden appears to be much less willing to forego the potential branding opportunities implied by badging gender-equality policies as Swedish. For Sweden, brand considerations may therefore trump policy effectiveness.

And last, a reflection on the Nordic case also indicates a third possible unanticipated implication, which is that ostensibly positive brands can easily turn negative, especially if the claimed knowledge brand appears arrogant or smug. For instance, the Nordic countries' proselytising about gender equality and general suggestion of moral superiority has sometimes left an impression that they are rather sanctimonious 'know it alls' (Moss 2018; 2021, 65–6; Ojanen and Raunio 2018), which may be one reason Norway is now more willing to take a less visible role, at least in the realm of gender equality. The Nordic countries, of course, are no stranger to this, with foreign perceptions of the region generally alternating between visions of utopia and dystopia. The point, though, is that, insofar as knowledge brands and attempts at good state nation branding through policy transfer can generate a certain amount of resentment and resistance, questions also arise as to whether embedding policy transfer within nation branding frameworks may actually be sub-optimal to solving global problems, at least in some cases. This is because – despite claims to benevolence – good state nation branding ultimately remains premised on hierarchical and competitive geopolitical imaginaries.

CASE ANALYSIS:
THE NORDIC GOOD STATE BRAND

To illustrate some of the points made above it is useful to expand further on the case of the Nordic states. The Nordic countries make a good case for several reasons. First, they have a long-standing reputation as benevolent actors in international politics, often referred to in public and academic discourse as 'norm entrepreneurs' (Ingebritsen 2002), 'moral superpowers' (Vik et al. 2018, 193), and 'good states' (Lawler 2005). In particular, this is connected to an enduring reputation that became crystallised during the Cold War for their embrace of pro-social agendas on environmentalism, welfarism at home, and solidarity with the developing world abroad via active humanitarian and development aid policies, and, not least, activist stances with respect to conflict mediation/resolution and peacekeeping (Mouritzen 1995). Second, since its first iteration in 2014, Denmark, Finland, Norway, and Sweden have featured consistently in and around the top ten place rankings of the Good Country Index, often topping it. For instance, the 2020 iteration placed Sweden first, Denmark second, Finland fifth, and Norway eleventh.[4]

Third, since 2000 each of the countries has actively developed official nation branding programmes; moreover, and the focus of this section, since 2015 they have also developed a collective region-wide branding programme. In part, this is in recognition that, like many small states, they are often confused with each other. However, unlike some other states in similar situations (for instance, the '*Stans* of Central Asia, or Ukraine, Moldova and Belarus with respect to Russia' [Saunders 2012, 54–5]), this lack of individual distinction has not necessarily been problematic because, in general, the notion of the 'Nordic' carries positive resonance. As such, rather than trying to escape from a regional identification, as evident in some countries' nation branding programmes (see chapter 6), in general the Nordic countries have seen their regional moniker and identification as beneficial and bolstering ontological security, status, and self-esteem.

It is important to recognise, however, that the story here is more nuanced than it may initially seem. Not least, the end of the Cold War resulted in a crisis of confidence across the region that in Bourdieuian terms derived from an apparent loss of distinction that touched on questions of identity, ontological security, status, and self-esteem. Specifically, key elements that lay at the heart of Cold

War claims about Norden as a region of exceptionalism and alternative European/global futures no longer held. On the one hand, the progressivist and egalitarian social democratic-infused notion of a future 'third way' combining the best elements of Western capitalism and Soviet socialism no longer appeared so convincing. Instead, the future seemed to have moved away, from a region now cast as increasingly statist and modernist, towards the promise offered by the postmodernist project of European integration, Anglo-American economic liberalism, and globalisation. Meanwhile, other established markers of distinction (e.g., the emphasis on being peaceful societies and bridge builders, on internationalist solidarism, and on environmentalism) no longer appeared particularly exceptional or distinctive (Laatikainen 2003). From being exceptional, the threat of normality loomed with claims about the 'death' of Norden (and various Nordic models[5]) widely aired (Browning 2007; Mouritzen 1995; Patomäki 2000; Wæver 1992).

The past decade, however, has seen an intriguing revival of notions of Nordic distinction, central to which has been a reframing of Nordic exceptionalism through practices of nation branding at both state and regional levels. While state-oriented nation branding programmes started earlier, it is notable that in 2015 the Nordic Council of Ministers – an intergovernmental forum for cooperation between the Nordic countries – published *Strategy for International Branding of the Nordic Region 2015–2018*, with this subsequently extended for 2019–2021 (Nordic Council of Ministers 2015; 2019).

The developing collective Nordic branding project includes much that one would expect to find in a typical nation or region branding programme. For instance, there is the requisite (and largely interchangeable) proliferation of inspiring and beautiful images (of people, places, and food); an emphasis on education, science, technology, and culture; and where a 'Nordic perspective' is described as one focused on 'openness, trust in each other, new ways of thinking, sustainable management, compassion and tolerance' (Nordic Council and the Nordic Council of Ministers n.d.). However, the *Strategy* is also interesting because it places notions of do-gooding at the heart of its branding strategy.

For instance, it explicitly addresses the question of what 'the Nordic region can offer the outside world', and it answers this by conceptualising the region as a 'knowledge society' – this itself indicating how the economic imaginaries identified by Sum and Jessop (2013) have become internalised – possessing solutions for pressing global problems, including in the areas of social, economic, and environmental sustainability, while placing particular emphasis on how the Nordic governance and welfare model distinguished itself following the 2008 economic crisis (Nordic Council of Ministers 2015, 16–7). Presented as a 'knowledge society', the region is in turn presented as possessing a range of policy-focused 'knowledge brands' for export, with these spanning everything from energy and environmental policy, gender politics, and education to criminal justice amongst others. The effect of this is to revive notions of Nordic exceptionalism and distinction. This not only reaffirms exceptionalism as a core part of the Nordic brand, with this demonstrated via the deployment of a range of global benchmarking indexes that in turn help serve to cultivate the idea that the Nordics possess expertise in specific policy areas, but also helps preserve the notion that there is such a thing as a Nordic model for the twenty-first century. It thereby reaffirms established Cold War geopolitical imaginaries that once again code the Nordic brand as green (through the focus on environmental policies), humane (through the focus on criminal justice and humanitarian policies), and egalitarian (through the focus on educational and gender-based policies).

However, to consider what happens when 'doing good' becomes subject to practices of nation/region branding it is useful to focus in on one particular element of the Nordic Council of Ministers' emphasis on good state branding – its specific embracing of 'peace'. Interestingly, peace did not feature explicitly in the 2015 Nordic branding *Strategy* document, yet by 2017 it had become central, with the Nordic Council of Ministers (2017) declaring '*Låt fred bli Nordens varumärke*' (Let peace become the Nordic brand/trademark). Following this a report was released to scope out the idea but that, notably, directly packages this as part of the more 'general branding efforts of the Nordics, "Nordic solutions to global problems"' (Hagemann and Bramsen 2019, 44). The report's starting point, of course, is to determine whether a Nordic peace 'brand' exists in the first place. Unsurprisingly it finds it does, seeing this as evidenced, on the one hand, by the longer history of intra-Nordic peace and, on the other hand, by the Nordic countries' historical record of trying to 'export peace'. In this regard the region is presented as both a region '*of* peace' and '*for* peace', with the Nordic peace brand explained in terms of a sense of shared culture, mind-set, and values (7, 9, 12, 15, 17, 36).

Several things are notable about this. First is how the framing represents the Nordic countries as an identifiable community with something distinct to offer the world based on their specific history and identity. In this respect, a nation/region building element is evident in which the identification of a Nordic peace brand also functions to reconstitute, rebind, and normalise the very idea of the Nordic community following a period when it had been put in question.

Second, it is of course important to recognise and reflect on the historical legacy and heritage upon which the branding of 'Nordic peace' draws, with this raising the question of what may be at stake in the application of the signifier 'brand' in this context. In this respect, the notion of Nordic peace is not new in and of itself. For instance, from the mid-nineteenth century through to the Second World War the idea of being 'peaceful' nations increasingly spread across the region, arguably becoming a significant element in at least some discourses of national self-identity and, as such, had started to become ontologically significant (Browning and Joenniemi 2013). For instance, from its early years of independence in 1905, being a 'peace nation' became embedded in Norwegian narratives of self-identity (Leira 2013). Internally, the region increasingly came to resemble a Deutschian (Deutsch et al. 1957) security community, that is, a community of nations amongst whom expectations of peaceful change had become established (see also Adler and Barnett 1998; Kupchan 2010). It is this that the commissioned report on a Nordic peace brand is referencing when describing the Nordic countries as constituting a 'region *of* peace'.

The Cold War period, however, saw some notable developments, and it is perhaps at this point that it might be argued that a discernibly Nordic peace 'brand' developed, if brand here refers simply to an identifying mark or characteristic. Specifically, it was during this period when the Nordic countries began to engage in more concerted efforts of peace promotion abroad – that is, becoming a 'region *for* peace' in the terms of the commissioned report. There were, however, a couple of drivers for this. On the one hand, geopolitical considerations were important in that engaging in visible peace activism – for instance, in terms of contributing to UN peacekeeping missions, offering services for East-West bridge building – beyond the region became a way of carving out a role for these countries in international politics and where doing so was designed to send a signal to both East and West that the status of the region as 'the quiet corner of Europe' should be preserved. Peace activism therefore functioned as a form of security policy, legitimising the Nordic region's somewhat distanced position outside the main vectors of the Cold War confrontation (Mouritzen 1995; Browning forthcoming). Insofar as this could be seen as a 'brand', it was one that conformed to a diplomatic logic. On the other hand, as the Cold War developed, this geostrategic rationale was supported by more emotive drivers. For instance, the developing reputation for peace promotion also had a status dividend for the Nordic countries, this transforming peace promotion into something virtuous, which in turn further enhanced a sense of moralism in the different nations' conceptions of self-identity – perhaps most notably in Sweden, where the notion of the country as the 'world's conscience' increasingly gained ground (Trädgårdh 2002, 152). In other words, peace activism was not just valued because it enhanced regional security and status but also because it had become internalised into notions of 'who we are'.

What marks out the contemporary context from the historical legacy on which it draws is the shift from the emergence of Nordic peace as a 'brand' towards more active strategies of 'branding' premised on increasingly economic logics of brand cultivation, with this arguably changing the relationship between Nordic peace and its role in national and regional identity. A sign of this is evident in the commissioned report's renewed emphasis on ideas of Nordic peace more as an instrumental asset and less as a fundamental virtue or manifestation of self-understanding. To quote one ambassador referenced in the report: 'We have a Nordic brand that we could possibly use more. It gives us a good profile when we go out together and perform together. In addition, visiting different countries together generates good press coverage and awareness of us' (quoted in Hagemann and Bramsen 2019, 36).

Framed as an asset of Nordic branding, Nordic peace is therefore revalued fundamentally for its potential for publicity, reputational impact, and status enhancement, and perhaps only secondarily in terms of either its centrality to ethically infused conceptions of self-identity or with respect to whether or not Nordic peace actions may actually be helping in the world. The quote therefore reflects a sentiment expressed by Jan Petersen, when in 2002 and as the Norwegian foreign minister, he stated: 'Peace processes make us interesting ... We need a few products like that' (quoted in Wohlforth et al. 2018, 540). Interesting in this respect, then, is whether the constitutive components of Nordic peace are being transformed by its current curation as a brand. As Nordic peace has become increasingly subject to imperatives of conspicuous do-goodism and the need to establish a sense of virtuous difference, arguably they are. In other words, for the Nordic peace brand to sell it has become especially important to establish its unique selling points and points of distinction, with this itself central to the very process of branding Nordic peace in the first place.

It is notable therefore that the previous Cold War emphasis on peacekeeping is being replaced by three specific areas of prioritisation. The first emphasises peace mediation and dialogue that draws on experiences and practices initially developed during the Cold War and where in recent years there has been a certain intensification of activities. Norway has led the way in this area by seeking to capitalise on its role in the Oslo peace process of the 1990s, thereby seeking to cultivate the idea that it possesses a 'knowledge brand' in this field. The second area is arguably more notable, with an evident shift away from more traditional peacekeeping operations, with their emphasis on neutrality and impartiality towards the combatant parties in any conflict, towards active military engagement in peace enforcement operations, a role that entails a willingness to actively take sides and where peace promotion and being 'good' is reframed more in terms of being a 'good ally' willing to accept sacrifices (Wohlforth et al. 2018). Interestingly, and despite their long heritage of neutrality and non-alignment, this is a role that has been embraced by Finland and Sweden as much as by NATO-allies Denmark and Norway.

Third, however, and perhaps most interestingly, has been an emerging focus on gender and, more specifically, on claimed connections between women, peace, and security and in which area the Nordics position themselves as 'leading by example' (Hagemann and Bramsen 2019, 19). The aim is therefore to capitalise on what is perceived to be an almost unparalleled reputation for gender equality and that elsewhere they have described as a 'knowledge product' (Nordic Council of Ministers for Gender Equality 2019). Specifically, internal achievements of gender equality are now depicted as one explanation for internal regional peace and a central component of a renewed Nordic model, the so-called 'Nordic gender effect', which is now to be offered to the world as part of the broader package of 'Nordic solutions to global challenges'. Framed as such, this becomes justification for actively promoting a Nordic understanding of gender mainstreaming abroad (Hagemann and Bramsen 2019, 19). As Wivel (2017, 494) supportively notes in an article discussing what has otherwise happened to the Nordic model for international peace and security, integrating gender into all aspects of Nordic peace support will provide a welcome boost to the rebranding of Nordic peace by 'providing a distinct Nordic voice internationally'. However, one reason this focus on gender as part of the constitution (and rebranding) of a new Nordic peace brand is interesting is because it plays strongly to Nordic notions of distinction and exceptionalism – or exclusivity and virtuous difference, in Bourdieu's terms. This is because, for cultural, structural, and developmental reasons, Nordic distinction in this realm is largely assured. The gender focus therefore resonates with Bourdieu's idea that, while performing distinction is central to establishing a sense of virtuous difference, and while the aim of such actions may be to encourage imitation, the enjoyment and satisfaction of virtuous difference (and good state branding) ultimately rests in its rarity, exclusivity, and remaining out of reach.

A couple of final points can also be made. First, it is notable that despite the aim of cultivating a common brand, this is not always straightforward. For instance, the commissioned report on branding Nordic peace itself recognised the potential for intra-Nordic competition, presuming that there will be incentives for individual countries to want to take sole credit for those initiatives on which they have led (Hagemann and Bramsen 2019, 37–8). Assumptions that good state nation branding will tend towards a shift away from competition towards more collaborative behaviours in the pursuit of the common good therefore should not be taken for granted – even in cases where this appears to be an explicit aim. Similarly, and to repeat a point made earlier, the imperative to 'be seen' to be doing good also means that there may always be a temptation to prioritise presentation and visibility over substance. In general, though, what we see in current practices of Nordic good state nation branding is a shift away from a focus on geopolitical considerations interlinked with the enactment of internalised claims about self-identity towards a valuing of Nordic peace more for its ability to generate status benefits, standing, and to enhance regional self-esteem via the repackaging of Nordic peace as a distinct (set of) knowledge brand(s) designed to establish which aspects of Nordic peace promotion stand out.

Finally, the Nordic case is also interesting because, intriguingly, it is one to which, at times, other countries and foreign actors have also become attached, or have at least seen reasons to reaffirm, often for distinctly strategic ends. For instance, the (re)production of pervasive utopian visions of 'the Nordics as a soft-focus paradise of welfare and well-being' (Crouch 2018, 30) and as a focal point for individual and collective flourishing have not been the preserve of the Nordics alone. In recent years, for instance, airport and high street bookshops have been piled high with books dedicated to various Nordic concepts seen to encapsulate fundamental wisdoms about the nature of the good life – the Danish concepts of *hygge* and *lykke*, the Swedish concepts of *lagom* and *fika*. Yet this phenomenon was actually conceived by London publishing houses seeking to capitalise on the flourishing market for books about lifestyle choices, thus showing how non-Nordic corporate interests have been able to capitalise on Nordic good state branding by actively promoting it (Higgins 2016). Likewise, however, images of the Nordic good state are also sometimes appropriated in (geo)political debates outside the region as a resource of political legitimation. For instance, in the US, Democrats like Bernie Sanders have sometimes embraced the progressivist notion of '*Nordic* socialism' when promoting more state-interventionist policies, the hope being that the 'Nordic' component might detoxify the 'socialist' component for some American voters (Dorfmann 2018). Less progressive, however, are cases where governments have invoked Nordic political decisions to justify more restrictive, othering, and populist policies on the grounds that, if the 'good' Nordics are doing this (e.g., Denmark's increasingly tough and arguably discriminatory policies towards migrants and refugees), then how bad could they possibly be (Browning 2021, 32–3)? In such cases, therefore, the cultivated good state brand is perversely mobilised by others to justify their own lack of humanitarian solidarity and misdeeds. In such cases, then, and arguably completely at odds with the expectations of advocates of good state nation branding, even when the Nordics are themselves falling short this might not necessarily sully the brand, at least if other governments see a strategic presentational interest in holding up the Nordics as a beacon of international do-gooding.

CONCLUSION

This chapter focuses on how, in recent years, nation branding has become actively inflected with normative agendas. Underpinning this is the suggestion that more traditional forms of nation branding emphasising 'country of origin' and 'place branding' dynamics are insufficient in themselves. To really stand out and succeed states, it is argued, need to embrace pro-social agendas that help cultivate reputations for being and doing 'good'. This is the world of good state nation branding where altruism is reframed as a competitive advantage.

The chapter identifies several drivers for this development. Of course, it is important to recognise that 'do gooding' in international politics is not a completely new phenomenon. Within international relations theorising, for instance, there is a long tradition discussing the potential for positive normative and pro-social behaviours, as evident, for example, in debates between 'idealists' and 'realists' (Carr 1946), in English School notions of internationalist solidarism (Bull 1977), and in the broader set of discussions around international regimes. In this regard, small and middle powers have often sought to act as 'norm entrepreneurs' for such developments, in so doing helping to carve out roles and reputations as useful actors, with this further securing recognition and enhancing status and standing. However, central to the emergence of good state nation branding is the prior emergence of practices of corporate social responsibility and the business community's recognition of the potential financial rewards to be gained through cultivating the 'market for virtue'. Here, the branding of ethical consumption tempts consumers into purchases by appealing to their desires to enact virtuous self-concepts and modes of being.

Fundamental, however, has been a shift in perspective of key nation branding consultants who have seen in this the potential for states to likewise appeal to such desires by emphasising the good that their states can do for the world. Altruism, it is argued, carries a competitive edge and, as such, should appeal to notions of enlightened self-interest. Doing good, it is argued, is now key to cultivating positive national images, and states should be interested in this because, as the argument goes, a positive national image is ultimately the fundamental factor in economic competitiveness. This chapter shows how, just as with nation branding in general, the discourse of good state nation branding has been promoted through persuasive modelling and benchmarking practices, but where one constitutive effect of the discourse is also to shift the focus of nation branding increasingly towards the cultivation of 'knowledge brands' and opportunities for policy branding (and potentially policy transfer).

While the consultancy pitch for good state nation branding appeals to notions of (economic) enlightened self-interest, it is argued that its appeal also lies in how it responds to Bourdieuian desires of the subject to establish a sense of virtuous difference. In short, there is enjoyment to be gained through securing recognition through acts of conspicuous do-goodism, and where the enjoyment and satisfaction derives through being admired, encouraging emulation, but remaining always just out of reach, elusive, and esteemed. In this respect, good state nation branding also appeals to states' desires to enhance feelings of ontological security, status, and self-esteem.

Despite its intuitive appeal, though, good state nation branding is also shown to manifest certain limitations and problems, some of which are then illustrated in a longer case analysis of the Nordic Council of Ministers' active embracing of such an emphasis in its recent internationally focused region branding programme. For instance, a key issue concerns who, and how to define what, constitutes the 'good' and the fact that, insofar as good state nation branding continues to operate in line with economic logics of nation branding, the good is hardly likely to extend so far as to fundamentally challenge the socio-economic structures of global capitalism that have been a cause of so many of the world's problems in the first place. Second, it is suggested that subjecting altruism to logics of nation branding may also affect the sorts of actions states may be tempted to undertake as, ultimately, it is imperative not only that such actions are seen and recognised but also that they are not controversial. On the latter point, it is unlikely that good state nation branding will encourage states to engage with sensitive moral and political issues. It may even have the opposite effect. On the former, the emphasis on *being seen to be doing good* itself has the potential to override the imperatives of *actually doing good* in some contexts, something evident in the different approaches of Sweden and Norway to the branding of initiatives promoting gender-based actions. Third, there are also questions to be raised as to whether good state nation branding will necessarily promote enhanced cooperation and collaboration in international politics, and where it is noted that the imperative to be able to take credit for do-gooding can sometimes create barriers in this regard. Last, the Nordic example also highlights that 'doing bad' may not necessarily have a negative impact on a state with an established good state brand, particularly in situations in which other governments are looking for cover through which to justify their own 'bad' behaviours.

Ultimately, however, the emergence of discourses and practices of good state nation branding has had an undeniable impact, becoming a key component of many countries' nation branding programmes. The following chapter builds on the progressive normative potentials claimed to be inherent within nation branding by exploring assertions that nation branding can also play fundamental roles in enhancing both international and national security.

5

Peaceful States

If the world's governments placed even half the value that most wise corporations have learned to place on their good names, the world would be a safer and quieter place than it is today.

Simon Anholt (2020, 20)

We call your new brand Love Korea ... You will be the first country in the world to have 'love' as your number one value as well as the name of your country. Let us know if you have any questions. Best regards, SNASK.

SNASK (http://www.love-is-korea.com)

In 2017, the Swedish branding agency SNASK did something a little unusual. In response to *Icon Magazine*'s ongoing Rethink feature, which invites design studios to reinterpret anything they choose, SNASK took as its target North Korea, one of the world's most despotic regimes and famously identified by US president George W. Bush in the aftermath of the terrorist attacks on the United States in 2001 as part of an 'axis of evil', along with Iraq and Iran (Tucker 2017). Departing from the idea that North Korea has an image problem, SNASK suggested a fundamental rebrand was in order. Clearly feeling that the country's current moniker, the Democratic People's Republic of Korea, was tarnished, SNASK proposed Pyongyang should adopt 'Love Korea' as the country's new official name and #loveiskorea as its strapline. A new flag was also proposed (see figure 5.1). The existing design of two horizontal blue stripes with a central red stripe separating them would be maintained, but the red star in a white circle would be replaced by a white heart inside of which would be a conjoined 'k' and 'o', also typographically restylised into a more abstract heart.

Figure 5.1 SNASK's redesign of the Democratic People's Republic of Korea

SNASK published these and various other rebranding tools and files on a website (http://www.love-is-korea.com) the front page of which also included an 'open letter' to North Korea. The letter laments how the world is witnessing an increasing amount of 'anger and hate' (North Korea had conducted a nuclear test the year before), with this 'the biggest enemy to a bright future'. Hate only begets more hate, but, as it notes, the same is also the case with love: 'So if you love someone, that person will be instantly drawn to loving you back'. This being the case, SNASK suggests that its rebranding (and renaming) of 'Love Korea' is itself being offered in a gesture of love, with SNASK stating that it is 'giving you this identity and branding for free' and that it will help North Korea 'implement this new identity for free 'on the one condition that North Korea proves 'to the world that you are a free democracy'.

What should we make of SNASK's bold and ambitious intervention? Should we even take it seriously? In respect of the latter, it is obviously important to be mindful that, aside from rebranding North Korea, in responding to *Icon Magazine*'s Rethink feature SNASK was also engaged in a deft bit of branding on its own behalf. What better way for a branding agency to generate a bit of self-publicity and potentially conjure up additional business than to itself cultivate an image as benign and pro-social but also as sharp, witty, and capable of thinking outside the box. The agency itself did not expect its campaign would work, something affirmed by the fact that it subsequently received an e-mail from the North Korean government requesting that it take down the site or risk potential cyber-attacks (Kerdsup 2017). Yet it did hope to show the potential it believes is extant within branding to promote positive change, even in the context of some of the most difficult and fractious of relationships. In this respect, the suggestion behind the offering was not simply that North Korea suffers from an image problem but that nation branding might itself offer up a chance for more peace and solidarity and less division, conflict, and war than currently exists internationally.

In this respect, SNASK's rebranding stunt reflects a more general claim, espoused not only by consultants but also by some analysts, that an emphasis on nation branding is likely to have dividends for peace and security. To interrogate this claim, this chapter is divided into five sections, with the first three focused on matters of international security. In this regard, the previous chapter already demonstrates how some countries (e.g., the Nordics) have tried to make their efforts at promoting peace/conflict resolution a key part of their national and regional branding campaigns. The claims addressed here, though, are more significant. The issue is not about mobilising contributions to peace to generate a competitive edge by cultivating the image and standing of a 'good state' but, rather, the much bigger claim that nation branding per se will promote a more peaceful international environment by signalling the end of classical geopolitical competition between states. Sections one and two engage this claim directly. Discussing the cases of North Korea and Russia they argue that, far from signalling an inevitable move away from traditional geopolitics and confrontation, the current upsurge in nation branding also has the potential to be co-opted in its service.

Section three extends this point by noting that we should also be cautious of the looser claim that nation branding will necessarily promote greater understanding between nations, a claim that essentially treats nation branding as a subset, or as unproblematically allied to, practices of public diplomacy. Again, while there are cases where such an alignment holds, there is nothing inevitable about this. In particular, the chapter highlights several cases where significant tensions between nation branding and public diplomacy can be identified, and even where nation-branding activities have appeared to operate obversely to the aims of public diplomacy, creating more tension, not less.

Sections four and five shift the focus to the domestic and national arena, where the potential for nation branding to play a role in facilitating national cohesion and security in (potentially) unstable states is discussed. Drawing on the cases of Colombia and post-apartheid South Africa, section four discusses claims that nation branding can have a pacifying effect at the domestic level through its ability to build community and enhance national self-esteem. At stake, therefore, is the potential link between nation branding and nation building that is initially unpacked in chapter 3. The analysis of the cases suggests a somewhat mixed picture. The pacifying nation building potentials of domestically directed nation branding campaigns should not be dismissed, yet in such campaigns problematic exclusions and limitations remain endemic.

The last section places particular focus on the constitutive effects of nation branding in non-democratic contexts. In doing so it considers an emerging literature that discusses the role of nation branding as a mechanism for manufacturing political legitimacy for existing regimes. Indeed, in such contexts it has been argued that it would be more accurate to speak of 'state branding' (Eggeling 2020) or even 'regime branding'. What this suggests is that presumptions evident in much of the literature that nation branding will support open, cosmopolitan, and democratic identities need to be challenged.

NATION BRANDING, PEACE, AND INTERNATIONAL SECURITY

In the broader literature on place/nation branding, questions of security feature in two distinct ways. First are challenges concerning the potential of place/nation branding to manage reputational risks associated with perceived insecurities and where several approaches can be identified. For instance, particularly in places that feel they suffer from a (now) undeserved reputation for insecurity, efforts may be made to counter this. This can take different forms. For example, in respect of Colombia (an example we return to later for different reasons) aspects of its 'Colombia is Passion' nation branding campaign from the early

2000s explicitly addressed the issue head on. Specifically, a series of promotional videos (no longer available on YouTube) sought to mock the stereotyped portrayal of the country in Western media and popular culture as a 'country peopled by dangerous Guerreros and drug smugglers', where violence was rampant and every day. Mobilising the refrain, 'Colombia – the only risk is wanting to stay', the videos instead emphasised the 'risk' that lay in enjoying the people's kindness, hospitality, food, passion for music, literature, sports, art, creativity, and development et cetera. Another approach is to try to avoid established images through 'name changing', or what we might term a 'hoodwinking' strategy of obfuscation. For instance, in the 1990s Belfast sought to shake off associations with terrorist violence in its development planning and promotional campaigning by avoiding direct references to 'Belfast' and instead emphasising the names of areas in the city less familiar to outsiders (Coaffee and Rogers 2008, 210). By contrast, London sought to turn the potential reputational damage of being a target of IRA bombings, and more recently Islamicist-inspired terrorist attacks, into an asset precisely by playing up security issues but emphasising the city's resilience and subsequent development of high-level security surveillance and mitigating measures, the aim being to convince companies and tourists that the city is actually a very safe place to visit and conduct business (211–13). In a similar vein, Anholt (2020, 71–2) advocates that countries like Mexico and Colombia that have become to some extent '*defined by their problems*' (emphasis in original) should adopt a 'victim to leader' strategy by directly emphasising their role in the fight against organised crime – that is, 'good states' helping to solve the global problem of drug trafficking.

Nation/place branding strategies for managing reputational risks associated with security problems are obviously important. Second, though, security also features in debates on nation branding in another and arguably even more significant way. This concerns the key claim that nation branding is fundamentally beneficial to promoting international peace and security in general. Key aspects of this claim are discussed in chapter 2 in respect of arguments that contemporary nation branding reflects and is further driving a paradigm shift from Hobbesian geopolitical imaginaries of the Westphalian 'territorial state' towards more Lockean geoeconomic imaginaries of the 'competition state'. A preoccupation with enmity, territorial conquest, and war is therefore being replaced by an emphasis on world politics as a global marketplace, with states reconstituted as corporate rivals competing for market share and investment in a context of global capitalism and the pervasive spread of neoliberal modes of governance. Under such an economic logic, it is assumed by many commentators and consultants that nation branding will promote more benign, cosmopolitan, and inclusive (even if competitive) identities, in contrast to chauvinistic nationalistic forms. For example, in van Ham's (2001, 3) view:

> State branding is gradually supplanting nationalism. The brand state's use of its history, geography, and ethnic motifs to construct its own distinct image is a benign campaign that lacks the deep-rooted and often antagonistic sense of national identity and uniqueness that can accompany nationalism. By marginalising nationalist chauvinism, the brand state is contributing greatly to the further pacification of Europe.

Aronczyk (2013, 78–9) concurs, arguing that 'branding appears as a benign form of national consciousness, because elements that are not benign are not permissible within a nation branding framework'. She suggests two reasons for this. First, because nation brands 'offer a version of nationalism rooted in the unifying spirit of benign commercial "interests" rather than in the potential divisions of political "passions"', and second, because nation branding is fundamentally a form of 'soft' power (17–18) – that is, it relies on the carrots of attraction rather than on the sticks of coercion. For Anholt (2006, 2), the market-based view of the world on which his own approach to nation branding is predicated is one in which markets will promote 'an inherently peaceful and humanistic model for the relationships between nations'. For him, this is because the nature of competition promoted is one based on 'consumer choice and consumer power', which in turn are linked to 'the freedom and power of the individual. For this reason, it seems far more likely to result in lasting world peace than a statecraft based on territory, economic power, ideologies, politics or religion'.

Claims like these are clearly enticing. Arguably, though, they betray a misplaced confidence in nation branding's powers of pacification. Not least, they are not fully reflected in the empirical record. As noted by Volčič and Andrejevic (2011, 606), there is no particular evidence to suggest that 'nation branding and violent forms of political nationalism are mutually exclusive, nor that the treatment of the state as an enterprise displaces or reduces political violence'. Indeed, the branding activities of terrorist organisations and wannabe states like ISIS clearly demonstrate the potential for nation branding practices to be mobilised for activities and political goals other than peace (Simons 2018). Analytically speaking, the problem with such claims is twofold. First, they essentially rely on accepting that a straightforward transition from Hobbesian to Lockean worlds is underway. As argued in chapter 2, the idea that the latter is replacing the former in toto is too simplistic. Rather, Hobbesian geopolitics and Lockean geoeconomics are increasingly intertwined (Cowen and Smith 2009, 42). Linked to this is the fact that such claims only tend to recognise 'economic logics' as a driver of nation branding, neglecting the role that 'cultural' and (not always so diplomatic) 'diplomatic' rationales may play. If nation branding is understood as a set of techniques and practices, there is no reason to think it might not also be used for less beneficent purposes.

Second, though, it is also important to avoid simplistic associations between economic logics, soft power, and peace that are evident in such claims. This itself reproduces typically liberal – but deeply problematic – assumptions that economic competition is inherently non-violent, that commercial interests are benign, something colonised peoples for one might find hard to stomach. Rather than innocently promoting international peacebuilding, nation branding is therefore just as likely to be mobilised by states seeking to secure sectoral and geopolitical advantages. In this respect, nation branding may entail both peace-enhancing and conflictual relations – whichever it is will be context dependent (Browning and de Oliveira 2017a, 495–6; Cho 2017, 602). At the same time, the argument linking nation branding to international peace and security implicitly draws upon two claims in liberal international relations theorising. The first is an assumption that economic imperatives of globalisation are creating increasingly entangled and complex interdependencies between states, where the benefits of maintaining such relations far outweigh the inevitable costs of breaking them through aggressive actions (Keohane and Nye 1977). Yet, as indicated by the fundamental breakdown in West-Russia relations following the latter's invasion of Ukraine in 2022, including the extremely costly and destabilising process of economic disentanglement, while the establishment of (complex) interdependence may create disincentives to conflict, it does not prevent it.

This feeds into the second liberal claim smuggled into nation branding discourse, the idea that alongside (or perhaps rather than) economic interdependence what really counts for the promotion of peace is regime type. Specifically, nation branding consultants like Anholt assume that nation branding supports democratic transition because democracy and (consumer) liberty and freedom are presumed to be especially attractive and therefore most likely to guarantee success. Understood this way, nation branding appears to bolster certain claims of (liberal) democratic peace theory (Doyle 1983; Owen 1994). Least robust is the suggestion that (liberal) democracies are less war prone than other states, something the military record of countries like the US and UK over the last century refutes. More robust is the claim that while (liberal) democracies may fight non-democracies, incidences of war between them are rare to non-existent, with this explained by the fact that they recognise other (liberal) democracies as legitimate and therefore will resolve disputes with each other via negotiation (Williams 2001). Of course, insofar as this may be the case, then it clearly begs the question as to whether nation branding, or the establishment of democracy, is the actual cause of peace in such cases. It is therefore worth noting that SNASK's confidence in the peace-enhancing potentials of its proposed rebranding of North Korea was ultimately limited, at least insofar as it stated that its further assistance was provisional on North Korea demonstrating its commitment to 'free democracy' *in advance*. In respect of international security, then, it is unclear whether the pacifying effects claimed for nation branding should (ever) be attributed to nation branding or whether, to the extent to which such correlations can be identified, they might be better attributed to regime type.

NATION BRANDING, ANTAGONISM, AND CONFLICT: NORTH KOREA AND RUSSIA

The presumed causal link between nation branding and the enhancement of international peace and security can be usefully challenged with reference to a couple of examples. These examples further illuminate how nation branding is often subject to needs of ontological security and desires to bolster status and self-esteem but where these are pursued through reinforcing antagonistic role identities and conflict rather than through seeking to meliorate them.

North Korea provides a rather dramatic case, and one that clearly suggests that the literature's emphasis on nation branding as a mechanism to enhance a state's global attractiveness and appeal can be overplayed. As noted by Cho (2017, 595), the nation branding policies of the hard-line communist regime in Pyongyang have never been designed 'to create a "favourable" self-image that would be acceptable to the outside world'. To the contrary, the aim has been to project a 'threatening' image to the international audience. In this respect, North Korean nation branding has been underpinned by cultural and diplomatic logics rather than economic logics seeking to make the country appear as attractive as possible to tourists, foreign workers, and international economic investment. Cho argues that nation branding has rather been directed towards ontological questions of the self-proclamation of the country's very *being* (600, 602). Central to this has been the desire to cultivate a nation brand emphasising that the country is strong and powerful, having the role identity of being able to stand up to the world's superpowers, principally the United States. Indeed, in many respects North Korea's nation brand is fundamentally premised on cultivating an antagonistic and oppositional stance to the West, and certainly not one emphasising cosmopolitanism and playful competition in capitalist markets.

North Korea's distinctiveness, however, also extends to its modes of nation branding. These can be nicely contrasted with those proffered by SNASK in its attempted rebranding (and renaming) of the country as 'Love Korea'. As noted, SNASK proposed a new name, a redesigned flag, a snappy hashtag logotype. Different templates were also offered, on which a stylised typography could be utilised, but there were also suggestions for a redesigned currency, a business card, shirt buttons, and the rebranding of Air Koryo, the national airline (http://www.love-is-korea.com/design#design1). SNASK's focus was therefore on re-imagining North Korea's visual identity. In many respects, of course, this reflected a rather 'cosmetic' approach to nation branding, although given that it was offering this for free this is perhaps not surprising. Notable, however, is how the rebranding package offered was fully in line with contemporary nation branding discourses pertaining to the reframing of countries as 'competition states' seeking global investment and market share through cultivating an aesthetically attractive set of brand images. However, far from being a 'competition state' (or even primarily a territorial state), North Korea has more recently been described by Kwon and Chung (2012) as a 'theatre state', a concept they take from anthropologist Clifford Geertz's (1980) work on the nineteenth-century Balinese Negara. Theatre states, Geertz argues, are governed by rituals and symbols rather than primarily by force, with particular emphasis placed on the spectacle, such as in the form of mass ceremonies and state-orchestrated productions. In North Korea, Kwon and Chung (2012, 1) argue that mass ritualised spectacles/performances have been central to building 'an aura of captivating charismatic power' around the Kim dynasty, with Cho (2017, 603) arguing that they have also become important for nation branding and nation building because of how they represent the nation and how citizens' participation emphasises ties of kinship and community.

For illustrative purposes, Cho (2017, 607–11) highlights two examples of North Korean theatre state nation branding. The first is the Arirang festival, a grand mass gymnastic/artistic performance that usually takes place throughout August/September, though not every year, in the 150,000-capacity May Day Stadium in Pyongyang. The performances can mobilise up to 100,000 citizens (including around thirty thousand young children) and are offered up in praise of the revolutionary lives of Kim Il-sung and the successes of the North Korean Workers Party. The second concerns North Korea's increasingly ritualised use of military spectacles, including not only parades of soldiers and equipment but also nuclear test demonstrations. These latter are far from usual forms of nation branding practice, but Cho argues that, combined, they are designed to promote images of the nation and of the robustness of the ruling regime, both at home and abroad. The timing of nuclear tests, for example, is often deliberately provocative (e.g., Pyongyang's first nuclear test was conducted on US Independence Day in 2006) and accompanied with bombastic language usually threatening South Korea, Japan, and the United States, often with pre-emptive nuclear strikes. The embedded narrative of such 'branding' is therefore that of a strong and powerful country standing up for its rights, and the rights of colonised peoples, against constitutive and identifiable imperialist 'evil' enemies while simultaneously dispelling more negative images of the country as 'poor', 'weak', and 'unequal' (604, 615). In this respect, North Korea's military and cultural spectacles are fundamentally a form of branded image competition, theatrical political performances explicitly designed to secure 'recognition and respect from others' and, in this respect, they are little different to 'the nation branding strategies of liberal capitalist countries' (609, 614).

Russia provides another example. Unlike North Korea, whose nation branding practices make a virtue out of being openly threatening, Russian nation branding strategies are interesting because they highlight tensions between competing logics (economic, diplomatic, cultural) of nation branding and their ability to promote a dominant strategic narrative of Russian self-identity that seeks to reassert Russia's global standing as a 'normal great power'. In this respect, Russian nation branding practices are significantly motivated by the desire to enhance national status and ontological security. However, as Szostek (2017) notes, the desire to appeal to both national and foreign audiences has entailed a certain amount of mixed messaging, the result being that Russia's nation branding over the last decade has been inconsistent and somewhat antagonistic at the international level. This latter has then been reaffirmed through revanchist Russian strategic actions, in particular in its near abroad and, not least, in Ukraine.

To understand the evident tensions in Russian nation branding efforts it is important to recognise how throughout the post-Cold War period Russian leaders have increasingly depicted international relations as a zero-sum and fundamentally geopolitical competitive struggle. Specifically, the Kremlin positions Russia as necessarily challenging a US-led Western hegemony that seems bent on obstructing Russia's rise and the pursuit of its legitimate interests (Szostek 2017, 571, 576). In this narrative, Russia is depicted as a great power and autonomous state, an idea with deep roots in Russian history (Trenin 2002). More particularly, contemporary Eurasianist accounts of Russian civilisational identity present the country as unique and therefore as possessing a developmental model distinct from that of Western democracy and neoliberal capitalism (Bassin and Aksenov 2006). Thus, although its European heritage and standing is emphasised, Russian identity is constituted largely in opposition to a specific representation of the West (Heller 2010). However, rather than recognising the country's claims to great power status, Russian leaders perceive the West as reluctant and constantly withholding recognition. Indeed, worse still, the West has increasingly been understood as seeking to undermine Russia, not least through its promotion of democratic forces and disregard of Russian 'rights' and 'privileged interests' in its near abroad, tensions that have been particularly evident over the eastern expansion of NATO and the political orientation (and sovereignty) of neighbouring countries like Ukraine (Szostek 2017, 577). Combined, this entails two things. First, that Russia feels no need to appease the West and conform to its normative prescriptions with respect to forms of governance and economy. Second, that, given its emphasis on world politics as a realm of zero-sum geopolitical competition, it also feels justified in seeking to undermine the West, with this most evident in its developing doctrine of hybrid warfare.

Yet, precisely because of its role as Russia's constitutive other, historically Russia has also remained locked into an inherently frustrating 'recognition game' (Ringmar 2002) with the West. In other words, while positioning itself as a contender/balancer of the West, Western recognition of its parity, inclusion, and equal status and standing remains constantly desired. For Zarakol (2011), this is to the extent that Russian national self-esteem and ontological security has become fundamentally dependent on Western recognition and acceptance, but recognition and acceptance that historically has been withheld leaving Russia frustrated and ontologically insecure. In the contemporary period, for instance, we see this in how Russia is frequently described in the West as stuck in history, as failing to modernise, always just lagging behind (Neumann 1996).

This somewhat schizophrenic relationship to the West and the international community more broadly is notably evident in Russia's nation branding actions. As Saunders (2017, 217–18) notes, the origins of a concerted Russian nation branding strategy lay in disaffection with prevailing negative images of the country that became common throughout the 1990s, images that by 2000 had become viewed as a potential threat to Russian security and economic well-being. In response, the Concept of the Foreign Policy of the Russian Federation that was issued that year emphasised the need to establish a more positive national image as a central component of foreign policy. In 2006, this was followed up by the hiring of American global PR firm Ketchum to represent Russia and help devise a branding strategy, a relationship that lasted until 2015 (Szostek 2017, 584). A central component of this strategy has been the bidding for and hosting of mega-events, most notable of which have been the World Student Games/Universiade (2013), the Sochi Winter Olympics (2014), the Ice Hockey World Championship (2016), the FIFA World Cup (2018), as well as the Russian Formula 1 grand prix, the World Aquatics Championship, and various other tournaments and events (Makarychev 2013, 1). The rationale for hosting such events has been to (re)position Russia as a 'normal' country, a country 'returning to the "premier league" of world politics', reclaiming its great power status, and just as capable as any other major state of running such large events and providing the security they demand (Makarychev and Yatsyk 2014). The hosting of such events is therefore as much about commanding respect and assuming a role identity (cultural/diplomatic logics) as it is about demonstrating Russia's attraction.

Of course, economic logics emphasising the power of attraction has not been completely absent. Part of the aim of 'normalisation' has also clearly been to cultivate images of 'Russia as a welcoming, modern country attractive to investors and visitors' (Szostek 2017, 572). So, while mega-events are seen as one way of communicating that Russia remains 'a force to be reckoned with' (Müller 2014), the strapline for the Sochi Games was 'Russia – Great, New, Open', a message that sought both to link hosting the games to a status claim about Russia's global standing that would boost Russian self-esteem and to position the country as non-threatening and cooperative – with this notably distinct from North Korean actions (Szostek 2017, 584–5). In this we can therefore detect an amalgamation of economic, cultural, and diplomatic logics of nation branding.

How compatible these are, though, has been questioned. For instance, Makarychev (2013, 2–3) identifies two points of tension. First, he notes how messages of love, harmony, peace, and universalism are often contradicted by a distinct emphasis on demonstrating Russia's national pre-eminence for fundamentally political purposes. For instance, he notes how the team that represented Russia at the World Student Games in 2013 included an unusual number of world-class athletes that won as many medals as all the other teams combined. The emphasis, he suggests, was less on the spirit of competition and more on 'boosting patriotic feelings of pride and glorification of "the Russian spirit"'. Of course, this has subsequently been reflected in the exposure of a systematic performance-enhancing doping programme of Russian athletes that has resulted in ongoing bans of the country's official representation at many sporting events, including the Olympics. Second, he notes how the messages of tolerance and openness typically central to sporting mega-events, and to which Russia has paid lip service, have been recurrently undermined by how such events have created opportunities for disaffected citizens and foreigners to protest about threats to human rights, including Russian discrimination against the LGBT community. For instance, prior to the Sochi Olympics Moscow had to give its informal assurance to the International Olympic Committee that a new law criminalising gay 'propaganda' would not be implemented during the Games. In the process of trying to demonstrate its normalisation and adherence to (Western) international standards through hosting mega-events, at times the exact opposite has therefore been achieved (Makarychev and Yatsyk 2014). Of course, in the case of the Sochi Games this was further compounded by how, in the months following, any possible nation branding dividends evaporated as its 'little green men' set about annexing the Crimean Peninsula (Saunders 2017, 224).

As Szostek (2017, 586–7) notes, Russia's use of mega-events for purposes of nation branding has therefore often failed to shift perceptions of international audiences, not least because these symbolic actions have clashed with the 'visible substance' of crackdowns against protestors and imperialising foreign policy adventures. However, she also argues that, ultimately, the Kremlin has concluded that the negative international reaction to the rhetorical positioning and nation branding of Russia as a great power, often implicitly (and sometimes explicitly) at the expense of others, is secondary to the sense of national collective self-esteem and status generated amongst Russians precisely by doing so. Contra Zarakol's foregrounding of international recognition as the basis of Russian ontological security and self-esteem then, she argues that today 'the Russian public and elite experience greater affirmation of their desired international status by defying Western criticism than by pursuing Western approval in Western terms' and interpret Russian 'defiance as evidence of their country's great power status'. In this respect, the 'acceptance which Russia would like from Western states pertains to its right to be "equal but different", not "equal and part of the liberal democratic club"' (Szostek 2017, 572, 588–9). Ultimately, this is what Russia's active engagement with bidding for and hosting global mega-events has fostered. International (read Western) criticisms around such events has therefore fed into ontological claims of Russia's identity, role, and global significance rather than fundamentally destabilising them, as might be expected.

NATION BRANDING VERSUS PUBLIC DIPLOMACY?

If the claim that nation branding is a fundamental force for international peace can be contested, so too can the looser claim that, on balance, nation branding is liable to enhance understanding between nations. Sometimes, of course, this may be the case, especially where the nation branding strategies of states appear to be in line with the pursuit and achievement of collective goods, as perhaps in some instances of 'good state' nation branding. However, there is nothing inevitable about this and there may also be times when nation branding has the opposite effect.

Insofar as nation branding is seen to support collective understanding it tends to be understood as closely related to and supportive of practices of public diplomacy, a concept that Tuch (1990, 3) defines as 'a government's process of communicating with foreign publics in an attempt to bring about understanding for its nation's ideas and ideals, its institutions and culture, as well as its national goals and policies'. In this respect, several defining characteristics are usually highlighted about public diplomacy. First, it targets foreign publics and non-official organisations as opposed to foreign governments and established international actors (traditional diplomacy). Second, it is about 'diplomacy', where communication with foreign publics (in idealised understandings) is viewed as a two-way process of persuasion and dialogue. Like propaganda, the aim is therefore to influence what people think, but it differs from propaganda in that public diplomacy 'also listens to what people have to say' (Melissen 2005, 18). As Cull (2019, 13) puts it, public diplomacy is based on 'truth' and 'listens to learn' while propaganda 'selects truth' and 'listens to target'. This also means that, in principle, the learning entailed in public diplomacy may change the initiating society as well as the target society, whereas propaganda is only interested in the latter. Third, public diplomacy is usually understood as limited in several respects. First, in that it is an activity typically limited to foreign policy practitioners. Second, that it is limited to generating international understanding for a government's policy positions. And third, that as a result its focus is largely restricted to political goals.

The exact ways in which nation branding differs from these characteristics of public diplomacy (and propaganda) is open to debate. As summarised in chapter 1, key distinctions include the fact that nation branding seeks to draw in a much broader range of participants, especially when it tries to co-opt citizens as 'brand ambassadors'. In this, nation branding also targets domestic as well as foreign audiences, while the mode of communication also differs since the aim is not to learn about what the other thinks about particular issues but to appeal to and shape their desires. It therefore operates at a more affective rather than cognitive or rational level (Saunders 2017, 50). Yet, insofar as appealing to (and anticipating) other's desires is central to nation branding, this also has the potential to have an impact on the brand identity that is to be cultivated. However, while public diplomacy is primarily concerned with policy, the core focus of nation branding is identity, something that arguably requires a more holistic and cross-sectoral approach (Anholt 2007a, 74; Melissen 2005, 19–21). Some analysts also draw a distinction between public diplomacy's focus on 'the political' and nation branding's focus on 'the economic', the argument being that this feeds into the former's focus on understanding (i.e., treating target audiences as concerned citizens) and the latter's emphasis on image management (i.e., treating target audiences as consumers) (e.g., Viktorin et al. 2018b, 10). However, this distinction only holds if nation branding is restricted to economic logics. When subject to cultural and diplomatic logics overt political goals are often also clearly in play.

Table 5.1 illustrates some of the differences between nation branding and public diplomacy – but also propaganda, since critics are prone to label both of the former as simply variations of the latter – in slightly more schematic form. The key point, though, is that, despite the differences, nation branding and public diplomacy are generally seen as complementary and mutually supportive, with Melissen (2005, 20) arguing that 'public diplomacy does not at all contradict nation branding'. This assessment, though, is too sweeping, with the relationship varying on a case-by-case basis and depending on the logic of nation branding primarily in play. For instance, the point about the underpinning logics of nation branding has been well made by Varga (2013), who charts the historical shift in Germany's nation branding practices from a Cold War emphasis on regaining trust (diplomatic logic) to a post–Cold War emphasis on commercial nationalism (economic logic). While the former was premised on identifying those 'cultural, historical, and political elements that were *shared*' with others, targeting 'individual members of foreign countries as *citizens*', in prioritising market rationalities the latter treats foreigners as '*consumers*' (emphasis in original). Questions of 'creating trust, political stability, and peaceful international relations' were notably downplayed in this shift (452–4).

Mordhorst (2015) identifies a similar dynamic with respect to another case, but one that is also interesting for another reason. Earlier it was noted how Russia's nation branding efforts have been significantly derailed by Russian actions. In contrast, Mordhorst highlights how governments sometimes deploy nation branding to divert international attention *away* from problematic diplomatic issues. His case focuses on the 'Mohammad Cartoon Crisis' that hit Denmark in the

Table 5.1
Propaganda, public diplomacy, and nation branding compared

	Goals	Mechanism	Self-serving/ other regarding	Target audience	Direction of communication
Propaganda	Political	Ideological persuasion/ manipulation	Self-serving	(Mainly) foreign publics	One way towards target
Public diplomacy	Political	Dialogue to promote mutual understanding	Other regarding	Foreign publics	Two-way
Nation branding	Economic and political	Cultivating an attractive brand identity	Self-serving (by appealing to desires of target)	Foreign and domestic publics	Practices of co-creation create possibilities for two-way communication

early 2000s following the publication in 2005 of twelve cartoons by the newspaper *Jyllands-Posten* that many Muslims viewed as blasphemous of the Prophet. The crisis itself needs to be set against the broader context of Denmark's adoption of a more activist foreign policy from the early 2000s, central to which was the government's willingness to become more closely engaged with American military adventures, especially after 9/11. Partially as a response to this, in 2003 the Danish-Arab Partnership Programme (DAPP) was established, a public diplomacy effort explicitly designed to strengthen 'dialogue, partnerships and mutual understanding between Denmark and the Middle East and North Africa' (quoted in Mordhorst 2015, 242). Initially, anger at the cartoons was confined to some Danish citizens (not only Danish Muslims). However, towards the end of 2005 the ambassadors of eleven major Muslim countries requested a meeting with the Danish government. Citing basic principles of free speech, the prime minister refused. This angered the foreign minister, who felt such an approach undermined the broader public diplomacy goal of promoting dialogue and understanding. From this the crisis grew. As anger spread across the Middle East a costly boycott of Danish products was announced while an estimated 150 people died in demonstrations (Rasmussen and Merkelsen 2014, 238). Images of Danish flags being burned flashed around the globe, with criticism of the Danish government's handling of the crisis spreading beyond the Islamic world.

With its reputation at stake, and with Danish companies also calling on Denmark to show more respect for other peoples, it is interesting to note that the government responded by eschewing mechanisms of public diplomacy and emphasising a nation branding programme instead. The programme itself aimed to demonstrate that the images being painted of Denmark were false not by addressing them directly (which would have entailed a nod in the direction of public diplomacy) but by ignoring the crisis in favour of a completely different set of images. Indeed, and as indicated by its title, the developed *Action Plan for the Global Marketing of Denmark*, to be implemented from 2007 to 2012, reframed the issue as a more general crisis of global marketing and notably shifted the focus away from the Middle East to instead emphasise global audiences and targeting, in particular, citizens in BRIC and OECD countries 'who were selected for economic rather than political reasons' (Mordhorst 2015, 246–51; Rasmussen and Merkelsen 2014, 241–2). Intriguingly, specific aspects of the developing nation brand seemed more likely to further offend Muslim populations than foster mutual understanding. This included the viral branding 'Karen' campaign, which was launched in 2009 by the tourism organisation Visit Denmark and which comprised a (fake) YouTube video featuring a young Danish woman who was searching for the tourist father of her baby following a one-night stand in Copenhagen. Another was the country's hosting of the 2009 World Outgames (the 'gay Olympics').

As Mordhorst (2015, 252–3) notes, irrespective of one's personal views, from the perspective of the public diplomacy unit in the Ministry of Foreign Affairs, 'whose main objective was to re-establish good relations with Muslim countries, the World Outgames [and Karen campaign] were problematic' but designed to appeal to commercial and political interests elsewhere. Thus, rather than trying to explain Denmark's policy choices and build mutual understanding, the nation branding campaign doubled down on the sense of differentiation with the Islamic world that many perceived as inherent in the initial publication of the cartoons. Analytically, Rasmussen and Mikelsen (2014) therefore argue that the case highlights how the application of a nation branding optic, particularly in contexts of unexpected and 'sudden crises', inevitably carries the danger of shifting the focus away from the issue at hand and, instead, directing it towards preserving the brand – the damage to which is ultimately only a secondary effect and, as such, should not constitute the primary concern. However, whenever nation branding is reached for, the complex causes and consequences of any crisis – in this case related to threats to national security and Danish exports to the Middle East – will be at risk of being displaced in favour of a simplified focus on brand crisis management (Rasmussen and Mikelsen 2014, 231).[1]

Similar effects were also evident during the Covid-19 pandemic, the reputational brand dynamics of which were reinforced through the widespread use of comparative indexes of infections, deaths, and vaccinations. Despite the context of widespread human suffering, economic damage, and social uncertainty, Covid-19 was also perceived by many states not only as (1) a potential threat to national brand standing but also as (2) a strategic opportunity for national brand enhancement. Regarding the former, poor performance on proliferating benchmarks, controversies over the speed and nature of government responses, or, in the case of China, the pejorative labelling of Covid-19 as the 'China/Wuhan virus' were perceived as genuine reputational concerns (Cull 2022, 19). In respect of the latter, various countries (e.g., China, Taiwan, South Korea) sought to leverage their Covid-19 experience and response to boost their global standing, be that through donations of protective equipment or through the cultivation of different knowledge brands for export through seeking to mobilise their own experiences and successes (Lee and Kim 2021). Again, though, there were dangers in this. First, internal to nation branding dynamics there was obviously the danger of branding efforts backfiring. For instance, Sweden became known for adopting a relatively lax response over lockdowns and social restrictions, a response that the government initially saw as an opportunity for national brand enhancement (Falkheimer and Raknes 2022; Rosamond et al. 2022). However, international criticism soon followed. Sweden was depicted as arrogant and irresponsible with this having a negative impact on the country's established nation brand as a pioneer and model, ultimately activating ontological and status anxieties in the country (Hagström et al. 2022). Second, though, and arguably more significant, is how these concerns with national brand standing further contributed to the nationalist and often geopolitically competitive framing of much of the pandemic response in ways sometimes detrimental to containing the virus, for instance, with the concern with comparative benchmarks affecting global vaccine distribution.

As the Cartoon Crisis and the case of Covid-19 demonstrate, then, there is no inherent alignment between nation branding and public diplomacy. Cases clearly do exist where nation branding has contributed to closing the gap between self and other, though when this happens – and absent a concomitant concerted emphasis on public diplomacy – it is often the result of diversionary tactics as opposed to fostering mutual recognition and understanding of underlying tensions. For instance, there are notable similarities between Denmark's response to the Cartoon Crisis and proliferating practices of 'sportswashing', where sport is used by countries to divert attention away from otherwise tarnished images and reputations and launder them through association with globally resonant sports and teams. This has clearly been evident in Russia's emphasis on hosting sporting mega-events. The same is true of Qatar's bid and hosting of the 2022 FIFA World Cup, although this has itself been tarnished by evidence of widespread human rights abuses of foreign construction workers. Other examples include Saudi Arabia's gaining rights to host a Formula One grand prix and its 2021 investment, through the country's Public Investment Fund, in the English Premier League football team Newcastle United, both of which have also proved controversial but where in each and every case the governments in question clearly perceive that such actions do more to detoxify the country's brand and reputation than they do to sully them. Indeed, in the case of Saudi Arabia's purchase of Newcastle United it is also clear that, despite some public opposition, the British government actively supported the deal, largely because it thought it would further cement the UK's close geostrategic relationship with the country (*Guardian* 2021). Of course, it is also important not to forget the status and self-esteem benefits that may be seen to flow from such actions domestically, something that we return to later.

NATION BRANDING AND NATIONAL SECURITY: SOUTH AFRICA AND COLOMBIA

The above discussion focuses on claims about nation branding's (limited) capacity to promote international peace and security and to foster understanding between nations. No less important, though, is whether nation branding can have a benign and pacifying effect at the domestic level, even in some of the most conflict-ridden and unstable societies. Insofar as it can, this is liable to be linked to its ability to foster national cohesion as well as a positive sense of community and to enhance self-esteem and ontological security. This is where the links between nation branding and nation building explored in chapter 3 become particularly salient. In related literature on place branding, for instance, Greenberg (2008) points to the potential to rejuvenate cities in crisis through the ability of place branding techniques to transcend divisive social issues of race and class to foster a sense of 'imagined consensus' (cited in Banet-Weiser 2012, 108). Central to this is the brand's ability to cultivate the belief that everyone (or at least enough people) stand to benefit not just from the campaign but also from their active engagement and co-option into the process – that is, by embracing notions of active citizenship and 'living the brand'. In this respect, citizens seeking to identify with where they live – be that at the level of the locale or nation – may well be amenable to branding techniques and liable to invest in place brands, at least insofar as these entail the promise of helping them feel good about their home identification (Turner 2016, 23). As such, the pacifying potentials of nation branding in conflict-affected societies should not be underestimated. However, nation branding's ability to provide a context for the peaceful resolution of societal tensions also has limits. This is not least because nation branding almost always entails problematic exclusions and typically works to the benefit of some more than others. It therefore also contains the potential to foster future grievances. Two cases highlight these varying dynamics well – post-apartheid South Africa and Colombia – both countries with deeply problematic histories of intercommunal violence but where nation branding has been actively invested with hopes of promoting resolution.

In South Africa, Cornelissen (2017, 526–7) argues that, aside from its perceived capacity to promote national economic goals, nation branding has also been embraced to cultivate political legitimacy and stability for the post-apartheid state and to reconstitute a more inclusive sense of society. Central to this has been the desire to use nation branding strategies to promote social harmony and racial unification. This was most notably captured in the 1990s through the popularisation of the imagery of South Africa as the 'Rainbow Nation' as the basis for post-apartheid nation building efforts, especially during the Mandela years (Cornelissen 2017, 531, 534; Browning 2016, 58). In turn, this became tied to a narrative of South Africa as a 'miracle nation' (Louw 2016), where the process of the peaceful transition from apartheid was seen to support a discourse and global role of the country as a moral leader able to teach others (Youde 2009, 129,

134–5). Such positioning was clearly designed to ward off potential shame at the historical legacy and to bolster the nation's global standing and societal self-esteem. In this respect, come the early 2000s the country was proclaimed as leading an 'African renaissance' (Louw 2016, 147).

In the late 1990s, South African nation branding was mainly conducted via the more corporate focused International Marketing Council. In 2000, though, this was reconstituted as Brand SA, whose first campaign was framed around the slogan 'South Africa ... Alive with possibilities' (Cornelissen 2017, 537). However, as with many other countries, emphasis was also placed on bidding for and hosting major sporting events. Amongst others, these included the 1995 Rugby World Cup and the International Cricket Council's World Cup in 2003, while a bid to host the 2004 Olympic Games was unsuccessful. Most significant, however, was South Africa's successful bid to host the 2010 FIFA World Cup, something it notably framed as of broader significance to the African continent and a further marker of the African renaissance (Alegi 2008, 399; Cornelissen 2017, 538–9).

Evidently, these efforts have had some success. For instance, Louw (2016, 156) notes that it was with the 2010 World Cup that the new post-apartheid national flag was finally 'naturalised', being displayed widely throughout society. Likewise, there is some evidence to suggest that nation branding operated to reduce emigration and, in particular, persuade white (and largely middle-class) South Africans to remain in the country and contribute to its regeneration (Cornelissen 2017, 537). However, there were also limits to these efforts, with Cornelissen concluding that 'domestic cleavages built on racial, class and other identities persist and social cohesion appears weak' (541). Similarly, Louw (2016, 148, 156) notes that the positive sense of national belonging fostered by the World Cup was largely temporary and was subsequently undermined by recurrent xenophobic attacks on African migrants, while Alegi (2008, 415) points to uneven distribution of the economic benefits of nation branding as a continued source of social disaffection (see chapter 6).

Colombia provides a possibly more dramatic example, a country that has experienced decades of military civil conflict and that, come the early 2000s, was widely depicted by analysts as a 'country teetering on the brink, with civil society in disarray, corruption rife in public and private institutions, and various bands of guerrillas, paramilitaries, and narco-traffickers fighting one another and the state' (Lobo 2017,

263). Over preceding decades, well over 200,000 people are believed to have been killed, with millions displaced outside their regions of origin (Bassols 2016, 315). In this context, a sense of Colombian national communion was widely seen as absent, potentially even impossible. In the early 2000s, however, the country embarked on a concerted set of nation branding initiatives. To date, most studies of Colombian nation branding have focused on its external orientation, the way it has been mobilised to try to overcome the reputational damage afflicting the country and its effect on foreign business investment, trade, and tourism. Indeed, earlier in the chapter it is noted how in the early 2000s external-oriented nation branding sought to emphasise that the only 'risk' facing visitors to Colombia was 'the risk of wanting to stay', a campaign that sought to downplay the everyday risks of violence. Arguably more significant is that Colombian nation branding from the early 2000s has also been fundamentally targeted internally, seeking to foster national cohesion. What matters here is less the perceptions of outsiders and more the perceptions of Colombians about themselves and the extent to which nation branding has been able to foster a sense of national unity, pride, and collective self-esteem and, in so doing, has potentially helped to foster moves towards peace. What we see in Colombia, however, is an intriguing combination of nation branding mechanisms being used alongside and in support of other (sometimes branded) security initiatives.

Before the 2000s, it is worth noting that already in the 1990s the Colombian government had realised that the country's poor reputation was a key obstacle to opening the economy to global markets and economic development. Thus, already in 1994, a report was commissioned that essentially focused on the need to promote a certain amount of consumer nationalism, encouraging Colombians to identify with Colombian products. However, the results of this and some other initiatives were limited (Sanín 2016, 48). The moment of change came in 2002, when Álvaro Uribe became president, serving two terms (2002–06, 2006–10) and adopting controversial policies that began to show some more positive results in respect of economic growth and internal security. Most controversial was his hard-line policy *Seguridad democrática* (Democratic security). The policy entailed a significant intensification of militarisation, the expansion of executive powers, restrictions on civil rights, the suppression and demonisation of dissent, and more concerted counter-insurgency operations, especially targeted at FARC guerrillas. As Ojeda (2013, 761–2) notes, all this was done in the name of the defence of democracy and political stability. While various armed groups were not completely subjugated – indeed, the policy generated some violent blowback – there was some success in regaining control of parts of national territory. Aspects of how this was achieved are interesting.

First, the enhanced mobilisation of the military against the guerrillas was not straightforward as, over the preceding years, the military had become viewed by large parts of the population as varyingly incompetent, dangerous, and not necessarily operating in the interests of the 'people'. An initial goal of the Uribe government was therefore 'to create the social basis to pursue the military option against the guerrilla' (Lobo 2017, 270). To achieve this, it was concluded the army needed a military makeover, with the advertising agency McCann Erickson contracted to undertake the task. The result was an emphasis on parades, rescue missions, and not least an advertising campaign *En Colombia sí hay héroes* (There are heroes in Colombia) that was played across newspapers, radio, television, and on billboards (Ojeda 2013, 763; Lobo 2017, 263). Specifically, the emotionally charged campaign emphasised the willingness of Colombian soldiers to die protecting fellow Colombians, even though they may be strangers. But as Lobo (2017, 266–9) notes, the context of the campaign was interesting since the advertisements showed Colombian soldiers lurking hidden in the background, watching over the people and waiting for the moment when they would be called into action to protect them. Of course, what Colombians would recognise was that the soldiers were deployed on Colombian soil and not to protect the country from foreign invaders but from the 'unseen enemy', other Colombians implicitly depicted as the guerrillas, the left wing, and those 'whose expressed intention is to overthrow the state and their (the viewer's) way of life' (269). Rebranding the military was therefore a process of making an identity claim about the nature of the nation, of who was in, and who the internal constitutive enemy other was. The identification of the enemy and the role of the army in protecting the nation and providing physical security was therefore crucial to justifying significant military mobilisation and deployment.

Alongside this rebranding of the military was a second initiative that provided a context in which the military could demonstrate its protective role. In 2002, the *Vive Colombia, viaja por Ella* (Live Colombia, travel through it) programme was also initiated, a programme that mobilised (mainly) domestic tourism and travel as a mechanism for promoting security, state building, and national identification. Specifically, tourism and travel became a route to extending the state's territorial penetration and control but arguably did more than that (Ojeda 2013, 763). A key element of *Vive Colombia* was to promote domestic travel throughout the nation, particularly to places and areas previously off limits due to their being under the control of rebel factions. However, guaranteeing safe travel required the intensive militarisation of travel routes and tourist destinations. The aim was to establish that it was now safe to travel around the country, to experience and live it. As part of the programme a series of convoys – *Caravanas Turísticas* – departed from the major cities. Thousands of people took part, travelling together into a landscape hitherto too dangerous to venture into. The irony, of course, was that this was only possible as part of police and military escorts, with helicopter gunships flying overhead (Ojeda 2013, 764). Despite this, the programme was a popular success and was extended over many years (Bassols 2016, 319). On the one hand, the programme further served to normalise the new framing of the military as protectors of the people and their role and presence in society. But the programme did two other things as well. First, it provided a context for people to experience the country as 'theirs', to (re)familiarise themselves with it, and for some to visit (former/holiday) homes previously out of reach. In ontological security terms, new routines were created, and the sense of territorial belonging expanded. In providing physical security the military was therefore also facilitating changing ontological security dynamics. Second, the many Colombians who over the years embraced the opportunity to explore the country were in turn also co-opted and mobilised into a form of active and participatory citizenship. As Ojeda (2013, 767–8) notes, embarking on these travels itself became part of 'retaking' the country, 'proof' that a new socio-spatial order was emerging. In this respect, travelling was actively encouraged and became a 'civil duty' and one way through which ordinary Colombians could participate in 'the war'.

Last, and building on these developments, in 2005 (and lasting until 2012) the country's first official nation branding programme was launched. Although it had an external dimension, the initial target was the domestic audience, the goal being to enhance Colombians' sense of national self-esteem and collective identity through promotional, commercial, and educational efforts – including via an extension of the *Vive Colombia* travel mechanism (Bassols 2016, 319;

Sanín 2016, 46–7). As Sanín (2016, 49–50) notes, underpinning the branding programme was a set of vested political and commercial interests, and, in this respect, it is 'difficult to consider the project's interests as those of "the people"' as opposed to a mix of public and private agendas. Yet there was also recognition that to succeed the nation brand would need to resonate with Colombians, who would themselves be encouraged to 'live the brand', internalise it as part of their own identity, and embrace the role of 'brand ambassadors'. The consultant David Lightle was hired to develop the brand, whose first task was to set about identifying (inventing) the Colombians' national character, something his team ultimately distilled in terms of 'passion' – a passion for everything in life (family, religion, sport, schooling, art, work etc.). The new brand's tagline therefore became 'Colombia is Passion', a brand that Sanín (2016, 50–2) notes at times risked reproducing certain sexualised Latino stereotypes. Considerable efforts were made to promote the brand. Key brand images proliferated, flags were flown, a pop song produced, pedagogical strategies deployed (including targeting school children), promotional videos aired widely, and a three-year campaign calling on Colombians to 'Show your Passion' organised (53, 55–6). Platforms were also developed to enable Colombians to directly engage with, internalise, and demonstrate their own personal commitment to the brand and, through this, loyalty to the country. For example, this included opportunities to buy branded products and services, with this indicating how 'Colombia is Passion' was imbued with logics of consumer nationalism and what Banet-Weiser (2012, 143) terms 'emotional capitalism'. In Sanín's (2016, 56) view, 'Colombia is Passion' was a clearly nationalistic project 'in which the brand worked as a tool for governance aimed to redefine what it meant to be Colombian and to teach people to be good citizens'.

The key question, of course is whether the 'Colombia is Passion' nation brand was effective. By some markers it was not. For instance, in 2010 FutureBrand ranked Colombia as having the worst national brand out of eighty-five countries assessed, but with this justified on the basis that the brand was primarily targeted domestically and only secondarily at international audiences (Bassols 2016, 320). This, of course, tells us something about the priorities of international consulting firms and the values embedded within global nation branding indexes. Seen in terms of its domestic impact, certain positive results were evident. For example, it appears clear that the brand captured the imagination of many citizens, becoming part of conceptions of self-identity. Public approval of the brand was broad, while companies who had paid to be able to use the brand logo as part of their marketing appeared to have fared well (Sanín 2016, 57–8, 61). Moreover, when in 2012 the government announced 'Colombia is Passion' would be replaced with the new brand *La Requesta es Colombia* (Colombia is the answer), with this justified on the basis that the situation of the country had now changed and the old brand was no longer needed, there was something of a revolt on social media networking sites, with thousands of citizens protesting, and with this indicative of the extent to which the brand had become a powerful symbol of the nation (46, 60). This illustrates two things. First, it reaffirms how while nation branding can feed into nation building the two are not synonymous. The new brand, for instance, was highly resonant of economic logics of nation branding and was geared more directly towards business and corporate interests. The embrace of the entrepreneurial subject evident in much contemporary (consulting) discourse on nation branding ultimately has little time for the sentimentality of national discourses of belonging. Second, the new brand was also interesting in how it sought to reposition Colombia as a 'good state', which in the Colombian context might also be considered as a declaration of 'normalisation', and with President Santos stating that 'Colombia is facing new times ahead in which it can be the solution to the world's problems' (quoted in Bassols 2016, 320).

This final point, of course, suggests that a significant transformation in the domestic security situation of the country had taken place. In this respect, levels of violence have declined and a peace process with FARC guerrillas has been ongoing. Exactly how much of this can be attributed to the Colombia is Passion nation branding campaign is open to question, and insofar as it can, then it also needs to be seen against the broader background of President Uribe's 'democratic security' initiative, the rebranding of the Colombian military, and the link between that and the *Vive Colombia* campaign. At the same time, insofar as Colombia is Passion contributed to building pride, self-esteem, and community at individual and national levels, then it certainly may have been a facilitating condition for a more peaceful domestic environment. Yet there is also need for caution and, as Ojeda (2013, 765) points out, there are several contradictions in such claims. First is the way in which democratic security and *Vive Colombia* were only able to demonstrate security, peace, and stability precisely through mass military deployments. Second is the fact that these initiatives all took place against massive amounts of forcible displacement and humanitarian crisis. In the decade from 1998 to 2008 this affected an estimated 4 million people (10 per cent of the population), who were removed from 5.3 million hectares of land across different regions. Thus, in the process of some citizens reconnecting with the Colombian homeland and bolstering their sense of ontological security through enhanced attachment to the nation, many others were experiencing the exact opposite. Third, there were distinct class, racial, and ideological elements to these processes, with peasants, Indigenous Peoples, Afro-Colombians, (left-wing) journalists, union workers, critical scholars, human rights advocates, and activists all targeted. For instance, the freedom to travel was largely reserved for privileged Colombians mainly residing in urban environments, travelling to places swept clean of anyone representing potential political opposition. In this context, disappearances, assassinations, and selective killings also increased throughout the period, with many victims from these groups (765–6, 772–3). And fourth, these processes were also grounded on an intense securitisation and dehumanisation of internal enemy others, not least FARC, with this justifying extensive state violence against them (769). In short, if nation branding has contributed to enhanced (ontological and physical) security for some, it has entailed a process not only of silencing but also of explicitly insecuritising others. In short, 'peace' – to the extent it exists – has been won less through promoting reconciliation between warring parties then through branding techniques being used to mobilise public support for concerted security actions, with disparate effects on different parts of the population.

NATION BRANDING OR REGIME/STATE BRANDING?

Finally, the Colombian example also begins to highlight how nation branding can function and be attractive to ruling elites as a mechanism for cultivating political legitimacy. Certainly, in democratic contexts it has already been argued that leaders will likely hope that positive foreign reception of an internationally well-crafted nation brand may 'boomerang' back home and help generate domestic consensus and support for government (Aronczyk 2013, 16). Yet amongst consultants and some analysts it is also often assumed that this itself is likely to promote further democratisation. This is because democratic systems – and the cosmopolitan and open identities they are seen to support – are presumed to be the most appealing and 'brandable', an assumption that has already been challenged in this chapter.[2] However, this criticism can be extended. Not only is the link between (successful) nation branding and democracy open to question, but nation branding may also be effectively mobilised to uphold non-democratic political systems.

For instance, Schwak (2018, 655–6) argues that, insofar as nation branding calls on citizens to 'live the brand', it can function as 'a powerful tool of domestic governance that works both towards political legitimisation of contested regimes, and towards governing domestic citizens' identities and behaviours' in ways that, in some contexts, may leave little room for dissent. This points to the disciplining mechanisms at play within some nation branding programmes (see chapter 3) and the way in which certain forms of citizenship become privileged as 'patriotic' and pro-social at the expense of others. For instance, Desatova (2018) highlights how in Thailand the government that followed the 2014 military coup explicitly mobilised nation branding strategies primarily in the service of political legitimisation and only secondarily in terms of trying to promote economic prosperity. Specifically, the Thailand 4.0 nation branding campaign was framed to encourage Thais 'to abandon their provincial identities and democratic and social aspirations in exchange for a semi-authoritarian rule under the traditional elites' (688). For instance, even ostensibly external tourism-focused messages had a clear domestic component, such as in directly reminding Thais of their duties to be good hosts, to help tourists, and not to take advantage of them, something that in turn reflected other messaging about the need for personal moderation, prudence, and respect for existing social hierarchies (690, 693). Desatova notes how the campaign branded the military in the role of national 'saviour', with the population essentially offered the deal of 'material benefits in exchange for popular recognition and legitimation' (690, 692). Fundamentally, the aim was to sell 'an appealing vision of their future selves to the Thai people in exchange for their support, trust and loyalty to the military government'. Nation branding was therefore mobilised to change the attitudes of the Thai people, both towards the military and towards the form of political order they desired. In contrast to the political stability and prosperity promised under military rule, democracy would only risk instability and economic decline (693).

In this respect, Eggeling (2020) pays particular attention to the role that nation branding has played in 'soft' authoritarian regimes over the last twenty years. Soft authoritarian regimes are characterised by their limited incorporation of democratic practices while falling short of being full procedural democracies. This contrasts with hard authoritarian regimes that are characterised by military dictatorships and next to no democratic elements. For Eggeling, at the heart of the distinction is a difference in how political legitimacy is gained, with soft authoritarian regimes reliant on persuasion and manipulating the discursive field by crafting images of the state for public consumption, as opposed to hard authoritarian regimes that are more likely to rely on coercion (48). A couple of points can be emphasised from Eggeling's work. First, at least when looking at soft authoritarian regimes, she suggests that it is important to specify more carefully exactly what is being branded and that, in this respect, the concept of 'nation branding' is too loose. Much of the time, she suggests, in these contexts it is not the nation that is being branded but the state and its ruling regime (51–2). In this respect, what practices of nation branding essentially do is elide the state/regime distinction such that the projection of the image of a successful state becomes conflated with and indistinguishable from the idea of a benevolent and legitimate governing regime. Insofar as nation branding is mobilised to produce an idealised reputation of the state, then this itself becomes 'inseparable from the policies, achievements, and vision of the regime ruling over it' (228–9).

Second, she challenges the tendency of analysts to distinguish between the internal and external aspects of nation branding programmes, emphasising how the internal and external dimensions of legitimation are often directly linked. For instance, the emphasis of soft authoritarian regimes on showcase global mega-events may serve two functions. First, to legitimise and normalise the state/regime to the international community. Second, in the absence of a democratic mandate, to act as a legitimation strategy domestically insofar as domestic audiences draw status, pride, and self-esteem from external recognition and adulation (Eggeling 2020, 48–9). The dynamic highlighted here is close to but not the equivalent of 'sportswashing'. In other words, regimes may seek to host mega-events not necessarily because they are seen as having the capacity to divert international (and domestic) attention from problematic aspects of regime governance and behaviour but because demonstrating the capacity of the regime to deliver can in turn reaffirm and stabilise dominant conceptions of state-identity and governance (230).

To demonstrate the argument, Eggeling draws on the cases of Kazakhstan and Qatar. While noting that each has deployed its fair share of 'cosmetic' nation branding programmes, she focuses on more institutionalised policies, in particular noting how both states have devoted considerable time and resource to hosting and partaking in global sports, constructing extravagant capital cities characterised by prestige architecture, as well as founding major hubs of higher education to help foster the idea that they are at the cutting edge of the knowledge-based economy. Again, the aim here is not simply to impress external audiences, to seek international recognition and secure investment, trade, and tourism, but, fundamentally, to signal to domestic audiences that the ruling regime remains the most appropriate for the society. As she puts it: 'a primary effect of engaging in the global branding circuit is the construction of idealised interpretations of state-identity that claim and (re)produce the naturalness and legitimacy of the incumbent political regime' (Eggeling 2020, 98–9, 228). Insofar as they succeed, though, it is likely to be because they have been successful at encouraging citizens to vicariously identify with the achievements of the state/regime – or indeed a particular leader (e.g., Nazarbayev in Kazakhstan) – to internalise them as their own and therefore enhancing their own sense of self-esteem, status, and ontological security.

In this respect, while Eggeling's distinction between state/regime branding and nation branding is useful in highlighting key aspects of the process in certain political contexts it might also be noted that, insofar as nations become defined in terms of their ruling regimes' ability to control the ideational and symbolic world, then the distinction she draws between state/regime branding and nation branding may itself start to collapse. For instance, it is notable that both her cases comprise relatively new 'artificial' states, which for different reasons – collapse of the Soviet Union (Kazakhstan), withdrawal of Britain from empire (Qatar) – found themselves facing a distinct problem of both nation and state building. While it is clearly the case that nation branding has been mobilised in the service of regime stability and endurance, principally by conflating the regime with the very idea of the independent state, it is also the case that these same practices have been fundamental to the process of constructing visions of national identity and the national story. In other words, in these particular instances regime branding, nation building, and nation branding have become notably aligned. However, this is not to suggest they are synonymous. Indeed, in situations in which citizens start to perceive regime branding as simply that, then this itself may expose fragilities and lack of a sense of common purpose and identity at the heart of society and the national (nation building) project. As a last point, though, the suggestion evident in the analysis that nation branding appeals to 'soft' authoritarian regimes because ultimately they rely on the power of persuasion in turn assumes that 'hard' authoritarian regimes have little need for nation branding, relying as they do solely on the power of coercion. However, North Korea's particular embrace of nation branding, also for purposes of domestic legitimation, indicates that, while hard authoritarian regimes may have less obvious need to adopt nation branding programmes, they still may do so, seeing this as providing for a stronger sense of legitimacy and consent than the simple use of coercion and fear.

Indeed, it is also worth noting how in recent years authoritarian regimes have demonstrated an ability to co-opt Western cultural producers into promoting their own nation branding and regime legitimation efforts. A case in point concerns China's growing ability to influence the plotlines, scripts, and representations of China in Hollywood blockbuster movies. As the world's biggest film market by revenue (Li 2021), under President Xi Jinping the Chinese government has placed increased censorship demands on any studio wishing to access the Chinese market. Films are therefore increasingly *preemptively* crafted with the Chinese audience (i.e., government) in mind to get them accepted by official Chinese censors (e.g., no Tiananmen, Tibet, Taiwan, or Xinjiang and the Uighurs). This includes attention to scripts, themes, plotlines, political messaging, and visual representations (Gross 2022). Increasingly, Hollywood has therefore become complicit in presenting China as a benevolent global actor, a world leader, even as a humanistic saviour, and land of the future, thereby reproducing narratives and images also characteristic of China's own developing film industry (Chao 2022).[3] In doing so, though, Hollywood has arguably further helped to legitimise the one-party system within China as well as to build legitimacy for China with global audiences. In other words, rather than promoting further democratisation, key (presumed) forces of Western influence and democratisation have become complicit in promoting precisely the opposite and doing the nation branding work of authoritarian regimes for them.

CONCLUSION

This chapter explores tempting claims that, aside from helping facilitate prosperity, nation branding is also a route to peace and reduced conflict in international politics. Thus, whereas the previous chapter points to potential advantages that may accrue to individual states for adopting pro-social nation branding platforms, the *nation branding = peace* claim is more significant, suggesting as it does a pacifying potential inherent in *all* nation branding strategies.

In general, be they consultants or academics, those making the claim are also those who see nation branding as a recent phenomenon, fundamentally connected to (and further promoting) economic transformations associated with globalisation and spurred on by the geopolitical changes wrought by the end of the Cold War. Inherent in these transformations, it is argued, is a shift in underpinning geopolitical imaginaries, a move from a Hobbesian world of enmity and geopolitical contestation towards an emphasis on competition for investment and market share. In turn, this is seen to promote more benign, cosmopolitan, and inclusive identities. Specifically, nation branding will see chauvinist nationalism supplanted by less antagonistic constructions of national identity. In Darwinian terms, this is because non-benign elements will be a losing strategy and will therefore be factored out.

This chapter argues that there are several problems with such claims. First, claims about geopolitical transformation are evidently too categorical and simplistic. Second, they fail to account for the different roles nation branding can play when subject to different logics, something clearly evident in the cases of Russia and North Korea in which nation branding functions, at least in part, to promote antagonistic role identities in opposition to the West (diplomatic logic). And third, even under economic logics the claim is overly optimistic in assuming the inherently benign nature of neoliberal market economics. Indeed, insofar as links between nation branding and peace can be identified it is argued they tend to rest on smuggled in (liberal) assumptions about (complex) interdependence and democratic peace theory. Yet the direction of the relationship between nation branding, interdependence, and democracy remains typically underspecified. If the claimed pacifying effects of nation branding are actually dependent on the prior existence of interdependence and/or democratic governance, then the constitutive effects of nation branding would appear to be negligible. Yet it may be that in *some* cases nation branding may further support the development of both, especially insofar as governments and populations have come to see cosmopolitan and democratic identities as especially attractive – and, of course, nation branding mobilises techniques that might be used to help foster such attitudes. However, the presumption of certain consultants and academics that such identities and forms of governance are by their nature more attractive arguably rests on a liberal delusion contradicted by some of the cases analysed.

For similar reasons, assumptions that nation branding will foster greater understanding between nations also need to be treated with caution as these amount to a claim that essentially treats nation branding as fully compatible with practices of public diplomacy. Without denying that this will sometimes be the case, it will not always be so. Ultimately, this is because, whereas public diplomacy is focused on promoting understanding of one's policy positions, nation branding is premised on promoting desired images. For instance, during the Mohammad Cartoon Crisis the Danish government ultimately appeared to give up on dialogic public diplomacy efforts targeted at the Arab/Islamic world in favour of a nation-branding campaign. Notably, this campaign was targeted at different audiences and framed in ways more likely to increase the perceptual gap with the Arab/Islamic world, with the latter tacitly positioned as a constitutive other marked by its difference to Denmark's embrace of liberal values. Moreover, even when aligned with public diplomacy and seeking to promote more positive relations with the other, nation branding might not actually do anything to foster greater understanding. Here nation branding may appear more as a diversionary tactic drawing attention away from points of contestation rather than addressing them directly, as is evident in practices of 'sportswashing'.

However, the chapter also explores claims that, irrespective of its actual ability to promote international peace and security, there might be a role for nation branding in promoting peace domestically. Central to this is the potential of nation branding to foster a sense of national community and cohesion that can override extant internal grievances. Focusing on South Africa and Colombia as examples, it is shown how nation branding has been actively embraced as a mechanism for enhancing national and individual self-esteem, essentially through encouraging citizens to vicariously identify with and draw a sense of ontological security through the (branded) nation. Nation branding's ability to do this, in part, rests on its ability to foster new routines and visions of home and community, reconnecting citizens to the homeland and each other in different ways. However, although positive elements can clearly be identified, the domestic pacifying potentials of nation branding also need to be treated cautiously. First, the Colombian case demonstrates how such effects are unlikely to be reducible to nation branding alone but, rather, need to be seen in terms of how nation branding can be mobilised in support of other policies. Second, it is also noted that in both cases nation branding was unable to fully resolve internal tensions. Indeed, particularly in Colombia, it is shown how the topography of 'peace' facilitated has been far from even and, in significant part, premised on intense processes of insecuritising internal others depicted as threats to an exclusivist conception of the nation.

Building on this, the chapter ends by noting how nation branding has become an important mechanism through which non-democratic regimes have increasingly sought to secure political legitimacy with their citizens. In this respect, nation-branding strategies have been mobilised to convince citizens not only that the current regime works but also that it can deliver global recognition and high status. In such cases nation branding segues into regime branding and provides a further demonstration of the problems with blanket claims about nation branding's democratising potentials. However, while developing literature has suggested that such strategies are likely to be most attractive for 'soft' authoritarian regimes that govern primarily through the power of persuasion, the case of North Korea suggests that 'hard' authoritarian regimes may (at times) also view such strategies as preferable to the use of coercive force. Insofar as this is the case, through its affective potential to enhance ontological security and resonate with citizens' desires for status and self-esteem, it is likely because nation branding has the capacity (or at least promises) to promote an altogether more robust quality of political legitimacy.

6

Stigmatised States

[Vilnius, a place of] economic chaos, gangsterism, and a diet reliant on horse meat.
    Jonathan Franzen, *The Corrections* (quoted in Saunders 2017, 231)

We have allowed others to monopolise our story to such an extent that we have come to see ourselves in those images. We have come to believe that indeed we are powerless and backward as we are portrayed.
    Thebe Ikalafeng (quoted in Versi 2012, 99)

Brand Africa is an intergenerational movement to inspire a brand-led African renaissance to drive Africa's competitiveness, connect Africa and create a positive image of the continent.
    Brand Africa (https://www.brandafrica.org)

In focusing on claims emphasising nation branding's ability to promote more pacific international relations and to contribute to national security the previous chapter implicitly foregrounds considerations of physical security. In so doing, though, it also emphasises how in the pursuit of such goals nation branding's appeal is generally seen in terms of its ability to respond to the desire of citizens and national communities for a sense of belonging, status, and ontological security that might potentially be found through the (re)branded nation. Irrespective of whether it works, at least part of nation branding's appeal in such cases rests in its promise to replace inadequacy with hope, shame with pride, and paralysis with the activation of a sense of agency. Building on similar themes, this chapter considers the extent to which nation branding may offer solutions to historically stigmatised states at the wrong end of global geopolitical and geoeconomic hierarchies. Specifically, it considers the extent to which nation branding can operate as a form of emancipatory geopolitics capable of rectifying long-standing global injustices. It does so by focusing on two interlinked issues.

In the first two sections it considers the extent to which nation branding offers potentials for escaping and transforming unwanted geopolitical associations and established geopolitical hierarchies. Focusing on a general level, the first section notes how, despite proclamations of issuing in a brand-new world transcending traditional geopolitics, nation branding campaigns remain fundamentally infused with the inventive politics of geographical imaging/imagining. Characteristic of many states' nation branding programmes, for instance, is either an attempt to (re)affirm a particular geopolitical signifier and location or replace one stigmatised identifier with another with more favourable connotations and resonances. Thus, while states may not be able to physically relocate themselves, geographical imaginations are far less constrained. Nation branding therefore provides opportunities to project new geopolitical imaginaries through which states may seek to secure recognition for new geographical identifications or status-enhancing roles.

To illustrate such practices, section 2 provides an analysis of the Brand Africa campaign. This campaign is interesting in several respects. First, because of its attempt to overturn established global geopolitical hierarchies and negative branding of 'Africa' via a concerted rebranding and reimagining of the continent. In this respect, Brand Africa manifests as an emancipatory form of subaltern geopolitics resisting the geographical framings of the metropole. Second, though, Brand Africa's emancipatory radicalism is also shown to be constrained, operating within limits largely conforming to the economic logics of the branding discourse within which Brand Africa is itself articulated and, as such, is at risk of reproducing a stigmatised geopolitical imaginary. Third, section 2 therefore explores alternative approaches and considers whether geopolitical stigmatisation is best addressed by seeking to rejuvenate/rebrand stigmatised geopolitical images or instead by seeking to replace them with entirely different geopolitical imaginaries.

The linked second issue concerns the extent to which nation branding may provide opportunities for economic empowerment through which developing countries may escape economic inequalities that are presented by industry consultants as resulting primarily from the fact that the proliferation of stigmatising negative images repels investors. Explicit here is a critique that labels development aid a fundamental part of the problem, yet this is also an analysis that links nation branding to a fundamentally status quo neoliberal development model. Thus, despite the bold claims of consultants that nation branding offers the elixir to long-term problems of underdevelopment, the medicine prescribed rests on an arguably problematic and limited understanding of the causes of underdevelopment and a restricted conception of what constitutes development in the first place. Whether nation branding provides the best path to economic justice and development is therefore questionable. Indeed, it may even be implicated in re-enforcing the structural dynamics of inequality.

The final section extends this point by noting how, while nation branding consultants criticise development aid as problematic (because of its inherent tendency to reproduce stigmatising images that repel international investment) they are also prone to advise clients seeking to escape economic stigmatisation to adopt visible development aid policies themselves. In this, we once again see how 'good state' nation branding itself is often dependent upon the reproduction of geopolitical hierarchies and stigmatisation that logics of nation branding seem more likely to embed than overcome (Sussman 2012, 40).

NATION BRANDING AND/AS (EMANCIPATORY) GEOPOLITICS

Contra the claims of various consultants and analysts that the proliferation of contemporary nation branding practices reflects and is further promoting the transcendence of geopolitics, previous chapters argue that nation branding remains firmly ensconced in a geopolitical world. Given that claims about geography – and geopolitical location in particular – are central to (most) nation branding campaigns, the claim is certainly puzzling. Yet the emancipatory impulse at the heart of the claim, the idea that geopolitics are not determinative, bears further consideration. Perhaps more accurately, therefore, the argument of this chapter is that nation branding is better understood as a potential strategic tool for the politics of geographical (re-)imaging/(re-)imagining, and one that its advocates argue state leaders and governments cannot ignore.

Why governments might want to be mindful of the geographical imaginations associated with their country can be illustrated with reference to Jonathan Franzen's US bestselling and Oprah Winfrey-recommended novel from 2001, *The Corrections*, a novel that depicts Lithuania in far from flattering terms, a country in the grip of crime and anarchy, afflicted by energy shortages, dismal freezing weather, and 'heavy dietary reliance on horsemeat' (Tracevskis and Bradley 2001). In Lithuania the depiction drew much criticism, with some citizens and commentators retorting with defensive and barbed comparisons to the US, Franzen's own country. In more official circles, the Lithuanian ambassador to the US wrote to Franzen expressing his 'sadness' and inviting the novelist to visit so that he could get a 'real picture' of the country – this following Franzen's admission that he had never travelled farther east than Prague (Tracevskis and Bradley 2001).

This last point, of course, is the most relevant. For Western/American readers Franzen's choice of location worked not because of anything they knew about Lithuanian realities but, rather, because of how the country's depiction conformed to embedded prejudicial stereotypes about the post-Soviet space in general. In this respect, Franzen's choice of Lithuania was moot: he could have picked another post-Soviet country and the story would likely have worked just as well. Saunders (2017, 3), for instance, points to numerous similar cases, noting how in the post-Cold War period countries of the post-Soviet world have been targeted by 'novelists, filmmakers, satirists, and other cultural producers who readily and often thoughtlessly besmirch the "brand" of the post-Soviet world through their own works of popular culture and artistic imagination'. Be it Borat or James Bond villains, the post-Soviet world has become a 'handy geopolitical setting for corruption, poverty, backwardness, intolerance, and – most importantly – self-righteous laughter' (7). And what goes for the post-Soviet world goes for other places too. To describe such practices, Saunders coins the term 'anti-branding', where a lack of geographical knowledge is no impediment to prejudice and stereotyping. Indeed, insofar as it plays on existing audience ignorance anti-branding may even serve to 'eradicate "genuine" geographical knowledge of foreign peoples, places, and spaces' (77).

From a nation branding perspective such practices are fundamentally problematic and damaging. Moreover, the greater the sense of cultural distance, foreignness, and general ignorance that exists about a country, arguably the more likely it is to find itself victim of such practices. Anti-branding and its tendency towards negative geopolitical stigmatisations, it is argued, therefore needs to be countered by active and adaptive nation branding strategies promoting 'correct' – or at least more favourable – images. The ability of states to do this, however, varies, and several different strategies can be identified (see table 6.1).

Most limited is a strategy of 'acceptance and accommodation' of the anti-branding practices of others. As Bardan and Imre (2012, 170) note, the ability of different countries to re-invent themselves as branded commodities varies significantly. States and corporate entities with already existing 'strong brands and established power positions within the global economic network' are typically much better placed to engage in rebranding exercises and to exert at least some level of control and influence over the proliferation of national brands globally. By contrast, the options of small and economically weak countries are more limited. They argue that such countries often find themselves forced 'to embrace and mobilize [the] negative stereotypes' assigned to them by outside actors. For instance, they note how international fascination with Romania's 'Draculescu' legacy, a term referencing Count Dracula and communist dictator Nicolae Ceauşescu, is constantly played upon and reinforced in international media and popular cultural references that the country has struggled to escape, despite nation branding programmes designed for this purpose. The vampiric and autocratic resonances operate to reinforce the sense of the country's East European otherness, appealing to Western tourists' desire to consume the exotic. Ultimately, the problem for Romania is that the considerable external investment in the promotion and consumption of this heritage – for example, with respect to Dracula consider the role of Hollywood films – has proved extremely difficult to overcome (Bardan and Imre 2012, 187; Light 2001). However, rather than seek to avoid a difficult history, legacy, or stigma, one response can be to embrace and seek to exploit it. This is particularly apparent in the market for 'dark tourism', something evident in Romania but also, for example, in various countries with war-torn pasts like Vietnam (Henderson 2000). The danger in such practices, though, is that, while they may potentially provide economic benefits, the commercialised form of national identification they promote also carries the risk of fostering practices of exoticised self-stereotyping verging on self-orientalism, thereby merely confirming the nation's/community's otherness (Comaroff and Comaroff 2009).

Rather than embracing and seeking to work with the anti-branding practices of others in the possible hope of rejuvenating an otherwise stigmatised geopolitical assignation, a second approach is a strategy of 'geopolitical escape', the aim being to move from a stigmatised

Table 6.1
Geopolitical nation-branding strategies in response to stigmatisation

Strategy	Approach	Examples
Acceptance and accommodation	Embrace and mobilise ascribed negative images, potentially through stigmatised self-stereotyping	'Dark tourism' e.g., Vietnam, Romania
Geopolitical escape	Replace stigmatised with more positive geopolitical signifiers	Estonia as 'Nordic'; Kazakhstan as 'Eurasian'
Geopolitical role enhancement	Mobilise geopolitical metaphors to ascribe one's geopolitical location with strategic significance	'Crossroads of Civilisations' (Kazakhstan, Turkey); 'Gateway' (South Africa)
Geopolitical resurrection	Overturn geopolitical hierarchies by reclaiming existing stigmatised geopolitical labels	Brand Africa

geopolitical location to one with more positive resonances in global imaginaries. Typically, this is to be done by appropriating and attaching to the nation alternative geopolitical signifiers. For example, in chapter 2 it is noted how the end of the Cold War generated significant anxieties across much of the former Soviet-dominated world as countries found themselves caught between a now stigmatised communist past and an unknown post-communist future, anxieties that were also played upon by the nation branding industry. In this context, Kaneva (2012b, 6–7) notes how the prevailing crisis of identity was to be managed through a branded process of 'transition' through embracing Western forms of governance, economy, modernity, and the West's presumed superior knowledge. Beyond this, though, aside from 'transition' being a process of seeking to close the political and economic gap between a stigmatised self and a desired other, at least amongst post-communist European countries, this was also generally accompanied by various attempts at geopolitical transition. In short, the now sullied designation of '*Eastern* Europe' was typically seen as something to be rejected and replaced with other signifiers locating these countries further 'West'. Particularly ambitious, for example, was Estonia's attempt to escape the perceived negative connotations as one of three post-Soviet East European Baltic States bordering Russia by unilaterally proclaiming itself to be a 'Nordic' country (Jansen 2012, 86), as such seeking to jump ahead of its Baltic neighbours through association with a geographical signifier carrying much higher resonance – interestingly, a geopolitical branding strategy that has more recently also been adopted by the Scottish National Party as part of its campaign for independence from the UK (Kennedy 2020; Scottish Government 2013). Further south, Slovenia has likewise undertaken significant efforts to distance itself from the idea that it is a 'Balkan' country, a signifier it sees as standing for backwardness and instability, instead seeking to place 'itself firmly within the broader center of the mainstream of European geography, culture, history, and economy' (Volčič 2012, 152).

Underpinning such practices, of course, is recognition of the existence of hierarchies within the geopolitical imaginaries of global politics, where the 'West' and 'Europe' are equated as privileged markers of civilisation and modernity. This has likewise been evident in countries beyond most people's conception of 'Europe', with Kazakhstan, for instance, preferring to identify itself in its nation branding efforts as 'Eurasian' rather than 'Central Asian'. Thus, while 'Central Asia' has been seen to carry Soviet and Islamic connotations of autocracy and authoritarianism (Saunders 2012, 59), the marker of Eurasia is seen to tone these down, not least insofar as it signifies some form of geographical connection with Europe, with one of its early nation branding straplines depicting the country as a 'Road to Europe' (Marat 2009, 1130). The effect of nation branding attempts to escape 'West' and move towards 'Europe' have, therefore, only played on and ultimately reinforced globally resonant geopolitical hierarchies and have done little to undermine them. Of course, while a strategy of 'geopolitical escape' offers the promise of enhanced status and self-esteem via a process of national geo-biographical renewal, it is also a strategy potentially fraught with geopolitical and ontological anxiety, reliant as it is upon securing international acceptance and recognition of such a move (e.g., Zarakol 2011). In a European context, this is one core reason EU and NATO membership became a central goal of the transitioning states. Aside from perceived economic and security benefits, membership has been seen as a de facto indicator of international recognition of successful geopolitical relocation while failure to secure membership has been seen as a marker not only of falling short but also of being in some sense lesser and outside core Europe (Schimmelfennig 2003).

A third and also quite common approach is to adopt a strategy of 'geopolitical role enhancement'. Central to this strategy is the mobilisation of new metaphors designed to ascribe a state's geographical location with enhanced geopolitical significance, the aim being to claim/carve out a role in global politics that garners international attention and hopefully praise and admiration. There are resonances here with 'good state' nation branding, but where such a strategy has tended to be popular particularly with peripheral and marginal states that have perceived an opportunity to reframe an otherwise unpromising or neglected location as one of strategic advantage. The mobilisation of metaphors indicating cross-cultural exchange and interaction is particularly common, with such metaphors also bolstering claims about the nation's globally resonant cosmopolitan identity, re-marking the state as a point of geopolitical confluence and centrality. For instance, Kazakhstan has not only emphasised itself as a 'road to Europe' but also as being positioned at the 'Crossroads of Civilizations' at the 'Heart of Eurasia', in this respect blending 'in a most harmonious way, all the contrasts between East and West' (Marat 2009, 1129). Other popular metaphors include those of 'bridge' and 'gateway'. The contrasting resonance of these metaphors is interesting since, while 'bridge' is arguably neutral and simply references a meeting point and place for connection, the latter serves to reinforce geopolitical hierarchies. For instance, be it South Africa's branding of itself as a 'gateway' into Africa in the 2000s (see below) or Finland's mobilisation of the metaphor of the country as a 'gateway to the East' in the 1990s (Berg 1995, 25), the notion of 'gateway' signifies a final place of familiarity, stability, and order, in contrast to the otherness and unpredictability that might lie beyond. As an economic strategy, the invocation is that the 'gateway' in question will provide a comfortable and reassuring base for anyone wishing to do business across this border.

At the same time, mobilising such geopolitical linking metaphors can also have unforeseen consequences, not least by activating ontological anxieties over self-identity. For instance, as noted by Rumelili and Suleymanoglu-Kurum (2017), setting aside a longer historical process of Westernisation, in the post-Cold War period Turkey has mobilised a range of linking metaphors including 'bridge', 'gate', and 'crossroads', most recently seeking to cultivate a nation brand as a mediator between civilisations. In this respect, rather than choose between an Eastern and Western identity it has sought to capitalise on a liminal identity, where being 'between' is reconceptualised as an asset that enables Turkey to emphasise its Eastern elements when talking to the East and its Western elements when talking to the West. As they note, though, despite viewing the mobilisation of a dual identity in the branding campaign as a purely strategic move, the result was actually to reignite debates both domestically and internationally as to Turkey's 'real' identity, Western or Eastern, thereby manifesting rather than salving ontological anxieties over identity in the country. The case therefore highlights the notable difficulty states can face in escaping certain geopolitical imaginaries, in this case, Turkey's difficulty in combining notions of 'East' and 'West' that in hegemonic geopolitical discourses tend to be presented as 'binary opposites' (Rumelili and Suleymanoglu-Kurum 2017, 550–1, 562–3; Browning and de Oliveira 2017a, 497).

GEOPOLITICAL RESURRECTION, SUBALTERN GEOPOLITICS, AND BRAND AFRICA

A fourth strategy can also be identified: 'geopolitical resurrection', where the aim is to rejuvenate and transform embedded stigmatised images associated with an existing geopolitical label and in so doing to overturn established geopolitical hierarchies. Africa provides an excellent example, subject as it has been to decades, even centuries, of negative 'anti-branding'. In this respect, Anholt (2007a, 72, 75) argues that Africa suffers from a negative 'continent brand effect', by which he means that even well performing parts of the continent suffer under a unifying scopic regime that stigmatises the whole of the continent as suffering from 'poverty, corruption, war, famine and disease' (see also Osei and Gbadamosi 2011). Africa's construction as the 'dark continent', functioning as a 'paradigm of difference' to 'civilised' Europe, has a long history indelibly connected to practices and experiences of colonialism and the racist and orientalist attitudes that underpinned them (Mudimbe 1994; Parker and Rathbone 2007; Jarosz 1992; Campbell and Power 2010). However, while the crude colonial practices of the past may be less apparent, the exploitation of negative images of Africa continues, even amongst the ostensibly altruistic claiming the only thing they wish to offer Africans is help. Specifically, this is apparent within the charity sector, with aid agencies competitively mobilising increasingly shocking images as a form of 'poverty porn' (Cameron and Haanstra 2008, 1477–9) to garner attention and donations (Polman 2010). Or we see it in the rise of 'celebrity humanitarianism' also peddling in similar imagery, with this in turn circulated across mainstream and social media (Brockington 2012; Kapoor 2013). As the marketing executive Melissa Davis notes, events and campaigns like Live Aid (1985), Live 8 (2005), Make Poverty History, or the Band Aid 30 re-release in 2014 of the song 'Do They Know It's Christmas' (in response to the Ebola outbreak in West Africa), promoted by celebrities like Bob Geldolf and Bono, have all had a reiterative effect of further embedding imaginaries of 'Africa as a continent that is beyond hope: too much poverty, too much death and an overwhelming sense of too many problems with too few solutions' (Davis quoted in Versi 2009; also Anholt 2007a, 76; 2020, 60–1; Richey and Ponte 2012).

The contention of the nation branding industry is that such anti-branding not only results in problematically skewed images in which the diverse experiences of a continent of over fifty states and a billion people are flattened out into a singular experience, but that these images themselves serve to keep the continent down. In this respect, branding for charity and branding for economic development are presented as incompatible opposites (Anholt 2007a, 76). What is needed instead are different images and a revived brand identity for Africa, one in which pictures of starving children and conflict are replaced, for instance, by those of 'African bankers driving Mercedes cars', to quote the Africa director of the Dutch development bank FMO (quoted in Versi 2009).

Throughout the 1990s and into the early 2000s initial ideas along these lines underpinned emergent concepts of 'Afro-modernity' and Thabo Mbeki's framing of an 'African Renaissance', an idea he expressed in terms of a 'journey of self-discovery and the restoration of our own self-esteem' (quoted in Cornelissen 2017, 533–4). Behind such notions of rebirth was therefore the desire to wrest control of the continent's image away from outsiders and thereby to gain control over their own destiny and reaffirm a sense of African pride. In 2010, and immediately following the South African FIFA World Cup, aspects of these ideas were then crystallised in the launch of the 'Brand Africa' initiative by the South African branding consultant Thebe Ikalafeng.[1] Brand Africa's proclaimed mission is to use cutting-edge branding techniques to transform perceptions of Africa from a continent of calamities into one of promising economic prospects and entrepreneurial populations, enabling Africans to take control of their own narrative and thereby shape a new future (Browning and de Oliveira 2017b, 641). The aim, in short, is to 'change the narrative around the continent, through the vehicle of brands' (Brand Africa 2022c). Underpinning the Brand Africa initiative, though, was also an accusation of auto-orientalism, the fact that Africans had for too long not only allowed others to 'monopolise our story' but had done so to such a degree that: 'We have come to believe that indeed we are powerless and backward as we are portrayed' (Ikalafeng quoted in Versi 2012, 99; see also Dambisa Moyo quoted in Brand Africa 2010, 10). In this respect, Brand Africa was presented as an opportunity for liberation and a chance to upend the hierarchies of established geopolitical imaginaries.

Several things can therefore be noted about Brand Africa. First is the desire to tackle negative images of Africa at the supranational level of continental representation. As various Brand Africa publications note, if everyone else has an agenda for Africa, then Africa itself should get one (e.g., Brand Africa 2010, 4). Here, Africa appears not only as a geographical marker but also (potentially) as a *geopolitical actor*, with this itself implying the existence of an identifiable Pan-African sensibility and community with sufficiently shared interests to pursue such a collective rebranding effort – but that may indeed also be forged through supranational branding (Browning and de Oliveira 2017b, 643). Second, the emphasis on African agency marks out the Brand Africa initiative as a manifestation of what Sharp (2011a; 2011b; 2013) terms 'subaltern geopolitics', a concept that emphasises how the weak, while marginalised and stuck in asymmetrical power relations and modes of representation, are rarely completely powerless. In particular, they can work to manipulate extant geopolitical scripts and secure a better position via practices of reproduction, mimicry, and subversion (Browning and de Oliveira 2017b, 644–5). Third, though, it is also evident that the subaltern geopolitics of Brand Africa is not simply about strategic and economic interests but is also connected with broader projects of postcolonial identity formation and the desire to address the detrimental impact of anti-branding on Africans' sense of ontological security and self-esteem.

To get a better sense of this, the first point about Pan-Africanism bears further consideration as it indicates some of the tensions and limitations evident within Brand Africa as a form of subaltern geopolitics and geopolitical resurrection. The key point is that the activist and emancipatory imperative behind Brand Africa is supported through drawing directly on the longer history and tradition of decolonial Pan-Africanism, where this heritage itself exists as evidence and inspiration for renewed Pan-African agency today. The tension is that historical decolonial discourses, movements, and thinkers generally framed an emergent Pan-Africanism in largely socialist terms. In contrast, the Pan-Africanism of Brand Africa has a distinctly capitalist framing, with this meaning that the links between the two are far from seamless but also implying that the subaltern geopolitical ambitions of the latter are far less radical than those of the former (Browning and de Oliveira 2017b, 642).

For instance, while it had different manifestations, from its emergence in the late nineteenth century and throughout the twentieth century, Pan-Africanism was characterised by a decolonial impulse to creatively reappropriate those 'paradigms of difference' that supported the colonial enterprise in Africa and that, not least, legitimised violence and oppression. For example, attempts were made to rescript 'blackness' and 'Africanity' from being racial markers of inferiority to being positive markers signifying the existence of a broad subaltern African imagined community. From being a category of alienation, race therefore gained a redemptive function, with Western 'knowledge' mobilised against the metropole and facilitating the imagining of alternative political geographies and projects of decolonisation. Rather than rejecting colonial categories, they were therefore subverted in a form of 'strategic essentialism' (Spivak 1987; Browning and de Oliveira 2017b, 646–8), with this reworking of conceptual categories to an emancipatory cause being what marks decolonial Pan-Africanism as a form of subaltern geopolitics. Western notions of national self-determination were similarly appropriated in the cause of national liberation. In the African context, though, national liberation was also framed as a step towards African liberation in general and the creation of a broader African community more specifically. In other words, the nationalism of the Pan-Africanists was notably far more inclusive/expansive and supportive of supranational projects and geopolitical visions than was that of the colonial powers. This sense of disruptive subaltern solidarity was in turn manifest in broad African support for the non-aligned movement, existing as it did as a challenge to the binary geopolitical scripts of the Cold War (Browning and de Oliveira 2017b, 648). The subaltern geopolitics of decolonial Pan-Africanism therefore emboldened a sense of agency by providing an alternative set of geopolitical visions that promised a renewed sense of pride, ontological security, and agency.

Given this, it is perhaps unsurprising that Brand Africa's architects have found the heritage of decolonial Pan-Africanism alluring and a source of legitimation for their own Pan-African ambitions – ambitions that they believe can be supercharged via the activation of the claimed world-making powers of nation branding. Links between the two are therefore openly proclaimed, with Brand Africa publications directly referencing and quoting key Pan-African figures, like Kwame Nkrumah (e.g., Brand Africa 2010, 4; Ikalafeng 2014). There are, of course, some obvious synergies, not least in terms of how both have sought to resurrect 'Africa' from a marker of denigration to one of dignity and pride. Beyond this, though, they differ markedly. For instance, while invoking and drawing legitimising succour from the forefathers of decolonial Pan-Africanism, Brand Africa publications avoid any detailed exploration of this heritage. The reason no doubt lies in the fact that Nkrumah and other key Pan-African thinkers (e.g., Amílcar Cabral, Julius Nyerere, Frantz Fanon, Sekou Touré) were heavily socialist and anticapitalist in political orientation (Martin 2012, chaps. 5 and 6), whereas Brand Africa clearly operates firmly within the confines of capitalist discourses of globalisation and the competition state.

In this respect, while the 'fathers of liberation' called upon African societies to reclaim their histories and to liberate themselves from a preoccupation with the perceptions of others, Brand Africa is much less radical. Indeed, it essentially accepts criticisms that African leaders have been complicit in perpetuating negative images of Africa,[2] and it calls on 'Western' knowledge – in the form of branding – to drive change by mobilising African people and leaders to take control of their brand and, through this, to attract global business and investment. The result, though, is that the geopolitical resurrection of Africa envisaged in Brand Africa is one that, while asserting Africa as an equal player and subject, with this to be done by mimicking prevailing branding tropes and technologies, is also one that ultimately reaffirms hegemonic Western notions of neoliberal subjectivity and conduct (Browning and de Oliveira 2017b, 650–1). Brand Africa therefore operates several initiatives within which this can be seen. One is an annual ranking competition of 'Africa's Best Places' in which 'best' is a euphemism for 'most competitive', the goal being to 'inspire, champion and celebrate best practices in Africa-focused initiatives and campaigns that successfully position, influence and drive competitive and sustainable Nation, City and Destination brands' (Brand Africa 2022b). Another is 'Brand Africa 100', which seeks to identify and rank Africa's top one hundred product brands, the belief being that – in line with 'country-of-origin' branding – people's perceptions of product brands influence their view of the country/continent within which they are produced (Brand Africa 2022a). The initiative is therefore one explicitly designed to actively educate Africans in the value of developing and valuing consumer brands. In both cases, Western knowledge and norms about 'development' is accepted largely without question (Browning and de Oliveira 2017b, 652).

In respect of subaltern geopolitics, Brand Africa is therefore double-edged. On the one hand, it represents a clear attempt at geopolitical resurrection in opposition to images of Africa prevalent in global imaginaries, with its subversiveness lying in how it mimics the practices of the coloniser precisely to challenge established geopolitical hierarchies. Yet, unlike the Pan-Africanism of the decolonial movement, it does this not by seeking to overthrow the underpinning logics and broader structural economic dynamics of those hierarchies but, rather, by seeking to reposition Africa within them and even reprioritising a concern with 'what they think of us', a concern that reinforces the demand to mould the self in line with the anticipated desires of others. Insofar as Brand Africa may enhance a Pan-African sense of pride, dignity, and ontological security, then, this is to be derived through fully embracing Western discourses of competitiveness privileging transnational markets and corporations, this itself standing in notable opposition to the historical legacies of Pan-Africanism on which it draws.

At the same time, Brand Africa's ability to promote the geopolitical resurrection/reimagining of 'Africa' and to promote a broader sense of Pan-African community and agency also warrants further consideration. This is because while Brand Africa is typically proclaimed to be a 'global African initiative *for Africa by Africa*' (Brand Africa 2015, 2, emphasis in original), a claim that assumes that a positive continental rebranding effort will be beneficial to all African nations – whether it will be is less clear. Indeed, it can be argued that the initiative is itself bound up in its own geopolitical machinations and liable to work to the benefit of some African nations more than others. Specifically, it is worth bearing in mind that Brand Africa has notable personal and institutional linkages to Brand South Africa, has its institutional home in South Africa, and has received its most significant state backing from South Africa (Browning and de Oliveira 2017b, 653–4). Indeed, in many respects the Brand Africa initiative emerged as part of South Africa's own attempts at geopolitically repositioning itself as the key representative of Africa's prospects in the world. This was evident already in its framing of the 2010 FIFA World Cup as the 'African' rather than specifically 'South African' World Cup. Notably, though, at the point at which Brand Africa was initiated in 2010, South

Africa's own nation branding programme was emphasising the need for South Africa itself 'to drive the rebranding of Africa' (International Marketing Council of South Africa 2011, 5; Brand South Africa 2012, 26) and to understand 'Africa' as an economic opportunity to be 'strategically leveraged'.

For instance, in the 2010s South Africa's own nation branding campaign began emphasising the country as a 'gateway' into Africa, with this itself an attempt to further emphasise its post-apartheid transformation (International Marketing Council of South Africa 2011, 5). The 'gateway' metaphor, of course, signifies a nation branding strategy of 'geopolitical role enhancement', with South Africa also depicted as a 'springboard, 'the powerhouse of a rising continent', and a 'catalyst' for growth elsewhere in Africa (Brand South Africa 2012, 8; 2013, 14; International Marketing Council of South Africa 2010, 4; 2011, 5). Yet the gateway metaphor also creates a certain amount of tension with Brand Africa's broader goal of continental 'geopolitical resurrection', the tension being that, in attempting to depict South Africa as a staging post for foreign investment in the rest of the continent, the metaphor tacitly reaffirms stereotyped prejudices of African instability and otherness, though this time positioned as beginning beyond South Africa's borders (Cornelissen 2017). Rather than driving uniform cross-continental development, such a strategy clearly had the potential to further exacerbate regional economic disparities, with Brand Africa's market-capitalist orientation liable to resonate better with, and benefit, some African countries more than others – for instance, those with more open economies and certain structural economic advantages (Browning and de Oliveira 2017b, 654–5).

For South Africa, the combining of nation branding strategies of 'geopolitical resurrection' (via supporting Brand Africa) and 'geopolitical role enhancement' (via Brand South Africa) has no doubt made strategic sense, enabling the country potentially to capitalise further on its already more positive global resonance and existing relative economic development when compared to many other African countries. On the other hand, rather than driving cross-continental development, the strategy clearly had the potential to further exacerbate regional economic discrepancies. This may explain why only a few other African countries have actively embraced the initiative as institutional partners. This points to two other things as well: first, the inherently competitive nature of nation branding (to be expanded on further below) and, second, the question of whether a strategy of geopolitical resurrection is necessarily the best response to the geopolitical stigmatisation of Africa for all African nations. With respect to the second, it is notable, therefore, that, rather than embrace a nation branding strategy of 'geopolitical resurrection' targeted at rejuvenating Africa's negative 'continent brand effect', some other African countries have instead placed their efforts on nation branding strategies of 'geopolitical escape'. For instance, Angola has emphasised its links to the Portuguese-speaking and transatlantic Lussophone community (especially Brazil and Portugal), with this, rather than Africa, being seen as the 'opportunity that must be leveraged' in the pursuit of investment, recognition, and geopolitical advantage (Scholvin 2016, 176–8). Rwanda, meanwhile, has attempted to reposition itself by casting its capital city, Kigali, as the 'Singapore of Africa'. Appropriating Singapore as a metaphor of (Asian) hyper-modernity is, as such, an attempt to replace embedded African associations with a more global imaginary and optic of Rwanda as a nodal point of globalisation, another stable investment gateway into Africa, but also a global player less constrained by continental boundaries (Robertson 2005; *Economist* 2012; Serlet and Martin 2021). As indicated, therefore, while it is understandable why countries, regions, and continents may be tempted to seek direct redress for geopolitical stigmatisations to which they find themselves subjected, other options promoting alternative positive visions and geopolitical imaginaries may also exist and, depending on context, may even be preferred (Browning and de Oliveira 2017b, 656).

NATION BRANDING AND DEVELOPMENT

The Brand Africa case also speaks to broader questions about the links between nation branding and the politics of development. As noted, industry diagnoses of the problems facing Africa and other underdeveloped countries and regions are relatively straightforward. Suffering from the negative anti-branding of others, these places lack sufficient attraction to entice investors, tourists, and trade, with particular ire reserved for the development/charity aid sector for 'mercilessly' promoting and 'milking' such images, with this seen as central to their very business model (Anholt 2020, 61). Nation branding consultants are obviously not alone in raising justified concerns about the constitutive effects of charity marketing campaigns, but they do draw very specific conclusions from this critique, the first being that charitable branding for aid is essentially pernicious, with this casting aid as fundamentally incompatible with long-term development because of the inherent economic stigmatisation it entails (Browning 2016, 55). Second, the key to addressing this problem is therefore for the developing world to mobilise around concerted nation branding actions to cultivate more positive images and brands. This reflects the industry argument outlined in chapter 2, that cultivating a competitive identity through practices of nation branding is the key to development and economic success. It also suggests that solutions to problems of underdevelopment are to be found principally from within the business sector and not the development community.

As framed, such an argument not only serves to neutralise criticisms of nation branding and consultancy practice but reframes these as instruments of social and global justice. As claimed by Anholt, who notably titled one of his books *Brand New Justice: How Branding Places and Products Can Help the Developing World* (2005), judiciously applied nation branding 'can be a powerful force for global wealth distribution and cultural as well as economic development' (Anholt 2002b, 59). As the Brand Africa case indicates, though, such a view is inherently status quo oriented, suggesting that poverty reduction is ultimately dependent on integrating poor countries into global markets, fostering consumer cultures, and cultivating their economic competitiveness (Cammack 2009). As such, the nation branding discourse clearly has the potential to socialise developing countries into accepting their need to compete in the global marketplace via the production of branded market identities (Pamment 2018, 404), a discourse that also notably shifts responsibility for development onto developing states themselves precisely by emphasising the imperative that they take control of their national brands (Browning 2016, 52).

Such messages have clearly been received, as evident in the proliferation of nation branding programmes throughout the developing world. One reason for this is no doubt that, rather than depicting the developing world as impotent, trapped in structurally embedded, exploitative, and self-reproducing economic relationships reinforcing dependency, the diagnosis of the problem and proposed cure is one that rejects powerlessness, promotes agency, and suggests that, through nation branding, a level of control and autonomy can be asserted over a country's development prospects (Wanjiru 2005, 84; Youde 2009, 127). It is understandable why such claims are tempting, yet whether nation branding is a magic bullet of poverty alleviation and development is a different question.

There is, of course, an intuitive reasonableness underpinning claims that good brands will foster development while weak and sullied images will be damaging. Given that most people would admit to being influenced by branding and marketing campaigns when making decisions about key purchases, it would be hard to deny that such considerations would not also feed into the destination preferences of tourists and students or the foreign investment decisions of companies, institutional investors, and governments. However, while a positive nation brand may support a country's development prospects at least to some degree, to extrapolate from this that underdevelopment is simply a product of poor brand management is much more problematic. For one thing, the claim itself rests on a problematic understanding of the historical operation of capitalism and neoliberal economics within which 'the market' is understood as fundamentally benign and where the aim is therefore to mobilise the neutral tools of nation branding to rebalance economic inequalities (Youde 2009, 132). Such a view assumes that actors have equal opportunities for access and that markets are not deeply influenced by historically embedded power dynamics and, as such, generally work in the interests of some more than others. This is obviously a view that sits at odds with the analyses of many postcolonial scholars, dependency theorists, and neo-Marxists, who rather see the operation of global markets as a structural problem and fundamental cause of global economic inequalities. In this respect, the 'market fundamentalism' (Jansen 2008, 131) championed by those advocating nation branding as a solution to problems of underdevelopment simply ignores the differential impacts of things like the historical imposition of IMF structural adjustment policies promoting privatisation, deregulation, and the removal of tariff barriers on the developing world, while these often remain in place in much of the developed world. Or the way in which parts of the developing world (not least Africa) are again being viewed as sites of raw materials and resource competition rather than manufacturing.

In this respect, despite claims that it is 'pragmatic and ideologically undogmatic' (van Ham 2002, 263), and that it is not only benign but also a mechanism for advancing emancipation and global social justice, in practice much contemporary nation branding is tied to a distinctly ideological view of the world. Indeed, the 'nation-branding-solves-(under)development' discourse is fundamentally depoliticising in that it directs attention away from deeper structural issues, naturalises market economics, and shifts responsibility onto developing countries by suggesting that one of the reasons poor countries are poor is that they have failed to sufficiently mobilise their entrepreneurial capacities (Lemke 2001, 201). The critically disarming effects of such a framing can, for instance, be seen in a statement by Mathias Akotia (2010), chief executive officer of the Brand Ghana Office. Accepting that a lack of branding is a 'reason there is such an ever increasing gap between the developing and developed countries', he notes that 'we [Ghana] continue to miss opportunities and blame others for our unfortunate situation'. Whether a country wins or loses, he suggests, is ultimately 'about nation brand strategy, discipline in execution and a focus on people [who] must deliver the strategy'. Such a call to adopt a claimed hitherto absent entrepreneurial spirit clearly has an empowering and potentially esteem-enhancing element to it, yet it is also one that locates success/failure firmly at the level of the developing state subject itself.

This points to another problem with the idea that nation branding offers a generalised solution to problems of global underdevelopment, which is that it ultimately sits at odds with the underlying economic logic of consultancy pitches. The issue is that while, on the one hand, nation branding consultants suggest that all a country needs to do to activate economic growth is to adopt a persuasive nation branding strategy, on the other hand, the economic logics of nation branding that drives their pitches depicts states as locked in a zero-sum game of winners and losers. Nation branding is necessary, it is argued, if states are to compete effectively in the 'supermarket of nations' for a sufficient share of the relatively fixed investment/tourism/status pie (Browning 2016, 60; Landau 2021), yet what this suggests is that not all nation branding strategies will be successful and that key to a successful strategy will be identifying and establishing a competitive edge. This precisely accounts for why South Africa embraced the notion of being a 'gateway' and Rwanda positions Kigali as the 'Singapore of Africa', brand messaging that is explicitly designed to establish their distinction from their fellow African partners/competitors and turn them into hubs sucking in a disproportionate amount of investment going into Africa. Thus, and setting aside arguments noted earlier pointing to the (at best) tenuous link between nation branding campaigns and a state's economic performance (see chapter 2), while nation branding might be beneficial in some cases, the zero-sum nature of the discourse suggests others will not be as fortunate (Mayes 2008, 130–1).

Moreover, questions can also be raised as to exactly who benefits from apparently 'successful' nation branding programmes. To really withstand scrutiny the claim that nation branding is a mechanism for tackling inequality and enhancing social justice needs to apply within states as well as between them. Raising a country's GDP is one thing, but whether this trickles down to alleviate the situation of the poorest in society and to iron out the gross economic inequalities that characterise many developing countries, or whether it rather disproportionately benefits big business, major corporations, and an already affluent elite, is another (Gertner 2007, 5). In this regard, marquee nation branding actions like the hosting of mega-events, which have been especially enticing to developing countries, have a particularly troubling track record. For instance, analyses of the preparations for the 2010 FIFA World Cup in South Africa have shown how this proved to be a considerable boon to big business and major construction companies that were tasked with building new stadia and infrastructure. By contrast, smaller enterprises were typically squeezed out in the tendering process while some of the new stadia were constructed against local opposition and – to provide the most appealing visual images of the country and best experience for visiting fans and media – were located in particularly picturesque places rather than where they would have the optimum impact for urban development (Alegi 2008, 404–8, 414; Louw 2016, 158).

The same has been the case in other places. For instance, the preparations for the 2016 Rio Olympics saw the demolition and clearance of favelas and the forcible relocation of residents who did not want to move, who were sceptical about the government's promises of rehousing, and who had resisted the action, arguing that the building of the Olympic Park was simply being used as an excuse to drive poorer communities from an area that developers had long been targeting for upscale compounds in the name of urban regeneration and renewal (Watts 2016). Meanwhile, while preparations for the Olympics were initially sold to residents as an opportunity to rejuvenate infrastructure and remake Rio into a 'city of the future', come the Olympics very little of this had been achieved, yet billions of dollars of taxpayer-subsidised revenues had by then been funnelled 'to a handful of Brazil's most powerful, well-connected families and their companies' (Cuadros 2016). Of course, these are not isolated cases and are also not specific to the developing world. Critics have long highlighted not only the nepotism and corruption surrounding mega-events but also how they strengthen a distinctly neoliberal conception of globalisation and global commerce while, in turn, fostering commercial and culturalized, as opposed to democratic or participatory, forms of nationalism and citizenship (Alegi 2008, 415; Louw 2016, 154). However, insofar as such practices are exposed, this may also serve to sully any potential positive brand effects that the hosting of such events might otherwise bring.[3] A good case can therefore be made that, in many cases, nation branding reinforces structural dynamics of domestic inequality rather than providing a clear strategy for resolving them.

Finally, it should also be clear that claims about nation branding's ability to resolve problems of (under)development typically serve to naturalise a market-based approach to development, measuring it in terms of capitalist consumption and the relative ranking of a state's GDP (Browning 2016, 61; Pamment 2018, 403–4). As Turner (2016, 20) notes, in much contemporary nation branding discourse modernisation is conflated with marketisation, with developing countries tempted to become globally competitive through re-enacting Western capitalist economic strategies. Or as Aronczyk (2013, 33) puts it, in the name of imagining themselves as 'unique, different and globally competitive, they first had to be reimagined as if they were all the same'. In this respect, nation branding is vulnerable to postcolonial critiques of orientalism. In other words, nation branding often looks like just the latest imposition of 'Western knowledge' privileging and normalising one development model over all other alternatives – alternatives, for instance, that instead of emphasising inward investment and market activity might potentially view development in terms of promoting 'self-realization, noninstrumental forms of community, [and] mutual respect' (Aronczyk 2008, 56; Escobar 1995).

DONOR NATION STATUS

To end, it is important to note that the juxtaposition between aid and nation branding in consultancy discourses is misleading at best, disingenuous at worst. Central to the claim is that development aid is not only ineffective but is fundamentally counter-productive, reinforcing negative images, stereotypes, and confirmatory biases that only dissuade inward investment while simultaneously disempowering developing states from asserting themselves on the global stage. By contrast, if aid is the problem the image makeover of nation branding provides the solution through its claimed ability to tackle prejudice and bolster pride and self-confidence, with this enabling the adoption of more proactive and agenda-setting approaches. The problem with this characterisation, however, is that the distinction drawn between aid and nation branding is far too categorical, not least because it misrepresents the advice consultants themselves often give to developing states and on whose advice such states have mobilised and subsumed international aid policies as constitutive parts of their nation branding strategies. As will be noted, at the very least this highlights a significant tension in claims that nation branding should be central to solving problems of global inequality and economic injustice. At worst it illustrates how, instead of offering a radical and disruptive alternative, nation branding plays an important role in reproducing the structural inequalities and hierarchies that industry consultants claim it can solve.

There are, of course, various reasons states develop overseas development aid programmes. For instance, they may be motivated by purely humanitarian concerns and the genuine desire to help those most in need in the global community. Former colonial nations may also be motivated by feelings of historical guilt and the desire to atone for their country's past exploitative actions, with this explaining why development aid provided by former colonial powers is often directed to those to whom a sense of historical responsibility manifests rather than to those regions and countries suffering most. After the terrorist attacks on the United States in 2001, the motivation behind much Western development aid gained a security imperative. In the new securitised environment aid was increasingly to be subordinated to strategic calculations about how it might be best targeted to fight terrorism, with US secretary of state Colin Powell (2001) describing humanitarian aid agencies as 'force multipliers' and 'an important part of our combat team'. The UK's Strategic Defence and Security Review from 2010 (HM Government 2010) therefore stipulated that spending to support fragile and conflict affected states was to increase from one-fifth to one-third of the total of the UK's Overseas Development Aid budget by 2014–15. In turn, aid spending shifted away from more traditional development activities (e.g., food, water, housing, education) and was increasingly targeted on 'security-enhancing' activities (e.g., police training, governance projects), with this leading to critical analyses of the constitutive effects of the securitisation of development (e.g., Beswick and Jackson 2014). And last, development aid may also be mobilised by states to promote economic interests. For instance, in the 2010s the UK development secretary suggested that UK overseas development aid to India was partly designed to influence the Indian government to purchase Typhoon fighter jets from the UK (Bidwai 2012).

However, be it for humanitarian, historical, security, or economic reasons, international development aid policies are also clearly tied up with concerns over national image and status dynamics. This is particularly the case for developing countries, some of whom have initiated their own international development aid policies as a constitutive part of nation branding strategies designed to escape their stigmatised status. For example, in the early 2000s the leaders of South Korea's nation branding programme concluded that the reason the country was still regarded by many global actors as poor was because the country 'had failed to provide sufficient contribution to the international community and has not been active in helping poorer countries' (Eu Yoon-dae quoted in Jeong-ju 2009). To rectify this, overseas development aid would increase as would the target number for South Korean volunteers working in the sector. According to the chairman of the country's nation branding council, such actions would 'contribute greatly to improving Korea's brand power' (quoted in Myo-ja 2009).

Framed through a nation branding lens, creating one's own development aid programme responds to and reinforces the image hierarchy between donors and recipients, the key aim being to situate one's own country on the right side of that divide. In part, of course, this may help cultivate the image of a benevolent 'good state', though arguably what counts more is the sense of category distinction and differentiation that this is seen to provide. For instance, Anholt (2020, 20–1) emphasises how he (successfully in his view) convinced the Slovenian government that the best way to establish a brand for itself as more stable, beautiful, and prosperous than its neighbours was not to undertake an advertising campaign to this effect but, rather, to become a donor to its more troubled Balkan counterparts. Doing so, he argued, would 'demonstrate to anyone paying attention that Slovenia was in a rather different financial position than some of its neighbours'. Possessing a development aid programme is therefore seen as a source of status and prestige and as signifying a state's transition from 'problematic' and undeveloped to 'normal' and developed (Kapoor 2013, 26, 64–5). Indeed, India's creation of its own aid agency in 2011 was greeted by the secretary general of the Federation of Indian Chambers of Commerce as signifying more than a transition to normality; rather, it was seen as a marker that the country was now operating in the upper echelons of the international community, a statement of confidence, and 'recognition by the Indian establishment that India ha[d] arrived as a global player with strategic interests' (quoted in Patel 2011). Concomitantly, the country has also discussed rejecting receiving international development aid itself, precisely because of the perceived stigmatising effect it is seen to have (Gilligan 2012).

Three concerns can therefore be noted about the incorporation of development aid as a strategy for nation branding. The first is how, rather than tackling global structural inequalities, insofar as the strategy relies on the idea that establishing a state's status as 'developed' is aided by – and possibly even dependent upon – the possession of an active overseas development aid programme, this is itself premised on the maintenance of structural inequalities between donor and recipient nations. The strategy, therefore, is just as likely to reproduce hierarchical geopolitical imaginaries and stigmatisations as it is to overcome them since the creation of the positive image of 'generous aid giver' is only meaningful in a context in which others continue to need such donations. The only difference is that mobilising development aid in the service of nation branding is seen to offer some developing states the chance to jump from one category to the other (Browning 2016, 67).

Linked to this is a second, more overtly ethical, concern. At face value, there is arguably something inherently progressive about how such strategies may have the effect of reinforcing the idea that the provision of development aid should be central to being able to claim the status and identity of a 'developed state'. To be clear, though, within the context of contemporary nation branding discourses of the competition state, status, self-esteem, and ontological security are understood as being derived from the ability to outcompete others in securing investment, tourists, foreign professionals, students, et cetera. Consequently, insofar as a state is successful in this game – a game characterised by the industry as an all-against-all competition for investment, prestige, and attention – the economic, status, and self-esteem benefits it experiences are inevitably to be achieved at the expense of others, with this itself potentially further fostering the superior/inferior dichotomy. As I therefore note elsewhere: 'Co-opting development aid into such strategies thus shifts the rationale from a focus on redistribution to viewing such disbursements as part of a longer-term strategy for the nation's enhanced accumulation of capital, attention, prestige and power to the detriment of others' (Browning 2016, 67).

In this respect, Pamment (2018) points to how, since the late 1990s, the link between nation branding and overseas development assistance has become increasingly strategic and directly tied to states' attempts to pursue broader political and economic interests in recipient nations. For instance, he points to how a German nation branding campaign directed towards India was explicitly targeted at promoting knowledge of German culture and language, such as through giving a million Indian schoolchildren the opportunity to learn the German language. On the face of it, the branding programme was designed to present '"German know-how, experience, products and service" across the fields of politics, business, education, research and science, and culture', but he notes that, in effect, the ultimate intention in such programmes of 'the deliberate and coordinated joining of international development activities with nation brands' is to influence 'the economic, cultural and political development of foreign countries' (397). As he puts it, 'aid funding is increasingly leveraged through brand identities to help stimulate growth, instigate infrastructural reform, assert ideational norms and promote the donor country as a partner of choice' (397). He refers to the conjoining of overseas development assistance and nation branding in this way as a form of 'postconditionality', the aim being to exert 'indirect social and diplomatic influence' in line with notions of 'soft power' and in contrast to the more direct 'command power over economic development' in recipient nations that has been characteristic of the conditionality mechanisms imposed by international financial institutions like the IMF and World Bank (397–401).

A third concern, and to reiterate a criticism levelled earlier with respect to good state nation branding, is that the linking of development assistance to nation branding can also corrupt the underlying impulses driving humanitarian actions by introducing issues of visibility and recognition. Once humanitarian assistance and development aid are subject to logics of nation branding then they are likely to be driven less by an ethical concern for others and more by the desire to promote a particular national image that solidifies the brand. This was evident in the South Korean example, where the decision to increase development aid spending and the number of volunteers was driven by concerns that the country's lack of visibility in this sector was a key reason for its inability to escape stigmatisation as a developing country. Helping needy foreigners was an instrumental second in this argument. As such, the subordination of development aid to logics of nation branding also carries the danger that, in future, it will be targeted primarily where it is believed it will have the optimum impact on brand enhancement rather than where its impact on human suffering will be greatest. As a signal of this, Anholt (2020, 159) himself reports how in conversations with the Austrian government the latter was clearly frustrated that it wasn't 'getting enough credit for [its] generosity', a frustration that could either lead to the cutting of aid – if this has become understood as its primary intended purpose – or its redirection to places or into forms that secure greater visibility and recognition.

CONCLUSION

This chapter considers claims that nation branding offers a unique way for states at the wrong end of global geopolitical and geoeconomic hierarchies to assert their agency, escape their historical stigmatisation, and, in so doing, re-establish a sense of self-esteem, status, pride, and ontological security. The idea that nation branding can function as a tool of emancipatory geopolitics for rectifying long-standing global injustices is certainly tempting and has clear intuitive appeal. Yet, despite this, the chapter argues that, in practice, nation branding's emancipatory potential is less radical and much more bounded than advocates claim.

The issue is addressed in two ways, first by considering the ability of nation branding to respond to and escape stigmatisations connected to a state's geographical location and the geopolitical imaginaries and metaphors with which it has become identified. In this context, nation branding's attraction lies in its promise to be able to rescript the nation since, while geographical location might be given, a state's location in global geopolitical imaginaries is potentially more fluid. Numerous cases are noted of states using their nation branding programmes to advance a range of 'transitional' geopolitical metaphors designed to signify and impress upon global audiences that the stigmas by which a country has become known should no longer apply. Often such metaphors promote a sense of enhanced geographical club status through association with historically privileged signifiers, for instance, by emphasising links to 'Europe' or the 'West'. Alternatively, they may also do so by metaphorically positioning the state as occupying a position of strategic importance or, by virtue of its geopolitical location, able to perform important geopolitical roles as sites ('bridges', 'gateways') for intercultural/civilisational exchange and communication.

In both cases, however, it is noted how any attempt to escape a geopolitical stigmatisation typically has the effect of reproducing it. Thus, even if a state is successful in its attempts to shift position its enhanced 'status' remains dependent upon the (re)activation of geopolitical hierarchies and the continued stigmatisation of those now deemed to lie outside and geopolitically 'lesser'.

More specifically, four geopolitical nation branding strategies in response to stigmatisation are identified. The best that may be possible for particularly weak and marginalised states is perhaps a strategy of 'acceptance and accommodation'. Other states may engage in strategies of 'geopolitical escape' or 'geopolitical role enhancement'. Perhaps most ambitious, though, is a strategy of 'geopolitical resurrection' whereby attempts are made to turn a currently stigmatised geopolitical marker into a much more positive one. To consider such an approach the Brand Africa initiative's attempt to overturn Africa's negative 'continent brand effect' is discussed. Brand Africa, it is argued, manifests as an ambitious form of subaltern geopolitics, mobilising and mimicking the geopolitical knowledge and branding techniques of the metropole to constitute 'Africa' as a geopolitical actor and in so doing manipulating and subverting extant geopolitical scripts. Yet Brand Africa's subaltern geopolitics is much less radical than the heritage of decolonial Pan-Africanism from which it draws some of its legitimacy and animating force. Instead of challenging prevailing global capitalist forms of governance and economy, Brand Africa reproduces them, the aim instead being to rise up the ranks and assert a sense of African pride, dignity, and ontological security, ironically by reinforcing a concern with market perceptions and what 'they think of us'. Moreover, Brand Africa is also seen to work in the interests of some African states more than others, with this perhaps accounting for why other African states seem to prefer strategies of geopolitical escape instead.

The chapter's second focus is on linked claims that nation branding offers the best option for states tarred with the stigmatisation of a lack of development. The claim itself is often framed through a direct critique of the 'anti-branding' practices of charities and aid agencies, who in the name of helping the world's poorest do so by seeking donations via the deployment of heart-rending and tragic images. Such images, it is argued, objectify and re-stigmatise developing countries as fundamentally abject. Instead of development aid, developing states are therefore called upon to embrace the redemptive power of nation branding, to take control of their nation brands, and thereby to promote more positive and proactive images. The 'nation-branding-equals-development' message is powerful, not least because it promises empowerment and promotes the possibility of exerting agency and control over the future. However, the claim also overlooks deeper problems that might be having an impact upon some countries' development prospects, for instance, problems connected to structurally embedded exploitative relationships between the developed and the developing world. Indeed, not only does it overlook such issues, but it arguably compounds them by ultimately fetishising and locking in developing countries to a model of development premised on globalised market capitalism. Moreover, it is also shown that the nation branding approach to development has often had problematic effects at the domestic level, something clearly evident in the experience of the differential (non)benefits experienced by citizens in countries tempted into bidding for and hosting symbolic mega-events. Finally, the chapter ends by noting that the *nation branding = good/development aid = bad* dichotomy of nation branding discourse and practice is itself counteracted by consultants' encouragement that developing states adopt their own overseas development aid policies precisely as a strategy to signify their distinction (in terms of prosperity and stability) from those around them.

Conclusion

Nation Branding and the Remaking of International Politics?

The preceding chapters demonstrate that engagement with proliferating practices of nation branding is important for a fuller understanding of contemporary international politics. While the sometimes crass and cringeworthy nature of some nation branding campaigns makes it tempting to dismiss nation branding as epiphenomenal and mere 'marketing', this book shows how nation branding intersects with international politics in often complex ways. Specifically, it argues that nation branding is having constitutive effects across a broad range of issue areas. While this might be expected in respect of states' economic orientations, nation branding has also been shown to be consequential not only in respect of the politics of security and community, the constitution of norms and global geopolitical imaginaries, but also in respect of the nature and role of the state. At the same time, the nature of nation branding's constitutive impact is often complex. Amongst industry consultants and analysts an intriguing dichotomy is often present. On the one hand, the significance of nation branding is played down, with nation branding presented as the application of marketing tools to campaigns of state promotion, a view that depicts nation branding as a largely technical and non-ideological exercise. In other contexts, though, nation branding is depicted as both responding to and further fostering a fundamental transformation in global politics from a world characterised by war and geopolitical rivalry to one characterised by states competing to attract attention and investment in global markets. Indeed, more than this, nation branding consultants and analysts have argued that nation branding provides a path to solving fundamental global problems of (inter)national peace and security, collective challenges such as those connected to various issues of social policy as states compete for reputation and standing based on how good they are, and, not least, that nation branding is an emancipatory vehicle for promoting global social and economic justice within and between states.

In subjecting such claims to critical analysis, this book argues that while important transformations connected to nation branding are taking place they are not necessarily as proclaimed by industry advocates and some analysts. For example, claims that nation branding is leading a change in the normative order, from a world dominated by geopolitical considerations in which preoccupations with territorial control and power, war and enmity, dominate to a new competitive yet pacific geoeconomic order, a 'postmodern world of images and influence' (van Ham 2001, 1), are exaggerated. Geopolitical worlds are not disappearing. Indeed, nation branding is often suffused with and mobilised in the name of geopolitics. Yet how this happens depends upon the logic of nation branding that is in play and where it has been argued that, aside from referencing a set of industry practices, nation branding also operates as a constitutive discourse of knowledge production, a way of understanding and apprehending the world that impinges on how geopolitical calculation and practice plays out in different contexts. Similarly, therefore, while claims that nation branding supports a more peaceful international politics and promotes global justice have intuitive appeal, the dynamics in play are complex, nuanced, and certainly not always inevitably pushing in a normatively progressive direction. In this respect, while nation branding may have positive impacts in certain situations, as a generalised practice there are also distinct limitations.

In particular, its transformational impact at the systemic level is questionable. Nation branding, for instance, is mobilised by traditionally geopolitical and revisionist states as well as by those seeking to uphold a (neoliberal) norms-based international order. Meanwhile, the inherently competitive logic of nation branding, with its emphasis on rankings and league tables, suggests something of a zero-sum mentality in which the aim is to secure as much as one can for oneself through emphasising one's distinction, inevitably to the cost of others. For instance, while it is hard to be against 'good state' nation branding on grounds of principle, in practice, with its emphasis on visibility (being *seen* to be doing good arguably over and above actually *doing* good) good state nation branding raises questions about its political motivation, its ethical implications, and, not least, about its actual efficacy in solving global problems. Likewise, while nation branding may offer a potential tool through which stigmatised and subaltern states can challenge and rectify their position, often such practices only reinscribe existing hierarchical geopolitical imaginaries or constitute new ones, the aim simply being to move the country into a better position. Not least, claims of ideological neutrality have also been problematised. At least when operating under economic logics nation branding accords to a distinctly ideological and status quo agenda, one in which nation branding is implicated in the reproduction of an environmentally (and often also socially) deeply destructive and divisive market-based approach to development, society, and politics.

At the same time, it has been argued that where nation branding may be playing an intriguing and potentially more notable transformative role is in respect of the politics of (national) identity, ontological security, and status dynamics. In one respect, nation branding has been shown to be potentially very destabilising for states, a source of anxiety and ontological insecurity, with the sales pitch of consultants and the underpinning constitutive discourse of nation branding preying on states' anxieties about their standing, status, and competitiveness. Yet nation branding also operates as a mechanism to respond to such concerns, the promise being that well-crafted nation branding programmes can enhance states' standing, status, and competitiveness through its potential to generate positive recognition from relevant global audiences, with this in turn potentially trickling down to have a positive impact on citizens' own sense of being. To do so, though, states need to make themselves attractive and admirable through the cultivation of particularly enticing identities, with national identity and culture understood as *the* core underpinning variable of national competitiveness. National identity and culture are therefore central to distinguishing national brands from the broader crowd, thereby establishing a sense of positive (and often virtuous) distinction, though only to a certain degree. In other words, while the imperative of nation branding is to stand out from one's competitors, to remain attractive and gain external recognition and praise, one's differentiation must necessarily be in line with the desires of salient global audiences. Therefore, inherent at least to the economic logics of nation branding, there is a notable disciplining element.

Similarly, interesting and important questions have also been raised about the relationship between nation branding and historically embedded practices of nation building and banal nationalism. The relationship is complex. Specifically, it has been argued that criticisms that nation branding entails the commodification, dehistoricisation, depoliticisation, hollowing out, and instrumentalisation of national identity need to be tempered. Such processes clearly are (often) evident and sometimes nation branding operates in opposition to broader processes of nation building. Conceptually, of course, one reason for this is that nation branding is targeted as much at external audiences as it is at national citizens. Its relationship to nation building is therefore always likely to be tricky. However, it has also been argued that nation branding is playing an (increasingly) important role in how citizens live through and imagine their nations. Insofar as it does, at least when it is operating in line with economic logics, it is also liable to affect how nations become a source of ontological security and self-esteem for citizens by shifting the focus away from an emphasis on kinship ties and the search for authentic narratives of selfhood (the imagined community) to an emphasis on securing recognition and status from global audiences for possessing a positive and desirable brand (the imaged community). Moreover, while it is tempting to view such a process as inherently alienating, in a context in which branding has become an all-pervasive cultural context and notions of consumer nationalism have become redolent and activating, it is unclear that this is (necessarily) the case (Banet-Weiser 2012; Volčič and Andrejevic 2016a). The notion of 'living the brand' and the cultivation of the citizen as a national 'brand ambassador' may sound crass when openly articulated, yet arguably taps into the way at least some citizens interact with and experience their national brands.

Nation branding, though, is also complex because it has different dimensions and manifestations. Throughout the book it is noted that it can be underpinned by different logics (cultural, diplomatic, economic), with the logic in play reflecting different motivations and arguably having different constitutive impacts. When driven by cultural logics the emphasis is largely on securing recognition for the state by educating and enlightening foreigners about the country. When driven by diplomatic logics nation branding operates more in the service of carving out and justifying role identities and is more closely aligned with notions of soft power. By contrast, economic logics entails a focus on the competition for trade and investment in a context of globalised markets. In practice, the logics are often intermingled with each other, with nation branding programmes infused with various aims and sometimes operating at cross-purposes. Yet, aside from being underpinned by different logics, it has also been shown how nation branding manifests different forms. Nation branding is most usually associated with broader practices of 'place branding' that are focused on selling the nation and enticing investment, trade, and tourists by emphasising the country's particularly attractive features. Alongside place branding, though, a concern with 'country-of-origin' promotion can also be identified. At least as significant as place branding, though, is the increasing emphasis on practices of 'corporate branding' and 'policy branding', where the former directs our attention to the relationship between nation branding programmes, citizenship, and (democratic) governance and the latter towards an intriguing expansion in the domains around which states are positioning themselves and seeking status and recognition in contemporary international politics.

NATION BRANDING IN CRISIS?

Bearing all the above in mind, the book concludes by noting that, as both a(n industry) practice and a constitutive discourse of knowledge, nation branding is facing something of a crisis, with emergent challenges raising important questions about the possibility, legitimacy, and direction of nation branding in the future. Unsurprisingly, the idea that nation branding may face crises of possibility and legitimacy is something that those involved in the industry, or those who see nation branding as promoting normatively progressive change, tend to avoid for obvious reasons. However, three challenges for contemporary and future nation branding can be noted in this regard.

The first is that, while industry dogma argues that nation branding is essential for states to survive and thrive in a world of global markets, its actual efficacy can be questioned. Indeed, even consultants have considered this issue, with people like Anholt (2007b) intriguingly sceptical. This is often seen as what lies at the heart of the analytical distinction drawn by Kaneva (2011, 118) between 'cosmetic' approaches, in which the emphasis is on the advertising techniques of marketing, and more 'institutionalised' forms of nation branding that entail more concerted action and investments in terms of the alignment of cross-sectoral policy agendas or infrastructural developments and urban planning, for instance. In practice, most states' nation branding programmes and activities will entail a mix of the two, although the typical criticism of nation branding consultants is that governments spend too much time on the former and not enough on the latter.

Typically, therefore, failures are attributed to a lack of client commitment to sufficiently implement plans (Olins 2005, 178; Teslik 2007; Da Silva 2010). What is needed is more nation branding, not less.

At the same time, though, the book argues that in most cases governments' willingness to undertake more concerted actions will rarely be motivated by nation branding considerations alone but are more likely to be influenced by broader political and economic concerns about self-identity, social justice, or security. In such contexts, any positive nation branding effects appear more incidental and secondary than fundamental to such processes. Despite its contested track record, though, the proliferation and (re)funding of more cosmetic nation branding campaigns has been the norm. One explanation as to why is the evident view that, despite failures, a sense pervades that if everyone else is doing it then so should we ... just in case it does work. In this respect, the rhetoric of consultants that the primary goal of political leaders is to keep the state's reputation intact (and enhanced) is powerful and persuasive, not least because it ties in with prevailing discourses of the inevitabilities of globalisation and neoliberal market economics (Browning 2016, 69–70). Moreover, at the end of the day, most cosmetic nation branding programmes are relatively cheap and can be sold to voters in terms of a proactive government taking action.

The second challenge is practical but entails further implications for the first and relates to the increasing difficulties states face in controlling nation branding messages, something evident with the rise of globalisation, digitalisation, and, in particular, the proliferation of social media platforms like Twitter, Facebook, Instagram, and TikTok. New technologies mean (potentially disruptive) 'branded' images and messages about nations can be produced from a multitude of sources and distributed globally in quick time, with the result being that nation brands are today better thought of as being 'continually negotiated' in a context of 'globalized media flows' involving an increasing range of often non-national narrators (Saunders 2012, 50). The result is that states are always at risk of losing control over the production of a coherent and clear brand, something that consultants frequently argue is essential for nation branding programmes to be effective and, hence, the increasing emphasis placed on practices of corporate branding designed to establish citizens' brand engagement. In this respect, nation branding programmes can be easily derailed – not simply through the reckless actions of governments (e.g., Russia's actions in Ukraine), the idiosyncrasies and personal ambitions of individual leaders (e.g., Donald Trump's use of Twitter to promote his own personal brand, arguably at the expense of that of the country of which he was president), or unexpected societal upheavals (e.g., Brexit in the UK – see introduction) but also through the deliberately disruptive actions of (non)citizens and advocacy groups as well (Pamment 2021; Jiménez-Martínez 2022). In this respect, Marklund (2015, 174) references the increasing '(im)possibility of purposive public diplomacy and image management' because the ability of states to control branding messages is now limited and often highly contingent.

By way of example, writing this conclusion in the weeks leading up to the 2022 FIFA World Cup in Qatar it became evident that even (soft) authoritarian regimes are unable to control nation branding messages. Qatar's bid to host the World Cup sat alongside several other significant and more concerted/institutionalised nation branding approaches the country has undertaken in recent years (e.g., emblematic architectural developments, the creation of a globally oriented universities education hub [Eggeling 2020]), most of which have drawn little negative international comment and might even be considered relatively successful at having cultivated generally positive impressions and images of the country. Interesting about the weeks prior to the start of the World Cup, however, was how this spectacular nation branding endeavour magnified several deeper issues related to human rights abuses and prevailing political and social values in Qatar that for many (often Western) onlookers were deemed unacceptable and an indictment of the decision to grant the World Cup to Qatar in the first place. In particular, these related not only to the harsh treatment – including many deaths – of migrant workers hired to build new infrastructure for the World Cup but also to Qatar's attitude towards people identifying as LGBTQI+. For instance, in respect of the latter, the Qatar World Cup ambassador called homosexuality 'damage in the mind' and 'harmful and unacceptable', with this reflecting the fact that homosexuality is illegal in Qatar and deemed immoral under Sharia law (BBC 2022).

Interesting about this is how in chapter 4 it is noted how nation branding generally steers clear of controversial social and political issues. Evidently, of course, it was not the Qatari government's intention that its hosting of the World Cup would become embroiled in such debates, with both the Qatari government and FIFA making pleas to fans, participating teams, media, and foreign governments not to disrupt the event and, rather, to show respect to the host country, 'focus on football', and avoid getting 'dragged into every ideological or political battle' (FIFA quoted in Roan 2022). The point, however, is that, while those undertaking nation branding programmes may wish to avoid controversial issues and the blowback and potential reputational damage this may entail, it is increasingly difficult to stop others using the attention generated by a state's nation branding actions as itself an opportunity for critique and counter 'anti-branding'. In the case of the Qatar World Cup this was typically framed in terms of accusations of 'sportswashing' (see chapter 5). To make a bigger point, though, cases like this arguably also reflect the nation branding industry's more recent identification of responding to global challenges as a potentially competitive edge and mark of distinction. In this respect, the shift towards an emphasis on cultivating nation brands as pro-social and ethically minded 'good states' might itself be seen as shifting the parameters of the nation branding game and creating new vulnerabilities and anxieties for states seeking to make a splash. In short, consultants' emphasis on making ethical concerns with 'the good' a point of focus and distinction within individual nation brands has itself created additional vulnerabilities – in the form of accusations of hypocrisy – for any government implementing such advice in its nation branding actions; but, perhaps more significantly, it has arguably also made nation branding *as a practice* (and those working within it) much more subject to ethical critique.

This, however, feeds into the third challenge. Contemporary advocates of nation branding generally assume an unproblematic moral universe and direction of travel, where transformation towards open multicultural, cosmopolitan Western liberal democracy is the destination. Such an assumption is rarely stated explicitly. Indeed, insofar as nation branding is presented as a largely technical exercise it is assumed to be inherently apolitical (though clearly not in its effects). For the most part, it is not that consultants subject their clients to explicit ideological arguments about Western liberal democracy as a fundamental good, rather, it is that it is simply assumed that such societies are more attractive and make for better and more desirable nation brands. The dispute over the Qatar World Cup, highlighting as it does fundamental differences in respect of political, religious, and social values, suggests that such a view is problematic and arguably complacent. Indeed, despite generally eschewing any overt political orientation it is evident that nation branding is becoming increasingly incorporated into often fierce and controversial political debates.

For example, the emergence of new geopolitically populist nation brands sits far out of line with the cosmopolitan identities nation branders generally assume their wares will foster. Likewise, we have seen that (soft) authoritarian regimes have also seen great potential in nation branding as a mechanism for promoting regime legitimacy and security at home, and through practices of sports/cultural/architectural washing doing likewise internationally. However, while concepts like sportswashing point to how nation branding may be used to divert attention from characteristics that are recognised as potentially problematic and unsavoury, and therefore unattractive to global audiences, it is worth reflecting on whether contemporary claims about an ongoing transformation away from a 'Western' towards a more 'postliberal' world order (Kagan 2017; Duncombe and Dunn 2018) will itself see the active embracing and revaluing of 'authoritarian' nation brands – and not only by overtly authoritarian states. For instance, across the democratic Western world admiration/fascination with authoritarian leaders has been on the rise, as evident, for instance, in favourable views of President Putin prior to (and even in some cases after) his decision to invade Ukraine in 2022 (Heath 2022). In turn, this has been reflected in the rising popularity of 'strong leaders' in otherwise democratic states (e.g., Donald Trump in the US, Viktor Orban in Hungary). Indeed, a recent poll found that 61 per cent of British people aged eighteen to thirty-four supported running the UK with 'a strong leader who doesn't have to bother with parliament/elections' (Hyde 2022). In turn, this comes on the back of the 2016 Brexit referendum in which the populist 'Leave' campaign was successfully able to mobilise alienated and disaffected citizens to reject a vision of Britain that had become perceived as only working to the benefit of a privileged metropolitan liberal elite, a vision that economic logics of nation branding have long championed and assumed to be the winning ticket (Browning 2019). As noted in this book's introduction, the post-Brexit rebranding of the UK as 'Global Britain' has been one way to respond to some of the fallout of the Brexit vote and the country's perceived loss of status and standing. In this respect, it is obviously tempting to see the UK's post-Brexit economic and image troubles as an implicit endorsement of nation branding. From this perspective, Brexit looks like a reckless instance of nation branding self-harm that merely confirms the imperative of governments to prioritise maintaining the country's nation brand above all else. Yet cases like this also highlight how a disjuncture has developed in many countries between citizens and the neoliberal framing of society that the economic logics of nation branding supports and promotes. In this respect, it is far from inconceivable that alternative ideologically inflected nation branding models might not emerge. The question, therefore, is what might nation branding look like in an increasingly post-liberal world, and might authoritarianism or populist nationalism become the new cool? Either way, the emergence of a post-liberal world is not self-evidently a threat to nation branding but may, instead, see a repositioning of the relative weight accorded to the economic, diplomatic, and cultural logics of nation branding and the forms of nation branding more likely to be invoked.

Notes

INTRODUCTION

1 There are some exceptions. See van Ham (2001; 2002; 2008), Browning (2015a; 2016), Eggeling (2020). Instead, most critically oriented work has been done in political geography (Saunders 2017) and media and communication studies (Aronczyk 2013; Kaneva 2011; 2012a). There are also some emerging historical studies (Clerc et al. 2015; Viktorin 2018a).

CHAPTER ONE

1 The distinction between imagined communities and imaged communities is drawn from Clerc and Glover (2015).
2 For another excellent historical engagement with nation branding, see Clerc, Glover, and Jordan (2015).
3 Indeed, until recently such negative perceptions of 'Made in China' also prevailed amongst Chinese consumers, though more recently that has begun to change (Shephard 2016).

CHAPTER TWO

1 Though prior to this, others had also talked about the need to bring marketing to the level of nations (e.g., Kotler et al. 1993; Kotler et al. 1997).
2 Indeed, it is worth noting that 'Competitive Identity' is the title of one of Anholt's (2007b) many publications on the theme and a book in which nation branding is to some extent supplanted by this term.

CHAPTER THREE

1 To quote Sussman (2012, 32), 'Nation is not a "branded" identity that can be organized by professional wordsmiths or image makers. It is a set of social, cultural, and political (not professional or economistic) relationships, a collective expression of its people'.
2 For a more detailed discussion of the distinction between more psychological and more sociological readings of ontological security, see Zarakol (2010).
3 Note how the earlier official 'GREAT Britain' branding campaign launched to coincide with the 2012 London Olympics hits some similar mnemonics for British and international audiences.
4 Noting links to ontological security, Lebow (2008, 25, 61) defines self-esteem as 'a sense of self-worth that makes people feel good about themselves, happier about life and more confident about their ability to confront its challenges'.
5 And such goals can work. Anecdotally, a Colombian master's degree student reported to me that it was only following the introduction of the 'Colombia Is Passion' nation branding programme in the early 2000s that he and his friends stopped feeling embarrassed about their national identity when travelling abroad.
6 The relationship between the nation and state in practices of nation branding is contested (e.g., Eggeling 2020) and is discussed in chapter 5.
7 Also see the growing work on public moods and rhythms in international relations (e.g., Solomon 2019).
8 From a psychoanalytical perspective, Solomon (2015, 63; 2013, 16–7) suggests that thinking about subjectivity in such a binary fashion is itself fundamentally problematic as it entails treating subjects and discourse as ontologically distinct realms. To the contrary, he argues that, rather than the individual and the collective being different levels, they are better viewed as 'interweaving and interdependent registers where no bright line is discernible between the subject and society'. In other words, insofar as people identify with a group, then the group exists as embodied within the individual, with all the psychological vulnerabilities that implies (also Mercer 2006, 297).
9 Viktorin et al. (2018a, 16) make a similar point in respect of Suriname, noting how nation branding was deployed as a way to try to 'address the nation's multicultural and pluralist makeup' with nation branding and nation building 'intertwined to (re)define a national identity' through enhancing state capacity.

10 Theoretically, there are resonances with Veblen's (1957, 28–9) analysis of how (self-)esteem is generated in consumerist societies and where he notes that the standing of 'the leisure class' has become less dependent on possessing superior force and is increasingly connected to its ability to engage in 'conspicuous consumption' – the demonstrative spending of excess wealth on fashionable adornments that may also be desired by others who cannot afford them, thereby demonstrating one's wealth and enhancing social standing. In a similar way, economic logics of nation branding likewise aims to entice consumers/investors and make the nation an object of desire and conspicuous consumption, with this in turn entailing a status and self-esteem dividend.

11 It is notable that Cameron's appeal to Britain's global brand standing failed to strike a chord with many Scottish voters – although it was a clear manifestation of the ontological and status anxieties prevalent amongst the political elite in London and also evident within the pro-Union press, where a constant theme recalled the UK's historical global achievements, principally those connected to Empire and the World Wars. In Scotland, by contrast, such arguments about brand value, global influence, and status fared poorly when stacked up against the nationalist argument. This appealed to an alternative identity narrative of Scotland in the world and central to which was making Scotland a complete/finished nation with self-determination, an equal subject amongst others, whilst also rejecting militarist arguments in favour of hinting at de-nuclearised Nordic neutralism as an alternative role identity (i.e., arguments closer to cultural and diplomatic logics of nation branding).

However, the 2014 Scottish Referendum obviously had other dimensions as well. For instance, Cameron's branding argument was also paralleled by concerted efforts to generate economic anxieties amongst Scottish voters that independence was financially unviable and by suggesting that an independent Scotland would not find a straightforward welcome into the EU. In other words, self-determination might not beget the status recognition desired. Interestingly, though, come the final week of campaigning one opinion poll put the pro-independence campaign ahead. At this point, the brand/status arguments of the 'no' to independence campaign were largely set aside, with leaders of all the major parties travelling to Scotland to strike a different note, this time also utilising arguments emphasising shared identity and kinship. Indeed, non-Scottish citizens were even actively encouraged by the 'no' campaign to undertake missions of personal diplomacy designed to emphasise common bonds (what we think of each other), thereby playing down the previous external focus on what others think of us. Whether this more traditional appeal to the kinship, history, and nation building practices of the *imagined community*, as opposed to the *imaged community* of the branded competition state, was decisive in shifting the vote against independence – as opposed to offers of enhanced devolution, for instance, or continued worries about the economic consequences of independence – is unclear. What the case does highlight, though, is how identity can be mobilised differently in the activation of different socio-psychological needs. Thus, in contrast to the nation branding discourse with its emphasis on status and self-esteem enhancement via appealing to the affective desires of outsiders, the shift towards appeals historically more central to nation building were rather more inward looking, appealing to deeper ontological questions of the nation's very being and, indeed, whether a collective British nation even existed.

12 For instance, Surowiec (2012, 135–6) notes how, in the case of Poland, the Saffron branding consultancy tasked with developing the country's nation brand seems to have built much of its work precisely on identifying and playing with existing foreign and domestic stereotypes, never questioning their origins or roots while failing to consult broader academic research into Polish national identity.

13 For instance, in 2006 the Slovenian branding committee ran a contest to create a new slogan for the country as part of the country's first long-term branding programme, ultimately settling on 'I feel *Slove*nia'. Yet it was soon discovered that the committee had pre-selected the slogan before going through the motions of holding the contest. As Volčič (2012, 154) comments, 'In the end, it appeared that the contest was little more than public relations: an attempt to make the people feel they had chosen a slogan, which had already been pre-selected for them'.

14 However, the line between 'authorised' dissent deemed positive for national image projection and 'unauthorised' dissent can be fine. For instance, a more recent Nordic example is Norway's official embracing of the Norwegian 'black metal' music scene, with 'black metal' characterised by its satanic themes and the neo-Nazi sympathies of some of its members. Throughout the 1980s and 1990s the authorities generally viewed the black metal scene as problematic, with its members identified with anti-social and criminal behaviour. For instance, fans of different bands fought each other and burned down ancient Stave churches, while the musician and figurehead, Varg Virkenes (otherwise known as Count Grishnackh), was imprisoned for murdering a musician from another band. Yet, come the 2000s, and with Norwegian black metal now gaining

foreign fans interested in visiting the country, Norwegian diplomats reportedly began to receive an introduction to the history and personalities of Norwegian black metal so they could wax lyrical while stationed overseas (Markessinis 2011). Despite its anti-establishment, anarchic, satanic (and racist) elements, Norwegian black metal was therefore rescripted and co-opted in the cause of national brand promotion and tourist consumption, which is nothing if not intriguing but presumably raises questions about the ethical boundaries of nation branding and national image promotion. This is especially so given that Varg Virkenes was also subsequently imprisoned in 2014 in France for inciting racial hatred against Jews and Muslims and who was also in possession of a copy of the manifesto of the mass murderer Anders Breivik (Bond 2013).

CHAPTER FOUR

1 For instance, see Anholt's (2020) *The Good Country Equation,* in which the consultant and policy adviser is unquestionably earnest about his desire to promote a better world.
2 On the redemptive power of apology and embracing shame, see Ahmed (2004, 101–21).
3 For example, Nordic Model Now! is a UK-based 'secular, feminist, grassroots women's group' set up in 2016 campaigning for the 'implementation of the Nordic model approach to prostitution' (https://nordicmodelnow.org/about).
4 Iceland has always been an outlier in the Good Country Index and in 2020 was ranked twentieth.
5 Although the term has historically tended to focus on the distinctiveness of socio-economic relations in the region, more recently the notion of the 'Nordic model' has expanded. As Byrkjeflot et al. (2021) note, today it often appears quite eclectic, being attached to issues ranging from culture (cuisine, design, cinema), to institutional design (political and economic), to foreign policy orientation.

CHAPTER FIVE

1 It is worth noting that the British branding consultant Simon Anholt was a 'central figure' in formulating both the nature of the problem facing Denmark and the solution. The problem was reframed by noting a decline in Denmark's performance on the Anholt-GfK Roper Nation Brand Index because of the crisis. A key part of the solution, as articulated in the

subsequent *Action Plan*, was to undertake actions that would improve Denmark's performance on this benchmark. As Rasmussen and Mikelsen (2014, 241–2) note, the effect was to turn a (somewhat arbitrary) measure of the impact of the crisis (impact on brand ranking position) into the key risk to be countered.

2 Of course, believing in the inherently democratising effects of nation branding may be one way in which (typically Western) nation branding consultants justify to themselves working for certain clients.

3 To give just one example, the 2018 film *Mortal Engines* (Universal Pictures) depicts a future world of predatory, mechanised, and largely Western cities (principally London) in a struggle of municipal Darwinism, tearing up the world and devouring all before them in a thin allegory of Western colonialism. That is, until London (Great Britain) tries to defeat and consume Shan Guo (formerly China), a territory that has rejected such practices in favour of an emphasis on place, tradition, and peaceful coexistence. Needless to say, Shan Guo prevails for the benefit of humankind.

CHAPTER SIX

1 Brand Africa is a private non-profit organisation but has historically received most support from South Africa. Other African countries have been engaged, not least through their own nation branding or marketing institutions (e.g., Kenya, Malawi, Zimbabwe).

2 For instance, speaking at the inaugural Brand Africa Forum event in 2010, the influential African economist Dambisa Moyo chastised African leaders for shamelessly going 'around the world perpetuating this idea of Africa being poor and pathetic' (Brand Africa 2010, 10).

3 Anholt (2020, 27) himself notes: 'Analysis of the NBI [Nation Brand Index] data before and after numerous major events showed that they are far more effective at drawing attention to the host country's failings and defects and reinforcing negative stereotypes than promoting its image. Even highly successful events – like London's 2012 Olympics – do little more than "pay the rent" on a highly respected country's image and can do little to enhance it. In the case of Brazil and South Africa, these hugely expensive events have set back both countries' image by many years'.

References

Adler, Emanuel, and Michael Barnett. 1998. *Security Communities*. Cambridge: Cambridge University Press.
Adler-Nissen, Rebecca. 2014. 'Stigma Management in International Relations: Transgressive Identities, Norms and Order in International Society'. *International Organization* 68, no. 1: 143–76.
Agnew, John. 2003. *Geopolitics: Revisioning World Politics*. London and New York: Routledge.
– 2009. *Globalization and Sovereignty*. Lanham: Rowman and Littlefield.
Ahmed, Sara. 2004. *The Cultural Politics of Emotion*. Edinburgh: Edinburgh University Press.
Akotia, Mathias. 2010. 'Nation Branding and Nation Image'. *Ghanaweb.com*. 14 November 2010. http://www.ghanaweb.com/GhanaHomePage/NewsArchive/artikel.php?ID=197380.
Alegi, Peter. 2008. '"A Nation to Be Reckoned With": The Politics of World Cup Stadium Construction in Cape Town and Durban, South Africa'. *African Affairs* 67, no. 3: 397–422.
'America First ... Slovenia Second (OFFICIAL)'. 2017. Uploaded 7 February 2017 by Ta teden z Juretom Godlerjem. YouTube video, 3:40. https://www.youtube.com/watch?v=UktXYuDQgSs.
Anderson, Benedict. 1991. *Imagined Communities: Reflections on the Origin and Spread of Nationalism*. London: Verso Books.
Anholt, Simon. 1998. 'Nation-Brands of the Twenty-First Century'. *Journal of Brand Management* 5, no. 6: 395–406.
– 2002a. 'Foreword'. *Journal of Brand Management* 9, nos. 4–5: 229–39.
– 2002b. 'Nation Branding: A Continuing Theme'. *Journal of Brand Management* 10, no. 1: 59–60.

- 2003. *Brand New Justice: The Upside of Global Branding*. Oxford: Elsevier Butterworth-Heinemann.
- 2005. *Brand New Justice: How Branding Places and Products Can Help the Developing World*. Oxford: Elsevier Butterworth-Heinemann.
- 2006. 'Is Place Branding a Capitalist Tool?' *Place Branding and Public Diplomacy* 2, no. 1: 1–4.
- 2007a. "Brand Africa: What Is Competitive Identity?' *African Analyst* 2, no. 2: 72–81.
- 2007b. *Competitive Identity: The New Brand Management for Nations, Cities and Regions*. Houndmills: Palgrave Macmillan.
- 2008a. 'From Nation Branding to Competitive Identity – The Role of Brand Management as a Component of National Policy'. In *Nation Branding: Concepts, Issues, Practice*, ed. Keith Dinnie, 22–3. Oxford: Butterworth-Heinnemann.
- 2008b. 'The Importance of National Reputation'. In *Engagement: Public Diplomacy in a Globalised World*. London: Foreign and Commonwealth Office, 30–43. http://uscpublicdiplomacy.org/sites/uscpublicdiplomacy.org/files/useruploads/u26739/Engagement_FCO.pdf.
- 2009. "Branding Places and Nations." In *Brands and Branding*, 2nd ed., ed. Rita Clifton and John Simmons, 213–26. London: The Economist with Profile Books.
- 2012. 'The Globalisation of Culture'. Talk given at University of Warwick, One World Week. Page discontinued, accessed 18 January 2013. http://www2.warwick.ac.uk/knowledge/culture/globalisationculture.
- 2020. *The Good Country Equation: How We Can Repair the World in One Generation*. Oakland, CA: Berrett-Koehler Publishers.

Araratyan, Aram. 2015. 'Simon Anholt: "Armenia Has to Do Something for Humanity"'. *Mediamax*, 3 February 2015. https://mediamax.am/en/news/interviews/13053.

Aronczyk, Melissa. 2008. '"Living the Brand": Nationality, Globality and the Identity Strategies of Nation Branding Consultants'. *International Journal of Communication* 2, no. 1: 41–65.
- 2013. *Branding the Nation: The Global Business of National Identity*. Oxford: Oxford University Press.

Banet-Weiser, Sarah. 2012. *Authentic: The Politics of Ambivalence in a Brand Culture*. New York and London: New York University Press.

Bardan, Alice, and Anikó Imre. 2012. 'Vampire Branding: Romania's Dark Destinations'. In *Branding Post-Communist Nations: Marketizing*

National Identities in the 'New' Europe, ed. Nadia Kaneva, 168–92. London: Routledge.

Barnett, Michael. 1999. 'Culture, Strategy and Foreign Policy: Israel's Road to Oslo'. *European Journal of International Relations* 5, no. 1: 5–36.

Barsade, Sigal G. 2002. 'The Ripple Effect: Emotional Contagion and Its Influence on Group Behaviour'. *Administrative Science Quarterly* 47, no. 4: 644–75.

Bassin, Mark, and Konstantin E. Aksenov. 2006. 'Mackinder and the Heartland Theory in Post-Soviet Geopolitical Discourse'. *Geopolitics* 11, no. 1: 99–118.

Bassols, Narcís. 2016. 'Branding and Promoting a Country amidst a Long-Term Conflict: The Case of Colombia'. *Journal of Destination Marketing and Management* 5, no. 4: 314–24.

BBC Sport. 2022. 'World Cup 2022: Qatar Ambassador Comments on Homosexuality as "Harmful and Unacceptable"'. 8 November 2022. https://www.bbc.co.uk/sport/football/63561340.

Beaumont, Paul. 2017. 'Status Hierarchies in World Politics'. Paper presented at the International Studies Association Annual Convention, Baltimore, MD.

– 2020. 'Grammar of Status Competition: International Hierarchies as Domestic Practice.' PhD diss., Norwegian University of Life Sciences.

Beaumont, Paul, and Ann Towns. 2021. 'The Rankings Game: A Relational Approach to Country Performance Indicators'. *International Studies Review* 23, no. 4: 1467–94.

Berenskoetter, Felix. 2010. 'Let's Think about Conditions: Controlling Anxiety and Creating Authenticity in International Relations'. Paper presented at the 52nd International Studies Association Annual Convention, New Orleans, LA.

Berg, Nils-Christian. 1995. 'Finland. The Business Center for the New Northern Europe'. In *Finland in Europe*. Helsinki: Finnish Ministry for Foreign Affairs.

Beswick, Danielle, and Paul Jackson. 2014. *Conflict, Security and Development: An Introduction*. London: Routledge.

Bidwai, Praful. 2012. 'Why India Needs Aid'. *Guardian*, 7 February 2012. https://www.theguardian.com/commentisfree/2012/feb/07/why-india-needs-aid.

Billig, Michael. 1995. *Banal Nationalism*. London: Sage.

Blaut, J.M. 1993. *The Colonizer's Model of the World: Geographical Diffusionism and Eurocentric History*. London: Guildford Press.

Bond, Anthony. 2013. 'Norwegian Neo-Nazi Musician Said to Be an "Anders Breivik Sympathiser" Arrested in France over Fears He Was Plotting a Similar Massacre'. *MailOnline*, 16 July 2013. https://www.dailymail.co.uk/news/article-2365720/Anders-Breivik-sympathiser-Kristian-Vikernes-arrested-France-fears-plotting-similar-massacre.html.

Bourdieu, Pierre. 1984. *Distinction: A Social Critique of the Judgment of Taste*. London: Routledge.

Brand Africa. 2010. *Brand Africa Forum 2010 Report*. http://www.brandafrica.net.

– 2011. *Brand Africa Forum 2011 Report*. http://www.brandafrica.net.

– 2015. *Brand Africa Brochure 2015*. Page discontinued. http://www.brandafrica.net/Documents/BrandAfricaBrochure2015.pdf.

– 2022a. 'Africa's Best Brands'. https://www.brandafrica.org/Home/Initiatives.

– 2022b. 'Celebrating Distinctive, Sustainable and Competitive Places in Africa'. https://www.brandafrica.org/Places#Content.

– 2022c. 'Future Proof: How Will African Brands Survive?' https://www.brandafrica.org/Home/MediaAfricanBrands.

Brand South Africa. 2012. *Annual Report 2011/2012*. Johannesburg: Brand South Africa.

– 2013. *Annual Report 2012/2013*. Johannesburg: Brand South Africa.

Brockington, Dan. 2012. 'Celebrity Interventions'. *Review of African Political Economy* 39, no. 131: 147–9.

Broome, André, and Joel Quirk. 2015. 'Governing the World at a Distance: The Practice of Global Benchmarking.' *Review of International Studies* 41, no. 5: 819–41.

Browning, Christopher S. 2007. 'Branding Nordicity: Models, Identity and the Decline of Exceptionalism'. *Cooperation and Conflict* 42, no. 1: 27–51.

– 2008. *Constructivism, Narrative and Foreign Policy Analysis: A Case Study of Finland*. Oxford: Peter Lang.

– 2015a. 'Nation Branding, National Self-Esteem, and the Constitution of Subjectivity in Late Modernity'. *Foreign Policy Analysis* 11, no. 2: 195–214.

– 2015b. 'Small-State Identities: Promotions Past and Present'. In *Histories of Public Diplomacy and Nation Branding in the Nordic and Baltic Countries: Representing the Periphery*, ed. Louis Clerc, Nikolas Glover, and Paul Jordan, 282–300. Leiden: Brill Nijhoff.

– 2016. 'Nation Branding and Development: Poverty Panacea or Business as Usual'. *Journal of International Relations and Development* 19, no. 1: 50–75.

- 2018. 'Brexit, Existential Anxiety and Ontological (In)Security'. *European Security* 27, no. 3: 336–55.
- 2019. 'Brexit Populism and Fantasies of Fulfilment'. *Cambridge Review of International Affairs* 32, no. 3: 222–44.
- 2021. 'Fantasy, Distinction, Shame: The Stickiness of the Nordic "Good State" Brand'. In *Do-Gooders at the End of Aid: Scandinavian Humanitarianism in the Twenty-First Century*, ed. Antoine de Bengy Puyvallée and Kristian Bjørkdahl, 14–37. Cambridge: Cambridge University Press.
- Forthcoming. 'Nordic Peace: Identity, Brand, Branding'. In *Nordic Peace Revisited*, ed. Christopher S. Browning, Marko Lehti, and Johan Strang. London: Routledge.

Browning, Christopher S., and Antonio Ferraz de Oliveira. 2017a. 'Introduction: Nation Branding and Competitive Identity in World Politics'. *Geopolitics* 22, no. 3: 481–501.

- 2017b. 'Reading Brand Africa Geopolitically: Nation Branding, Subaltern Geopolitics and the Persistence of Politics'. *Geopolitics* 22, no. 3: 640–64.

Browning, Christopher S., and Pertti Joenniemi. 2013. 'From Fratricide to Security Community: Re-theorising Difference in the Constitution of Nordic Peace'. *Journal of International Relations and Development* 16, no. 4: 483–513.

- 2017. 'Ontological Security, Self-Articulation and the Securitization of Identity'. *Cooperation and Conflict* 52, no. 1: 31–47.

Browning, Christopher S., Pertti Joenniemi, and Brent J. Steele. 2021. *Vicarious Identity in International Relations: Self, Security, and Status on the Global Stage*. New York: Oxford University Press.

Budnitskiy, Stanislav. 2012. *Lost Tribes of Nation Branding? Representations of Russian Minority in Estonia's Nation Branding Efforts*. Budapest: Central European University.

Bull, Hedley. 1977. *The Anarchical Society*. London: Macmillan.

Byrkjeflot, Haldor, Mads Mordhorst, and Klaus Petersen. 2021. 'The Making and Circulation of Nordic Models: An introduction'. In *The Making and Circulation of Nordic Models, Ideas and Images*, ed. Haldor Byrkjeflot, Lars Myøset, Mads Mordhorst, and Klaus Petersen, 1–10. London: Routledge.

Cameron, David. 2014. 'The Importance of Scotland to the UK'. Prime minister's speech, Lee Valley VeloPark, 7 February 2014. https://www.gov.uk/government/speeches/the-importance-of-scotland-to-the-uk-david-camerons-speech.

Cameron, John, and Anna Haanstra. 2008. 'Development Made Sexy: How It Happened and What It Means'. *Third World Quarterly* 29, no. 8: 1,475–89.

Cammack, Paul. 2009. 'Poverty Reduction and Universal Competitiveness'. *Labour, Capital and Society* 42, no. 1: 32–54.

Campbell, David. 1992. *Writing Security: United States Foreign Policy and the Politics of Identity*. Manchester: Manchester University Press.

Campbell, David, and M. Power. 2010. 'The Scopic Regime of Africa'. In *Observant States: Geopolitics and Visual Culture*, ed. F. MacDonald, R. Hughes, and K. Dodds, 167–98. London: IB Tauris.

Carah, Nicholas, and P. Eric Louw. 2016. 'The Apologetic Brand: Building Australia's Brand on a Postcolonial Apology'. In *Commercial Nationalism: Selling the Nation and Nationalizing the Sell*, ed. Zala Volčič and Mark Andrejevic, 27–45. Basingstoke: Palgrave Macmillan.

Carr, E.H. 1946. *The Twenty Years' Crisis, 1919-1939: An Introduction to the Study of International Relations*. London: Macmillan.

Castells, Manuel. 2000. *The Rise of the Network Society*. Oxford: Blackwell.

Cerny, Phillip G. 1990. *The Changing Architecture of Politics: Structure, Agency and the Future of the State*. London: Sage.

– 2010. 'The Competition State Today: From Raison d'État to Raison du Monde'. *Policy Studies* 31, no. 1: 5–21.

Chao, Jenifer. 2022. 'The Visual Politics of Brand China: Exceptional History and Speculative Future'. In *Place Branding and Public Diplomacy*. https://doi.org/10.1057/s41254-022-00270-6.

Chao, Maggie, Elaine Chow, Gil Kerbs, and Kate Long. 2012. '"Thanks, But No Thanks" to Made in China'. *Knowledge@Wharton*, 3 January 2012. https://knowledge.wharton.upenn.edu/article/thanks-but-no-thanks-to-made-in-china-2.

Cho, Eun Jeon R. 2017. 'Nation Branding for Survival in North Korea: The Arirang Festival and Nuclear Weapons Tests'. *Geopolitics* 22, no. 3: 594–622.

Clegg, Stewart R., and Martin Kornberger. 2010. 'An Organizational Perspective on Space and Place Branding'. In *International Place Branding Yearbook 2010*, ed. Frank M. Go and Robert Govers, 3–11. Houndmills: Palgrave Macmillan.

Clerc, Louis, and Nikolas Glover. 2015. 'Representing the Small States of Northern Europe: Between Imagined and Imaged Communities'. In *Histories of Public Diplomacy and Nation Branding in the Nordic and Baltic Countries: Representing the Periphery*, ed. Louis Clerc, Nikolas Glover, and Paul Jordan, 3–20. Leiden and Boston: Brill Nijhoff.

Clerc, Louis, Nikolas Glover, and Paul Jordan, eds. 2015. *Histories of Public Diplomacy and Nation Branding in the Nordic and Baltic Countries: Representing the Periphery*. Leiden and Boston: Brill Nijhoff.

Clunan, Anne L. 2014. 'Why Status Matters in World Politics'. In *Status in World Politics*, ed. T.V. Paul, Deborah Welch Larson, and Willian C. Wohlforth, 273–96. Cambridge: Cambridge University Press.

Coaffee, Jon, and Peter Rogers. 2008. 'Reputational Risk and Resiliency: The Branding of Security in Place-Making." *Place Branding and Public Diplomacy* 4, no. 3: 205–17.

Comaroff, John L., and Jean Comaroff. 2009. *Ethnicity, Inc.* Chicago: University of Chicago Press.

Cornelissen, Scarlett. 2017. 'National Meaning-Making in Complex Societies: Political Legitimation and Branding Dynamics in Post-Apartheid South Africa'. *Geopolitics* 22, no. 3: 525–48.

Country Brand Report. 2010. *Mission for Finland: How Finland Will Solve the World's Most Intractable Problems*. Helsinki: Tehtavasuomelle. https://www.tehtavasuomelle.fi/documents/TS_Report_EN.pdf.

Cowen, Deborah, and Neil Smith. 2009. 'After Geopolitics? From the Geopolitical Social to Geoeconomics'. *Antipode* 41, no. 1: 22–48.

Craib, Ian. 1998. *Experiencing Identity*. London and Thousand Oaks, CA: Sage.

Cross, Gary. 2000. *An All-Consuming Century: Why Commercialism Won in Modern America*. New York: Columbia University Press.

Crouch, David. 2018. 'From Fika to Fake News'. *Nordicom-information* 40, no. 2: 29–33.

Cuadros, Alex. 2016. 'The Broken Promise of the Rio Olympics: How a Chance to Remake the City for Ordinary Brazilians Ended up Lining the Pockets of the Rich Instead." *Atlantic*, 1 August 2016. https://www.theatlantic.com/international/archive/2016/08/building-barra-rio-olympics-brazil/493697.

Cull, Nicholas J. 2008. 'Public Diplomacy: Seven Lessons for Its Future from Its Past'. In *Engagement: Public Diplomacy in a Globalised World*, ed. Jolyon Welsh and Daniel Fearn, 17–29. London: Foreign and Commonwealth Office. https://www.uscpublicdiplomacy.org/sites/uscpublicdiplomacy.org/files/useruploads/u26739/Engagement_FCO.pdf.

– 2019. *Public Diplomacy: Foundations for Global Engagement in the Digital Age*. Cambridge: Polity Press.

– 2022. 'From Soft Power to Reputational Security: Rethinking Public Diplomacy and Cultural Diplomacy for a Dangerous Age'. *Place Branding and Public Diplomacy* 18, no. 1: 18–21.

Da Silva, Issa Sikiti. 2010. 'Branding, a Deceitful Word – Simon Anholt'. *BizCommunity.com*, 21 September 2010. https://www.bizcommunity. africa/Article/410/82/52358.html.

Davenport, Thomas H., and John Beck. 2001. *The Attention Economy: Understanding the New Economy of Business*. Boston: Harvard Business School.

de Carvalho, Benjamin, and Iver B. Neumann, eds. 2015. *Small State Status Seeking: Norway's Quest for International Standing*. London: Routledge.

de Carvalho, Benjamin, and Jon Harald Sande Lie. 2015. 'A Great Power Performance: Norway, Status and the Policy of Involvement'. In *Small State Status Seeking: Norway's Quest for International Standing*, ed. Benjamin de Carvalho and Iver B. Neumann, 56–72. Abingdon: Routledge.

Dembek, Agata, and Renata Włoch. 2014. 'The Impact of a Sports Mega-Event on the International Image of a Country: The Case of Poland Hosting the UEFA Euro 2012'. *Perspectives* 22, no. 1: 33–47.

Desatova, Petra. 2018. 'Thailand 4.0 and the Internal Focus of Nation Branding'. *Asian Studies Review* 42, no. 4: 682–700.

Deutsch, Karl, Sidney A. Burrell, Robert A. Kann, Maurice Lee, Martin Lichterman, Raymond E. Lindgren, Francis L. Loewenheim, and Richard W. van Wagenen. 1957. *Political Community and the North Atlantic Area*. New York: Greenwood Press.

Dinnie, Keith. 2008. *Nation Branding: Concepts, Issues, Practice*. Oxford: Elsevier Butterworth-Heinemann.

Dorfman, Jeffrey. 2018. 'Sorry Bernie Bros But Nordic Countries Are Not Socialist'. *Forbes Magazine*, 8 July 2018. https://www.forbes.com/sites/ jeffreydorfman/2018/07/08/sorry-bernie-bros-but-nordic-countries-are-not-socialist.

Doyle, M. 1983. 'Kant, Liberal Legacies and Foreign Affairs'. *Philosophy and Public Affairs* 12, no. 3: 205–35.

Duncombe, Constance, and Tim Dunne. 2018. 'After Liberal World Order'. *International Affairs* 94, no. 1: 25–42.

Economist. 2012. 'Africa's Singapore?' 25 February 2012. http://www. economist.com/node/21548263.

Edensor, Tim. 2002. *National Identity, Popular Culture and Everyday Life*. Oxford and New York: Berg.

Eggeling, Kristin Anabel. 2018. 'Brand New World: The Politics of State-Branding in Kazakhstan and Qatar'. PhD diss., University of St Andrews.

– 2020. *Nation-Branding in Practice: The Politics of Promoting Sports, Cities and Universities in Kazakhstan and Qatar*. London: Routledge.

Elliot, Edward. 2018. '#Global Britain and the Value of a Nation Brand'. *British Foreign Policy Group*, 20 March 2018. https://bfpg.co.uk/2018/03/globalbritain-and-the-value-of-a-nation-brand.

Escobar, Arturo. 1995. *Encountering Development: The Making and Unmaking of the Third World*. Princeton: Princeton University Press.

Falkheimer, Jesper, and Ketil Raknes. 2022. 'Nordic Neighbours in Pandemic Crisis: The Communication Battle between Sweden and Norway'. *Place Branding and Public Diplomacy* 18, no. 1: 26–9.

Fan, Ying. 2006. 'Branding the Nation: What Is Being Branded?' *Journal of Vacation Marketing* 12, no. 1: 5–14.

Finnemore, Martha, and Kathryn Sikkink. 1998. 'International Norm Dynamics and Political Change'. *International Organization* 52, no. 4: 887–917.

Foucault, Michel. 1977. *Discipline and Punish: The Birth of the Prison*. New York: Vintage Books.

Fougner, Tore. 2006. 'The State, International Competitiveness and Neoliberal Globalisation: Is There a Future Beyond the "Competition State"'? *Review of International Studies* 32, no. 1: 165–85.

Freire, Joao R. 2005. 'Geo-Branding, Are We Talking Nonsense? A Theoretical Reflection on Brands Applied to Places'. *Place Branding and Public Diplomacy* 1, no. 4: 347–62.

Fukuyama, Francis. 1992. *The End of History and the Last Man*. New York: Free Press.

Geertz, Clifford. 1980. *Negara: The Theatre State in Nineteenth-Century Bali*. Princeton, NJ: Princeton University Press.

Gertner, David. 2007. 'Place Branding: Dilemma or Reconciliation between Political Ideology and Economic Pragmatism'. *Place Branding and Public Diplomacy* 3, no. 1: 3–7.

Giddens, Anthony. 1984. *The Constitution of Society*. Cambridge: Polity.

– 1991. *Modernity and Self-Identity*. Cambridge: Polity.

Gilady, Lilach. 2018. *The Cost of Prestige: Conspicuous Consumption in International Relations*. Chicago and London: University of Chicago Press.

Gilligan, Andrew. 2012. 'India Tells Britain: We Don't Want Your Aid'. *Telegraph*, 4 February 2012. https://www.telegraph.co.uk/news/worldnews/asia/india/9061844/India-tells-Britain-We-dont-want-your-aid.html.

Glover, Nikolas. 2015. 'A Total Image Deconstructed: The Corporate Analogy and the Legitimacy of Promoting Sweden Abroad in the 1960s'. In *Histories of Public Diplomacy and Nation Branding in the Nordic and*

Baltic Countries: Representing the Periphery, ed. Louis Clerc, Nikolas Glover, and Paul Jordan, 123–44. Leiden and Boston: Brill Nijhoff.

Greenberg, Miriam. 2008. *Branding New York: How a City in Crisis Was Sold to the World*. New York: Routledge.

Greenfeld, Liah. 1995. *Nationalism: Five Roads to Modernity*. Cambridge: Harvard University Press.

Grix, Jonathan, and Barrie Houlihan. 2014. 'Sports Mega-Events as Part of a Nation's Soft Power Strategy: The Cases of Germany (2006) and the UK (2012)'. *British Journal of Politics and International Relations* 16, no. 4: 572–96.

Gross, Terry. 2022. 'Hollywood Relies on China to Stay Afloat: What Does That Mean for Movies?' *NPR Fresh Air*, 21 February 2022. https://www.npr.org/2022/02/21/1081435029/china-hollywood-movies-censorship-erich-schwartzel.

Guardian. 2021. 'Newcastle Fans Think They've Got Their Club Back: But at What Cost?' *Today in Focus*, 15 October 2021. https://www.theguardian.com/news/audio/2021/oct/15/newcastle-fans-think-theyve-got-their-club-back-but-at-what-cost-podcast.

Güney, Aylın, and Fulya Gökcan. 2010. 'The "Greater Middle East" as a "Modern" Geopolitical Imagination in American Foreign Policy'. *Geopolitics* 15, no. 1: 22–38.

Gustafsson, Karl, and Nina C. Krickel-Choi. 2020. 'Returning to the Roots of Ontological Security: Insights from the Existentialist Anxiety Literature." *European Journal of International Relations* 26, no. 3: 875–95.

Guzzini, Stefano. 2000. 'A Reconstruction of Constructivism in International Relations'. *European Journal of International Relations* 6, no. 2: 147–82.

Hagemann, Anine, and Isabel Bramsen. 2019. *New Nordic Peace: Nordic Peace and Conflict Resolution Efforts*. Copenhagen: Nordic Council of Ministers.

Hagström, Charlotte Wagnsson, and Magnus Lundström. 2022. 'Logics of Othering: Sweden as Other in the Time of COVID-19'. *Cooperation and Conflict*, 23 July 2022. https://doi.org/10.1177/00108367221110675.

Heath, Nicola. 2022. 'What's behind Putin's Popularity in the West? Family Values, Nationalism, and a Strongman Persona'. *ABC News*, 1 April 2022. https://www.abc.net.au/news/2022-04-02/putin-s-supporters-in-united-states-europe/100944412.

Heller, Peggy. 2010. 'The Russian Dawn: How Russia Contributed to the Emergence of "the West" as a Concept'. In *The Struggle for the*

West: A Divided and Contested Legacy, ed. Christopher S. Browning and Marko Lehti, 33–52. Abingdon: Routledge.

Helsingin Sanomat International Edition. 2012. 'Small Group Demonstrates in Helsinki against Proposed Guggenheim Museum'. 12 March 2012.

Henderson, Joan C. 2000. 'War as a Tourist Attraction: The Case of Vietnam'. International Journal of Tourism Research 2, no. 4: 269–80.

Higgins, Christine. 2016. 'The Long Read: The Hygge Conspiracy'. Guardian, 22 November 2016. https://www.theguardian.com/lifeandstyle/2016/nov/22/hygge-conspiracy-denmark-cosiness-trend.

HM Government. 2010. Securing Britain in an Age of Uncertainty: The Strategic and Defence Security Review. London: The Stationery Office.

Homolar, Alexandra. 2015. 'Human Security Benchmarks: Governing Human Wellbeing at a Distance'. Review of International Studies 41, no. 5: 843–63.

House of Commons Foreign Affairs Committee. 2018. Global Britain. Sixth Report of Session 2017–19. 6 March 2018. https://publications.parliament.uk/pa/cm201719/cmselect/cmfaff/780/780.pdf.

Huntington, Samuel P. 1996. The Clash of Civilizations and the Remaking of World Order. New York: Simon and Schuster.

Hyde, Marina. 2022. 'Cronyism, Donors, Wily MPs: Johnson's Honours Glorify All That Is Wrong with His Party'. Guardian, 8 November 2022. https://www.theguardian.com/commentisfree/2022/nov/08/cronyism-donors-mps-johnson-honours-scandals-tories.

Hymans, Jacques E.C. 2010. 'The Arrival of Psychological Constructivism'. International Theory 2, no. 3: 461–67.

Ikalafeng, Thebe. 2014. 'New Brand Afrika'. Samsung Magazine, October 2014. http://www.ikalafeng.com/Article/2014/10/new_brand_afrika.

Ilves, Toomas Hendrik. 1999. 'Estonia as a Nordic Country'. Speech by the Estonian minister of foreign affairs to the Swedish Institute for International Affairs. 14 December 1999. https://www.vm.ee/en/news/estonia-nordic-country.

Ingebritsen, Christine. 2002. 'Norm Entrepreneurs: Scandinavia's Role in World Politics'. Cooperation and Conflict 37, no. 1: 11–23.

International Marketing Council of South Africa. 2010. Annual Report 2009/2010. Page discontinued. http://www.imc.org.za/annual-report/668-annual-report-2010.

– 2011. Annual Report, 2010/2011. Page discontinued. http://www.imc.org.za/annual-report/704-annual-report-2010-2011.

Iriqat, Dalal. 2019. 'Palestinian Nation Branding via Public Diplomacy'. *International Relations and Diplomacy* 7, no. 5: 202–16.

Irshaid, Faisal. 2017. '"America First" But Who Will Be Second'. BBC *News*, 9 February 2017. https://www.bbc.co.uk/news/world-38921918.

Jansen, Sue Curry. 2008. 'Designer Nations: Neo-liberal Nation Branding – Brand Estonia'. *Social Identities* 14, no. 1: 121–42.

– 2012. 'Redesigning a Nation: Welcome to E-stonia, 2001–2018'. In *Branding Post-Communist Nations: Marketizing National Identities in the 'New' Europe*, ed. Nadia Kaneva, 79–98. London: Routledge.

Jarosz, Lucy. 1992. 'Constructing the Dark Continent: Metaphor as Geographic Representation of Africa'. *Geografiska Annaler. Series B. Human Geography* 74, no. 2: 105–15.

Jeong-ju, Na. 2009. 'Interview with Chairman of Korea's Nation Branding Council'. *Nation-branding.info*, 28 January 2009. https://nation-branding.info/2009/01/28/interview-korea-nation-branding-council.

Jiménez-Martínez, César. 2017. 'Making Chile Visible: Purposes, Operationalisation and Audiences from the Perspective of Nation Branding Practitioners'. *Geopolitics* 22, no. 3: 502–24.

– 2022. 'The Public as a Problem: Protest, Public Diplomacy and the Pandemic'. *Place Branding and Public Diplomacy* 18, no. 1: 33–6.

Jordan, Paul. 2015. 'Walking in Singin: Brand Estonia, the Eurovision Song Contest and Estonia's Self-Proclaimed Return to Europe, 2001–2002'. In *Histories of Public Diplomacy and Nation Branding in the Nordic and Baltic Countries: Representing the Periphery*, ed. Louis Clerc, Nikolas Glover, and Paul Jordan, 217–36. Leiden and Boston: Brill Nijhoff.

Kagan, Robert. 2017. 'The Twilight of the Liberal World Order'. *Brookings Report*, 24 January 2017. https://www.brookings.edu/research/the-twilight-of-the-liberal-world-order.

Kaneva, Nadia. 2011. 'Nation Branding: Toward an Agenda for Critical Research'. *International Journal of Communication* 5, no. 1: 117–41.

– ed. 2012a. *Branding Post-Communist Nations: Maketizing National Identities in the 'New' Europe*. London: Routledge.

– 2012b. 'Nation Branding in Post-Communist Europe: Identities, Markets, and Democracy'. In *Branding Post-Communist Nations: Marketizing National Identities in the 'New' Europe*, ed. Nadia Kaneva, 3–22. London: Routledge.

– 2012c. 'Who Can Play This Game? The Rise of Nation Branding in Bulgaria, 2001–2005'. In *Branding Post-Communist Nations:*

Marketizing National Identities in the 'New' Europe, ed. Nadia Kaneva, 99–123. London: Routledge.

– 2016. 'Nation Branding and Commercial Nationalism: Notes for a Materialist Critique'. In *Commercial Nationalism: Selling the Nation and Nationalizing the Sell*, ed. Zala Volčič and Mark Andrejevic, 175–93. Basingstoke: Palgrave Macmillan.

Kaneva, Nadia, and Delia Popescu. 2011. 'National Identity Lite: Nation Branding in Post-Communist Romania and Bulgaria'. *International Journal of Cultural Studies* 14, no. 2: 191–207.

Kania-Lundholm, Magdalena. 2016. 'Nation for Sale? Citizen Online Debates and the "New Patriotism" in Post-Socialist Poland.' In *Commercial Nationalism: Selling the Nation and Nationalizing the Sell*, ed. Zala Volčič and Mark Andrejevic, 106–30. Basingstoke: Palgrave Macmillan.

Kapoor, Ilan. 2013. *Celebrity Humanitarianism: The Ideology of Global Charity*. London: Routledge.

Kennedy, Joe. 2020. '"Of Course, It Didn't Work – That Kind of Scheme Never Does": Scotland, the Nordic Imaginary, and the Mid-Twentieth-Century Thriller'. *Nordic Journal of English Studies* 19, no. 5: 311–33.

Keohane, Robert O., and Joseph S. Nye Jr. 1977. *Power and Interdependence: World Politics in Transition*. TBS The Book Service.

Kerdsup, Paphop. 2017. 'Love-is-Korea'. *Art4d*. 6 July 2017. https://art4d.com/2017/07/love-is-korea.

Kierkegaard, Soren. 1980. *The Concept of Anxiety*. Princeton, NJ: Princeton University Press.

Kinnvall, Catarina. 2004. 'Globalization and Religious Nationalism: Self, Identity, and the Search for Ontological Security'. *Political Psychology* 25, no. 5: 741–67.

Kinnvall, Catarina, and Jennifer Mitzen. 2018. 'Ontological Security and Conflict: The Dynamics of Crisis and the Constitution of Community'. *Journal of International Relations and Development* 21, no. 4: 825–35.

Klein, Naomi. 2000. *No Logo*. London: Flamingo.

Kotler, Philip, Donald H. Haider, and Irving J. Rein. 1993. *Marketing Places: Attracting Investment, Industry, and Tourism to Cities, Regions, States, and Nations*. New York: Free Press.

Kotler, Philip, Somkid Jatusripitak, and Suvit Maesincee. 1997. *The Marketing of Nations: Strategic Approach to Building National Wealth*. New York: Free Press.

Krolikowski, Alanna. 2008. 'State Personhood in Ontological Theories of International Relations and Chinese Nationalism: A Sceptical View'. *Chinese Journal of International Politics* 2, no. 1: 109–33.

Kulcsár, László, and Young-ok Yum. 2012. 'On Nation, One Brand? Nation Branding and Identity Reconstruction in Post-Communist Hungary'. In *Branding Post-Communist Nations: Marketizing National Identities in the 'New' Europe*, ed. Nadia Kaneva, 193–212. London: Routledge.

Kupchan, Charles A. 2010. *How Enemies Become Friends: The Sources of Stable Peace*. Princeton, NJ: Princeton University Press.

Kwon, Heonik, and Byung-Ho Chung. 2012. *North Korea: Beyond Charismatic Politics*. Rowman and Littlefield.

Laatikainen, Katie Verlin. 2003. 'Norden's Eclipse: The Impact of the European Union's Common Foreign and Security Policy on the Nordic Group in the United Nations'. *Cooperation and Conflict* 38, no. 4: 409–41.

Laffey, Mark. 2000. 'Locating Identity: Performativity, Foreign Policy and State Action'. *Review of International Studies* 26, no. 3: 429–44.

Laing, R.D. 1959 (2010). *The Divided Self*. Tavistock Publications.

Landau, Joanna. 2021. 'In the Supermarket of Nations, Israel Needs Better Branding'. *eJewishPhilanthropy.com*, 15 January 2021. https://ejewishphilanthropy.com/in-the-supermarket-of-nations-israel-needs-better-branding.

Larsen, Deborah Welch, T.V. Paul, and William C. Wohlforth. 2014. 'Status and World Order'. In *Status in World Politics*, ed. T.V. Paul, Deborah Welch Larsen, and William C. Wohlforth, 3–29. Cambridge: Cambridge University Press.

Lawler, Peter. 2005. 'The Good State: In Praise of "Classical" Internationalism'. *Review of International Studies* 31, no. 3: 427–49.

Lebow, Richard Ned. 2008. *A Cultural Theory of International Relations*. Cambridge: Cambridge University Press.

Lee, Seow Ting, and Hun Shik Kim. 2021. 'Nation Branding in the COVID-19 Era: South Korea's Pandemic Diplomacy'. *Place Branding and Public Diplomacy* 17, no. 4: 382–96.

Leira, Halvard. 2013. '"Our Entire People Are Natural Born Friends of Peace": The Norwegian Foreign Policy of Peace'. *Swiss Political Science Review* 19, no. 3: 338–56.

– 2021. 'Afterword: Gendering the Brand?' In *Gendering Equality and Nation Branding in the Nordic Region*, ed. Eirinn Larsen, Sigrun Marie Moss, and Inger Skjelsbæk, 207–11. London: Routledge.

Lemke, Thomas. 2001. 'The Birth of Biopolitics: Michel Foucault's Lecture at the College de France on Neo-Liberal Governmentality'. *Economy and Society* 30, no. 2: 190–207.

Leonard, Mark. 1997. *Britain TM: Renewing Our Identity*. London: Demos.

Li, Shirley. 2021. 'How Hollywood Sold Out to China'. *Atlantic*, 10 September 2021. https://www.theatlantic.com/culture/archive/2021/09/how-hollywood-sold-out-to-china/620021.

Light, Duncan. 2001. 'Tourism and Romania's Communist Past: Coming to Terms with an Unwanted Heritage'. In *Post-Communist Romania: Coming to Terms with Transition*, ed. Duncan Light and David Phinnemore, 59–75. New York: Palgrave.

Lindemann, Thomas. 2010. *Causes of War: The Struggle for Recognition*. Colchester, UK: ECPR Press.

Lobo, Gregory. 2017. 'Spectacular 'Nationism' in Modern Colombia: Mediating Commitment to the Military Option'. *Media, War and Conflict* 10, no. 3: 261–72.

Lorenzini, Daniele. 2015. 'What Is a "Regime of Truth"'? *Le foucauldien* 1, no. 1. http://doi.org/10.16995/lefou.2.

Louw, Eric. 2016. 'South African Nation Branding and the World Cup: Promoting Nationalism, Nation Branding, and the Miracle Nation Discourse'. In *Commercial Nationalism: Selling the Nation and Nationalizing the Sell*, ed. Zala Volčič and Mark Andrejevic, 147–61. Basingstoke: Palgrave Macmillan.

Luttwak, Edward. 1990. 'From Geopolitics to Geoeconomics: Logic of Conflict, Grammar of Commerce'. *National Interest* 20: 17–23.

Makarychev, Andrey. 2013. 'The Politics of Sports Mega-Events in Russia: Kazan, Sochi, and Beyond'. *PONARS Eurasia policy memo* no. 288 (September 2013): 1–6.

Makarychev, Andrey, and Alexandra Yatsyk. 2014. 'Sochi Olympics – the Dangers of Rebranding.' *Opendemocracy*, 3 February 2014. https://www.opendemocracy.net/en/odr/sochi-olympics-dangers-of-rebranding.

Mälksoo, Maria. 2015. '"Memory Must Be Defended": Beyond the Politics of Mnemonical Security'. *Security Dialogue* 46, no. 3: 221–37.

Marat, Erica. 2009. 'Nation Branding in Central Asia: A New Campaign to Present Ideas about the State and the Nation'. *Europe-Asia Studies* 62, no. 7: 1123–36.

Markessinis, Andreas. 2009. 'South Africa's Nation Brand a Mess Says Expert'. *Nation-branding.info*, 13 June 2009. https://nation-branding.info/2009/06/13/south-africa-nation-brand-a-mess.

– 2011. 'Norway to Use Black Metal for Nation Branding'. *Nation-branding.info*, 15 June 2011. https://nation-branding.info/2011/06/15/norway-to-use-black-metal-for-nation-branding.

Marklund, Carl. 2015. 'American Mirrors and Swedish Self-Portraits: US Images of Sweden and Swedish Public Diplomacy in the USA in the 1970s and 80s'. In *Histories of Public Diplomacy and Nation Branding in the Nordic and Baltic Countries: Representing the Periphery*, ed. Louis Clerc, Nikolas Glover, and Paul Jordan, 172–94. Leiden and Boston: Brill Nijhoff.

– 2017. 'The Nordic Model on the Global Market of Ideas: The Welfare State as Scandinavia's Best Brand'. *Geopolitics* 22, no. 3: 623–39.

Marlow, Jim. 2002. 'Governmentality, Ontological Security and Ideational Stability: Preliminary Observations on the Manner, Ritual and Logic of a Particular Art of Government'. *Journal of Political Ideologies* 7, no. 2: 241–59.

Marsh, David, and Paul Fawcett. 2011a. 'Branding and Franchising a Public Policy: The Case of the Gateway Review Process 2001–2010'. *Australian Journal of Public Administration* 70, no. 3: 246–58.

– 2011b. 'Branding, Politics and Democracy'. *Policy Studies* 32, no. 5: 515–30.

Martin, Guy. 2012. *African Political Thought*. Houndmills: Palgrave Macmillan.

Matola, Miller. 2012. 'The Importance of Protecting Our Nation Brand As a Key Strategic Asset'. *Brand South Africa*, 29 October 2012. https://www.brandsouthafrica.com/south-africa-fast-facts/news-facts/the-importance-of-protecting-our-nation-brand-as-a-key-strategic-asset.

May, Rollo. 1977. *The Meaning of Anxiety*. New York: W.W. Norton and Company.

May, Theresa. 2017. 'The Government's Negotiating Objectives for Exiting the EU'. Speech delivered on 17 January 2017. https://www.gov.uk/government/speeches/the-governments-negotiating-objectives-for-exiting-the-eu-pm-speech.

Mayes, Robyn. 2008. 'A Place in the Sun: The Politics of Place, Identity and Branding'. *Place Branding and Public Diplomacy* 4, no. 2: 124–35.

Meade, Rosemary. 2012. 'Our Country's Calling Card: Culture as the Brand in Recessionary Ireland'. *Variant* 43 (Spring): 33–5.

Melissen, Jan. 2005. 'The New Public Diplomacy: Between Theory and Practice'. In *The New Public Diplomacy: Soft Power in International Relations*, ed. Jan Melissen, 3–27. Basingstoke: Palgrave Macmillan.

Mercer, J. 2006. 'Human Nature and the First Image: Emotion in International Politics'. *Journal of International Relations and Development* 9, no. 3: 288–303.

Metahaven. 2008. 'Brand States: Postmodern Power, Democratic Pluralism, and Design'. *e-flux journal* 1 (December): 1–13.

Milliken, Jennifer. 1999. 'The Study of Discourse in International Relations: A Critique of Research and Methods'. *European Journal of International Relations* 5, no. 2: 225–54.

Ministry for Foreign Affairs, Finland. 2010. 'The Country Brand Delegation Sets Tasks for Finland'. Press release. 25 November 2010. http://www.formin.finland.fi.

Mitzen, Jennifer. 2006. 'Ontological Security in World Politics: State Identity and the Security Dilemma'. *European Journal of International Relations* 12, no. 3: 341–70.

Moilanen, Teemu, and Seppo Rainisto. 2009. *How to Brand Nations, Cities and Destinations: A Planning Book for Place Branding*. Houndmills: Palgrave Macmillan.

Moisio, Sami. 2008. 'From Enmity to Rivalry? Notes on National Identity Politics in Competition States'. *Scottish Geographical Journal* 124, no. 1: 78–95.

Mor, Ben D. 2012. 'Credibility Talk in Public Diplomacy'. *Review of International Studies* 38, no. 2: 393–422.

Mordhorst, Mads. 2015. 'Public Diplomacy vs Nation Branding: The Case of Denmark after the Cartoon Crisis'. In *Histories of Public Diplomacy and Nation Branding in the Nordic and Baltic Countries: Representing the Periphery*, ed. Louis Clerc, Nikolas Glover, and Paul Jordan, 237–56. Leiden and Boston: Brill Nijhoff.

– 2019. 'Nation Branding and Nationalism'. In *Nationalism and the Economy: Explorations into a Neglected Relationship*, ed. Stefan Berger and Thomas Fetzer, 189–208. Budapest: CEU Press.

Moss, Sigrun Marie. 2018. 'Representing Nordicity through Gender "Exports"'. Paper presented at the workshop 'Nordic Exceptionalism in the High and Low Politics of Justice-Making Elsewhere'. University of Oslo, 1–2 March 2018.

– 2021. 'Applying the Brand or Not? Challenges of Nordicity and Gender Equality in Scandinavian Diplomacy'. In *Gender Equality and Nation Branding in the Nordic Region*, ed. Eirinn Larsen, Sigrun Marie Moss, and Inger Skjelsbæk, 62–74. London: Routledge.

Mouffe, Chantal. 1994. 'For a Politics of Nomadic Identity'. In *Travellers' Tales: Narratives of Home and Displacement*, ed. George Robertson,

Melinda Mash, Lisa Tickner, Jon Bird, Barry Curtis, and Tim Putnam, 103–13. London: Routledge.

Mouritzen, Hans. 1995. 'The Nordic Model as a Foreign Policy Instrument: Its Rise and Fall'. *Journal of Peace Research* 32, no. 1: 9–21.

Mudimbe, V.Y. 1994. *The Idea of Africa*. Bloomington: Indiana University Press.

Müller, Martin. 2014. 'Introduction: Winter Olympics Sochi 2014 – What Is at Stake?" *East European Politics* 30, no. 2: 153–7.

Myo-ja, Ser. 2009. 'Building "Korea the Brand" Will Take Years'. *Korea JoonAng Daily*, 28 July 2009. https://koreajoongangdaily.joins.com/2009/07/28/people/In-depth-interview-Building-Korea-the-brand-will-take-years/2908004.html.

Neumann, Iver B. 1996. *Russia and the Idea of Europe: A Study in Identity and International Relations*. London: Routledge.

Neumann, Iver B., and Benjamin de Carvalho. 2015. 'Introduction: Small States and Status'. In *Small State Status Seeking: Norway's Quest for International Standing*, ed. Benjamin de Carvalho and Iver B. Neumann, 1–21. Abingdon: Routledge.

Nordic Council and the Nordic Council of Ministers. n.d. 'Det Nordiska Perspectivet'. https://www.norden.org/en/news-and-events/videos/the-nordic-perspective.

Nordic Council of Ministers. 2015. *Strategy for International Branding of the Nordic Region 2015–2018*. Copenhagen: Nordic Council of Ministers.

– 2017. 'Låt fred bli Nordens varumärke' [Let peace become the Nordic brand/trademark]. 4 April 2017. https://www.norden.org/en/node/4403.

– 2019. *Strategy for International Branding of the Nordic Region, 2019–21*. Copenhagen: Nordic Council of Ministers.

Nordic Council of Ministers for Gender Equality. 2019. 'Declaration of Support towards the Role of UN Women in the Realisation of the 2030 Agenda for Sustainable Development'. 10 March 2019. https://www.norden.org/en/declaration/declaration-support-towards-role-un-women-realisation-2030-agenda-sustainable.

Nye, Joseph S. 2004. *Soft Power: The Means to Success in World Politics*. New York: Public Affairs.

Ohmae, Kenichi. 1995. *The End of the Nation State: The Rise of Regional Economies*. London: Harper Collins.

Ojanen, Hanna, and Tapio Raunio. 2018. 'The Varying Degrees and Meanings of Nordicness in Finnish Foreign Policy'. *Global Affairs* 4, nos. 4/5: 405–18.

Ojeda, Diana. 2013. 'War and Tourism: The Banal Geographies of Security in Colombia's "Retaking"'. *Geopolitics* 18, no. 4: 759–78.

Olins, Wally. 2002. 'Branding the Nation: The Historical Context'. *Journal of Brand Management* 9, nos. 4/5: 241–8.

— 2003. *On Brand*. London: Thames and Hudson.

— 2005. 'Making a National Brand'. In *The New Public Diplomacy: Soft Power in International Relations*, ed. Jan Melissen, 169–79. Houndmills: Palgrave Macmillan.

Osei, Collins, and Ayantunji Gbadamosi. 2011. 'Re-branding Africa'. *Marketing Intelligence and Planning* 29, no. 3: 284–304.

Owen, J.M. 1994. 'How Liberalism Produces Democratic Peace'. *International Security* 19, no. 2: 87–125.

Pamment, James. 2015. '"Putting the GREAT Back into Britain": National Identity, Public-Private Collaboration and Transfers of Brand Equity in 2012's Global Promotional Campaign'. *British Journal of Politics and International Relations* 17, no. 2: 260–83.

— 2018. 'Towards a New Conditionality? The Convergence of International Development, Nation Brands, and Soft Power in the British National Security Strategy'. *Journal of International Relations and Development* 21, no. 2: 396–414.

— 2021. 'Does Public Diplomacy Need a Theory of Disruption? The Role of Nonstate Actors in Counter-Branding the Swedish COVID-19 Response'. *Journal of Public Diplomacy* 1, no. 1: 80–110.

Parker, John, and Richard Rathbone. 2007. *African History: A Very Short Introduction*. Oxford: Oxford University Press.

Parker, Owen. 2017. 'Commercializing Citizenship in Crisis EU: The Case of Immigrant Investor Programmes'. *Journal of Common Market Studies* 55, no. 2: 332–48.

Patel, Nishika. 2011. 'India to Create Central Foreign Aid Agency'. *Guardian*, 26 July 2011. https://www.theguardian.com/global-development/2011/jul/26/india-foreign-aid-agency.

Pathak, Sriparna. 2015. 'The "Peace" in China's Peaceful Rise'. *E-International Relations*, 15 October 2015. https://www.e-ir.info/2015/10/15/the-peace-in-chinas-peaceful-rise.

Patomäki, Heikki. 2000. 'Beyond Nordic Nostalgia: Envisaging a Social/Democratic System of Global Governance'. *Cooperation and Conflict* 35, no. 2: 115–54.

Paul, T.V., Deborah Welch Larson, and William Wohlforth, eds. 2014. *Status in World Politics*. Cambridge: Cambridge University Press.

Peterson, J.E. 2006. 'Qatar and the World: Branding for a Micro-State'. *Middle East Journal* 60, no. 4: 732–48.

Philo, Chris, and Gerry Kearns. 1993. 'Culture History, Capital: A Critical Introduction to the Selling of Places'. In *Selling Places: The City as Cultural Capital, Past and Present*, ed. Gerry Kearns and Chris Philo, 1–32. Oxford: Pergamon Press.

Polman, Linda. 2010. *War Games: The Story of Aid and War in Modern Times*. London: Viking.

Porter, Michael E. 1990. 'The Competitive Advantage of Nations'. *Harvard Business Review* (March/April). https://hbr.org/1990/03/the-competitive-advantage-of-nations.

Powell, Colin. 2001. 'Remarks to the National Foreign Policy Conference for Leaders of Nongovernmental Organizations'. 26 October 2001. https://2001-2009.state.gov/secretary/former/powell/remarks/2001/5762.htm.

Prime Minister's Office. 2012. *Action Plan on External Economic Relations*. 16 May 2012. Helsinki: Government Resolution.

Rasmussen, Rasmus Kjærgaard, and Henrik Merkelsen. 2014. 'The Risks of Nation Branding as Crisis Response: A Case Study of How the Danish Government Turned the Cartoon Crisis into a Struggle with Globalization'. *Place Branding and Public Diplomacy* 10, no. 3: 230–48.

Rice-Oxley, Mark. 2012. 'Vorsprung durch Technik – Ad Slogan That Changed How We Saw Germany." *Guardian*, 18 September 2012. https://www.theguardian.com/world/2012/sep/18/vorsprung-durch-technik-advertising-germany.

Richey, Lisa Ann, and Stefano Ponte. 2012. 'Brand Aid and Africa'. *Review of African Political Economy* 39, no. 131: 136–7.

Ringmar, Erik. 1996. *Identity, Interest and Action: A Cultural Explanation of Sweden's Intervention in the Thirty Years War*. Cambridge: Cambridge University Press.

– 2002. 'The Recognition Game: Soviet Russia against the West'. *Cooperation and Conflict* 37, no. 2: 115–36.

Roan, Dan. 2022. 'World Cup 2022: A Desert World Cup Blighted by a Dust-Storm of Controversy." *BBC News*, 14 November 2022. https://www.bbc.co.uk/sport/football/63570556.

Robertson, C. 2005. 'Rwanda Is Sure to Be the Singapore of Africa by 2020'. *Rwanda Development Board*. Website discontinued, accessed 5 March 2015. http://www.rwandainvest.com.cn/DetailA.asp?ID=296&intMaxID=9.

Rosamond, Annika Bergman, and Elsa Hedling. 2022. 'Celebrity Diplomacy during the Covid-19 Pandemic? The Chief State Epidemiologist as "the Face of the Swedish Experiment"'. *Place Branding and Public Diplomacy* 18, no. 1: 41–3.

Rossdale, Chris. 2015. 'Enclosing Critique: The Limits of Ontological Security." *International Political Sociology* 9, no. 4: 369–86.

Royal Government of Bhutan. 2010. *Economic Development Policy of the Royal Kingdom of Bhutan 2010*. http://admin.theiguides.org/Media/Documents/Economic%20Development%20Policy,%202010_1.pdf.

Rumelili, Bahar, ed. 2015a. *Conflict Resolution and Ontological Security: Peace Anxieties*. London: Routledge.

– 2015b. 'Ontological (In)security and Peace Anxieties: A Framework for Conflict Resolution'. In *Conflict Resolution and Ontological Security: Peace Anxieties*, ed. Bahar Rumelili, 10–29. London: Routledge.

Rumelili, Bahar, and Rahime Suleymanoglu-Kurum. 2017. 'Brand Turkey: Liminal Identity and its Limits'. *Geopolitics* 22, no. 3: 549–70.

Sanín, Juan. 2016. 'Colombia Was Passion: Commercial Nationalism and the Reinvention of Colombianness'. In *Commercial Nationalism: Selling the Nation and Nationalizing the Sell*, ed. Zala Volčič and Mark Andrejevic, 46–64. Basingstoke: Palgrave Macmillan.

Saunders, Robert A. 2008. 'Buying into Brand Borat: Kazakhstan's Cautious Embrace of Its Unwanted "Son"'. *Slavic Review* 67, no. 1: 63–80.

– 2012. 'Brand Interrupted: The Impact of Alternative Narrators on Nation Branding in the Former Second World'. In *Branding Post-Communist Nations: Maketizing National Identities in the 'New' Europe*, ed. Nadia Kaneva, 49–75. London: Routledge.

– 2017. *Popular Geopolitics and Nation Branding in the Post-Soviet Realm*. London: Routledge.

Schimmelfennig, Frank. 2003. *The EU, NATO, and the Integration of Europe: Rules and Rhetoric*. Cambridge: Cambridge University Press.

Scholvin, Sören. 2016. *The Geopolitics of Regional Power: Geography, Economics and Politics in Southern Africa*. London: Routledge.

Schwak, Juliette. 2018. 'All the World's a Stage: Promotional Politics and Branded Identities in Asia'. *Asian Studies Review* 42, no. 4: 648–61.

Scottish Government. 2013. *Scotland's Future: Your Guide to an Independent Scotland*. 26 November 2013. https://www.gov.scot/publications/scotlands-future.

Searle, John R. 1995. *The Construction of Social Reality*. London: Penguin.

Serlet, Thibault, and Preston Martin. 2021. 'Could Rwanda Be the Next Singapore?' *Site Selection Magazine*. November 2021. https://siteselection.com/investor-watch/could-rwanda-be-the-next-singapore.cfm.

Sharp, Joanna. 2011a. 'A Subaltern Critical Geopolitics of the War on Terror: Postcolonial Security in Tanzania'. *Geoforum* 42, no. 3: 297–305.

– 2011b. 'Subaltern Geopolitics: Introduction'. *Geoforum* 42, no. 3: 271–3.

– 2013. 'Geopolitics at the Margins? Reconsidering Genealogies of Critical Geopolitics'. *Political Geography* 37, no. 1: 20–9.

Shephard, Wade. 2016. 'How "Made in China" Became Cool'. *Forbes Magazine*, 22 May 2016. https://www.forbes.com/sites/wadeshepard/2016/05/22/how-made-in-china-became-cool.

Simons, Greg. 2018. 'Brand ISIS: Interactions of the Tangible and Intangible Environments'. *Journal of Political Marketing* 17, no. 4: 322–53.

Skilbrei, May-Len, and Charlotta Holmstrom. 2014. *Prostitution Policy in the Nordic Countries: Ambiguous Sympathies*. Aldershot: Ashgate.

Solomon, Ty. 2013. 'Resonances of Neoconservatism'. *Cooperation and Conflict* 48, no. 1: 100–21.

– 2015. *The Politics of Subjectivity in American Foreign Policy Discourses*. Ann Arbor: University of Michigan Press.

– 2019. 'Rhythm and Mobilization in International Relations'. *International Studies Quarterly* 63, no. 4: 1001–13.

Spivak, Gayatri. 1987. *In Other Worlds: Essays in Cultural Politics*. London: Taylor and Francis.

Ståhlberg, Per, and Göran Bolin. 2015. 'Having a Soul or Choosing a Face? Nation Branding and the Concept of "Identity"'. Research seminar presentation, the Centre for Baltic and East European Studies. Södertörn University. 9 February 2015.

Steele, Brent J. 2008. *Ontological Security in International Relations*. London and New York: Routledge.

Sum, Ngai-Ling, and Bob Jessop. 2013. *Towards a Cultural Political Economy: Putting Culture in Its Place in Political Economy*. Cheltenham, UK, and Northhamton, MA: Edward Elgar.

Surowiec, Pavel. 2012. 'Toward Corpo-Nationalism: Poland as a Brand'. In *Branding Post-Communist Nations: Marketizing National Identities in the 'New' Europe*, ed. Nadia Kaneva, 124–44. London: Routledge.

Sussman, Gerald. 2012. 'Systemic Propaganda and State Branding in Post-Soviet Eastern Europe'. In *Branding Post-Communist Nations:*

Marketizing National Identities in the 'New' Europe, ed. Nadia Kaneva, 23–48. London: Routledge.

Szostek, Joanna. 2017. 'Defence and Promotion of Desired State Identity in Russia's Strategic Narrative'. *Geopolitics* 22, no. 3: 571–93.

Teslik, Lee Hudson. 2007. 'Nation Branding Explained'. *Council on Foreign Relations*, 9 November 2007. https://www.cfr.org/backgrounder/nation-branding-explained.

Tillich, Paul. 2014. *The Courage to Be*. New Haven and London: Yale University Press.

Tracevskis, Rokas M., and Bryan Bradley. 2001. 'Lithuanians Shudder in Disbelief at Bestseller'. *Baltic Times*, 12 June 2001. https://www.baltictimes.com/news/articles/5794.

Trädgårdh, Lars. 2002. 'Sweden and the EU: Welfare State Nationalism and the Spectre of "Europe"'. In *European Integration and National Identity: The Challenge of the Nordic States*, ed. Lene Hansen and Ole Wæver, 130–81. London and New York: Routledge.

Trawińska, Anna Maria. n.d. "Case of Poland." *Institute for Cultural Diplomacy*. Accessed 30 August 2021. http://www.culturaldiplomacy.org/academy/content/articles/events/nationbranding/participant-papers/anna-maria-trawinska.pdf.

Trenin, Dmitri. 2002. *The End of Eurasia: Russia on the Border Between Geopolitics and Globalization*. Washington, DC: Brookings Institution Press.

Tuathail, Gerard. 1996. *Critical Geopolitics: The Politics of Writing Global Space*. Minneapolis and St Paul: University of Minnesota Press.

Tuathail, Gerard, and Jon Agnew. 1992. 'Geopolitics and Discourse: Practical Geopolitical Reasoning in American Foreign Policy'. *Political Geography* 11, no. 2: 190–204.

Tuch, Hans. 1990. *Communicating with the World: US Public Diplomacy Overseas*. New York: St Martin's Press.

Tucker, Emma. 2017. 'Snask Rebrands North Korea as Love Korea with Heart-Focused Identity." *Dezeen*, 8 May 2017. https://www.dezeen.com/2017/05/08/snask-rebrand-north-korea-love-korea-heart-motif-identity-design-graphics.

Turner, Graeme. 2016. 'Setting the Scene for Commercial Nationalism: The Nation, the Market, and the Media.' In *Commercial Nationalism: Selling the Nation and Nationalizing the Sell*, ed. Zala Volčič and Mark Andrejevic, 14–26. Basingstoke: Palgrave Macmillan.

van Ham, Peter. 2001. 'The Rise of the Brand State: The Postmodern Politics of Image and Reputation'. *Foreign Affairs* 80, no. 5: 2–6.
– 2002. 'Branding Territory: Inside the Wonderful Worlds of PR and IR Theory'. *Millennium: Journal of International Studies* 31, no. 2: 249–69.
– 2005. "Branding European Power." *Place Branding and Public Diplomacy* 1, no. 2: 122–6.
– 2008. 'Place Branding: The State if the Art'. *Annals of the American Academy of Political Science* 616, no. 1: 126–49.
Varga, Somogy. 2013. 'The Marketization of Foreign Cultural Policy: The Cultural Nationalism of the Competition State'. *Constellations* 20, no. 3: 442–58.
Veblen, Thorstein. 1957. *The Theory of the Leisure Class.* London: George Allen and Unwin.
Versi, Anver. 2012. 'No More Negative Images Please'. *Kenya Airways Msafiri Inflight Magazine* 80 (March-April): 92–100. http://www.brandafrica.net.
Vik, Hanne Hagtvedt, Steven L.B. Jensen, Linde Lindkvist, and Johan Strang. 2018. 'Histories of Human Rights in the Nordic Countries'. *Nordic Journal of Human Rights* 36, no. 3: 189–201.
Viktorin, Carolin, Jessica C.E. Gienow-Hecht, Annika Estner, and Marcel K. Will, eds. 2018a. 'Beyond Marketing and Diplomacy: Exploring the Historical Origins of Nation Branding'. In *Nation Branding in Modern History*, ed. Carolin Viktorin, Jessica C.E. Gienow-Hecht, Annika Estner, and Marcel K. Will, 1–26. New York and Oxford: Berghahn Books.
– 2018b. *Nation Branding in Modern History.* New York and Oxford: Berghahn Books.
Vogel, David. 2005. *The Market for Virtue: The Potential and Limits of Corporate Social Responsibility.* Washington, DC: Brookings Institution.
Volčič, Zala. 2012. 'Branding Slovenia: "You Can't Spell Slovenia without Love …"' In *Branding Post-Communist Nations: Maketizing National Identities in the 'New' Europe*, ed. Nadia Kaneva, 147–67. London: Routledge.
Volčič, Zala, and Mark Andrejevic. 2011. 'Nation Branding in the Era of Commercial Nationalism'. *International Journal of Communication* 5, no. 1: 598–618.
– eds. 2016a. *Commercial Nationalism: Selling the Nation and Nationalizing the Sell.* Basingstoke: Palgrave Macmillan.

– 2016b. 'Introduction'. In *Commercial Nationalism: Selling the Nation and Nationalizing the Sell*, ed. Zala Volčič and Mark Andrejevic, 1–13. Basingstoke: Palgrave Macmillan.

Wæver, Ole. 1992. 'Nordic Nostalgia: Northern Europe after the Cold War'. *International Affairs* 68, no. 1: 77–102.

– 2002. 'Identities, Communities and Foreign Policy: Discourse Analysis as Foreign Policy Theory'. In *European Integration and National Identity: The Challenge of the Nordic States*, ed. Lene Hansen and Ole Wæver, 20–49. London and New York: Routledge.

Wanjiru, Evalyne. 2005. 'Branding African Countries: A Prospect for the Future'. *Place Branding and Public Diplomacy* 2, no. 1: 84–95.

Watts, Jonathan. 2016. 'Brazil: Home of Favela Resident Fighting Eviction over Olympics Razed'. *Guardian*, 9 March 2016. https://www.theguardian.com/world/2016/mar/09/brazil-demolishes-home-of-slum-resident-fighting-eviction-over-olympic-development.

Weidner, Jason R. 2011. 'Nation Branding, Technologies of the Self, and the Political Subject of the Nation-State'. Paper presented at the ISA Annual Convention, Montreal, 16–19 March 2011.

Welch, David A. 2010. 'A Cultural Theory Meets Cultures of Theory.' *International Theory* 2, no. 3: 446–53.

Wendt, Alexander. 1999. *Social Theory of International Politics*. Cambridge: Cambridge University Press.

Williams, Michael C. 2001. 'The Discipline of Democratic Peace'. *European Journal of International Relations* 7, no. 4: 525–53.

Winch, Peter. 1990. *The Idea of a Social Science and its Relation to Philosophy*. London: Routledge.

Wivel, Anders. 2017. 'What Happened to the Nordic Model for International Peace and Security'. *Peace Review: A Journal of Social Justice* 29, no. 4: 489–96.

Wohlforth, William. 2010. 'A Matter of Honor'. *International Theory* 2, no. 3: 468–74.

Wohlforth, William C., Benjamin de Carvalho, Halvard Leira, and Iver B. Neumann. 2018. 'Moral Authority and Status in International Relations: Good States and the Social Dimension of Status Seeking'. *Review of International Studies* 44, no. 3: 526–46.

World Economic Forum. 2018. 'Finnish Lessons'. 15 January 2018. https://twitter.com/wef/status/952935161531912192.

York, Peter. 2011. 'The Brand Called Wally Olins'. *Adweek*, 3 May 2011. http://www.adweek.com/print/131125.

Youde, Jeremy. 2009. 'Selling the State: State Branding as a Political Resource in South Africa'. *Place Branding and Public Diplomacy* 5, no. 2: 126–40.

Zarakol, Ayşe. 2010. 'Ontological (In)security and State Denial of Historical Crimes: Turkey and Japan'. *International Relations* 24, no. 1: 3–23.

– 2011. *After Defeat: How the East Learned to Live with the West*. Cambridge: Cambridge University Press.

Index

Africa, 14, 81, 106, 154, 155, 161, 162–9, 171–2, 180, 198n2; African renaissance, 140, 154, 163
altruism, 8, 89, 96, 106, 116, 117, 118
Anglo-America, 110
Angola, 169
Anholt, Simon, 4, 14–15, 25, 43, 44, 46, 51–3, 81, 87, 94, 95–8, 101, 105, 107, 119, 123, 126, 162, 170, 176, 179, 193n2, 197n1, 198n3; Nation Brand Hexagon, 46–7
anti-branding, 157–8, 162, 164, 169, 180, 189
anxiety, 58, 60–1, 64–6, 160, 164; normal versus neurotic, 61
apartheid, 122, 139–40, 168
architecture, 24, 73, 95, 149
Armenia, 87
attention economy, 21, 43
Australia, 92–3
authoritarian regimes/states, 10, 147, 148, 150, 160, 188, 190–1; soft versus hard authoritarian regimes/states, 148, 150, 153

Baltic States, 20, 24, 159
banal nationalism, 59–60, 69–70, 80–4, 184
Belarus, 109
Belfast, 123
benchmarking, 40–1, 45, 49, 89, 98, 104, 106–7, 117; indexes, 40, 45–9, 51, 55, 60, 89, 97, 98–100, 111, 137, 144
Bhutan, 76–7
Billig, Michael, 69
Blair, Tony, 49
Borat, 14
Bourdieu, Pierre, 103–4
Brand Africa, 154, 155, 159, 162–9, 180, 198n1
Brazil, 80, 169, 173, 198n3
Brexit, 3–5, 13, 63, 188, 190
Bulgaria, 51, 73
Bush, George W., 119

Cameron, David, 3, 5–6, 74, 195n11
capitalism, 18, 52, 54, 57, 59, 78, 91, 102, 105, 110, 118, 124, 129, 171, 189; emotional capitalism, 144

Ceaușescu, Nicolae, 158
celebrity humanitarianism, 162-3
Central Asia, 14, 106, 109, 160
Cerny, Philip, 36-7
charity, 98, 162, 163, 169
China, 5, 13, 23, 137, 150, 193n3, 198n3
citizenship, 26, 59-60, 70, 80-4, 139, 143, 147, 174, 186; commercialising citizenship, 70
clash of civilisations, 34
Cohen, Sacha Baron, 14
Colombia, 79-80, 95, 108, 122-3, 138, 140-6, 152-3, 194n5; democratic security, 141-3; Colombia is Passion, 79, 122-3, 144-5, 194n5
colonialism, 13, 92, 162, 165, 175, 198n3
commercial nationalism, 21, 53, 79, 134. *See also* consumer nationalism
communication studies, 28, 193n1
communications, 7, 15, 43, 83. *See also* social media; digitalisation
competition state, 8, 19, 30-56, 74-6, 78, 88, 123-4, 127, 166, 177
competitive identity, 32, 51-4, 57, 78, 95, 101, 170, 193n2
conspicuous consumption, 87, 195n10
conspicuous do-goodism, 88-90, 103, 106-7, 113-14, 117
consultants, 43-51, 94-100
consumer nationalism, 59, 76-80, 83, 85, 141, 144, 185. *See also* commercial nationalism
consumerism, 90-1

consumption, 79, 85, 90, 92, 105; ethical consumption, 88, 117. *See also* conspicuous consumption
continent brand effect, 162, 169, 180
corporate social responsibility, 88, 91-2, 97, 117
Covid-19, 137
culture, 15, 32, 59, 170; commodification of, 76-80, 85, 92; and competitive identity, 40, 51-8, 184; counter-culture, 90; and soft power, 17

democracy, 24, 81, 126, 147, 151; democratic co-creation, 78, 80; democratic peace theory, 126; Western democracy, 129, 189
democratic peace theory, 126, 151
Democratic People's Republic of Korea. *See* North Korea
Denmark, 99, 109, 114, 134-7, 138, 152, 197n1
development, 156, 163, 169-74, 180-1; development aid, 109, 155-6, 174-9, 180, 181; underdevelopment, 14, 156, 171-2
digitalisation, 52, 69, 82-3, 86, 187
discourse, 33-4
dissent, 60, 80, 82-3, 147, 196n14
distinction, 89, 100, 103-4

Eastern Europe, 20, 50-1, 56, 58, 60, 64, 72, 73, 106, 158, 159; transition, 50, 56, 60, 159, 160
end of history, 35
English School, 117

entrepreneurialism, 36, 64, 163, 172; entrepreneurial subject, 59, 64, 78, 85, 145; norm entrepreneurs, 94, 109, 117
Estonia, 20, 70, 71–2, 79, 159
Eurasianism, 129, 156, 160
European Management Fund, 40
European Union (EU), 3, 4, 5, 13, 72, 160, 195n11
Eurovision song contest, 67, 71

feminism, 90, 197n3. *See also* gender
Finland, 20, 53, 67, 77, 95, 99, 101, 104, 114, 161
formative moment, 34, 56
France, 18, 197n14
franchising, 26, 101–2
Franzen, Jonathan, 154, 156–7

gender, 26, 71, 88, 91, 107, 108, 111, 114–15, 118
geopolitics, 8–9, 19, 34–8, 58, 121, 125, 155, 156, 162, 179, 183; geopolitical imaginary, 32, 34–8, 155; geopolitical resurrection 159, 162, 164, 166–9, 180; Hobbesian geopolitics versus Lockean geoeconomics, 35–6, 55, 75, 123, 125, 151; subaltern geopolitics, 155, 162, 164–5, 167, 180
Germany, 20–1, 23, 78, 99, 134, 178
Ghana, 81, 172
Giddens, Anthony, 38, 61–3
globalisation, 18–19, 21, 24, 35–8, 54–5, 187; challenge to subjectivity, 74–5

good states, 8, 87–118, 123, 132,145, 156, 161, 176, 178, 183–4, 189; Good Country Index, 98–100, 103, 106–7, 109, 197n4
governmentality, 26, 59–61, 80–6
Great Britain, 5, 194n3, 198n3; Cool Britannia, 25, 49; Global Britain, 3–5, 13, 63, 190. *See also* United Kingdom
greenwashing, 91, 105

Hollywood, 150, 158
Hungary, 190

Iceland, 197n4
Identity. *See* competitive identity; national identity; ontological (in)security; self-identity; role identity
Ikalafeng, Thebe, 154, 163
imaged community, 16, 58, 72, 85, 185, 193n1, 195–6n11
imagined community, 16, 58, 72, 74, 85, 165, 185, 193n1, 195–6n11
indexes. *See* benchmarking
India, 4, 175–7, 178
interdependence (complex), 36, 95, 125, 151

Kazakhstan, 14, 15, 72–3, 149–50, 159, 160, 161
Kierkegaard, Søren, 61
knowledge brand, 32, 42–51, 55–6, 60, 90, 101, 108, 114, 115

Laing, R.D., 61–2
league tables, 48, 183. *See also* benchmarking

legitimacy, 9, 19, 41, 50, 122, 139, 146, 148–50, 153, 180, 186, 190
Leonard, Mark, 24, 49
Lithuania, 157
London, 5, 6, 24–5, 116, 123, 195n11, 198n3; Olympics, 6, 74, 194n3, 198n3

market for virtue 90–4, 117
May, Theresa, 3
Mbeki, Thabo, 163
mega-events, 80, 130, 131–2, 138, 148–9, 173–4, 181
Middle East, 135–7
Mohammad Cartoon Crisis, 134–7, 152
Moldova, 109
morality, 89, 91, 97, 106–7
Moyo, Dambisa 198n2
Muslims, 135–6, 197n14

nation brand, 10–18
nation branding, 10–29; brand ambassador, 81, 82, 85, 133, 144, 185; corporate branding, 25–6, 82, 85, 88, 90, 96, 186, 187; cosmetic versus institutionalised, 15, 25, 27, 43, 52, 94, 127, 149, 186, 197; country of origin, 22–3, 27, 40, 79, 88, 96, 116, 166, 186; cultural, diplomatic and economic logics, 19–22; formal/official versus informal/unofficial, 28–9, 83–4; 'living the brand', 81, 139, 185; nation branding versus state branding, 72–3, 122, 146–50; place branding, 24–5, 123, 139, 186; policy branding, 26, 88, 89, 96, 100–2, 117, 186; regime branding, 122, 146–50, 153
nation building, 16, 19, 58–9, 69–75, 84–5, 122, 128, 139, 145, 150, 184–5, 194n9, 196n11
national identity, 15–16. *See also* nation building
national image, 12–13, 18, 52, 94, 97, 105, 117, 176, 196–7n14
nationalism, 50, 53, 65–6, 124, 151, 165, 174, 191. *See also* banal nationalism; commercial nationalism; consumer nationalism
NATO, 114, 129, 160
neoliberalism, 19, 36, 37, 49, 50, 64, 78, 103, 124, 129, 151, 156, 166, 171, 173, 187, 191
New Labour, 49
Nkrumah, Kwame, 166
Nordic Council of Ministers, 110–11, 118
Nordic countries, 20, 89–90, 102–3, 107–16, 118, 195n11, 196n14; Nordic brand, 109–16; Nordic distinction/exceptionalism, 109–11, 114–15, Nordic gender effect, 114; Nordic model(s), 90, 102–3, 110, 111, 114, 197n3, 197n5; Nordic peace, 90, 111–15
North Korea, 20, 119–21, 126–8, 131, 150, 151, 153; Arirang festival, 128; nuclear tests, 120, 128; theatre state, 127–8
Norway, 108–9, 114, 118, 196n14
Nye, Joseph, 17

Olins, Wally, 18, 23, 44–5, 51, 57, 69, 79

ontological (in)security, 57–69, 73–5, 79–80, 84–6; biographical narratives, 62–4, 68; routines, 63, 143, 153; physical versus ontological security, 63, 143, 146; securitising subjectivity, 63–4

Orban, Viktor, 190

Orientalism, 158, 163, 174

Pan-Africanism, 164–7, 180; decolonial Pan-Africanism, 164–6, 180; 'fathers of liberation', 166

Poland, 51, 78–9, 82, 196n12

populism, 116, 190–1

Porter, Michael, 39–40

postcolonialism, 37, 92, 106, 164, 171, 174

post-liberal world, 190–1

poverty porn, 162

Powell, Colin, 175

propaganda, 16–17, 131, 133–5

psychological constructivism, 66

public diplomacy, 16–18, 121–2, 132–8, 152, 188

Putin, Vladimir, 190

Qatar, 15, 20, 24, 72, 138, 149; FIFA World Cup, 188–9

realism, 34–7, 65, 66, 75, 93, 117

recognition, 58, 60, 61, 65–8

Rio Olympics, 80, 173

role identity, 127, 131, 197

Romania, 83, 158, 159

Russia, 21, 66, 71–2, 125, 128–32; Sochi Olympics, 130–2

Rwanda, 169, 172

Sanders, Bernie, 116

Saudi Arabia, 138

Scotland independence referendum, 3, 5–6, 74, 195n11; Scottish National Party, 160

security dilemma, 63

self-esteem, 64–9

self-identity, 60, 61–4, 65, 68, 91, 94, 113, 115, 144–5, 161, 187

shame, 50, 60, 62, 66, 67, 68, 140, 154, 197n2

Singapore, 81, 169, 172

Slovenia, 4, 81, 84, 160, 176, 196n13

SNASK, 119–21, 127

social media, 82–3, 86, 145, 162, 187

soft power, 6, 10, 11, 16, 17–18, 43, 53, 58, 124, 125, 178, 185

South Africa, 81, 95, 108, 122, 138–40, 159, 161, 163, 167–8, 172, 173, 198n1, 198n3

South Korea, 49, 76, 128, 137, 176, 178

Soviet Union, 34, 35, 50, 56

Spain, 24, 49

sportswashing, 138, 148, 152, 189, 190

status, 64–9; club status, 65, 179; positional status, 65

stereotypes, 14, 51, 144, 157, 158, 174, 196n12, 198n3; self-stereotyping, 77, 158, 159

stigmatisation, 9, 58, 66, 67, 83, 154–81, 184

Sweden, 82, 99, 108, 109, 113, 114, 118, 137

symbolic actions, 96, 107, 132

territorial state, 8, 19, 31, 36, 55, 123, 127

Thailand, 147
Tillich, Paul, 62, 65
tourism, 4, 25, 47–7, 136, 141, 142–3, 147, 149, 172; dark tourism 158, 159; ethical tourism, 92–3
transnational promotional class, 38–9, 41
Trump, Donald J., 83, 188, 190
Turkey, 66, 95, 159, 161–2

Ukraine, 109, 125, 129, 187, 190
United Kingdom (UK), 3–6, 48, 63, 74, 126, 138, 160, 175–6, 188, 190, 195n11, 197n3. *See also* Great Britain
United States (US), 25, 83, 102, 116, 119, 126, 127, 128, 129, 156–7, 175; America, 102, 116, 135, 157; 'America first ...', 83–4
Uribe, Álvaro, 141–2, 145
Uzbekistan, 70

vicarious identification, 73, 83
Vietnam, 158, 159
virtuous difference, 89, 90, 103–4, 113–14, 115, 117

World Economic Forum, 101; Global Competitiveness Index/Reports, 41, 48, 51
World Intellectual Property Organisation, 54, 98

Zimbabwe, 46, 81, 198n1